How Students Learn

MATHEMATICS IN THE CLASSROOM

D1531257

Committee on *How People Learn*, A Targeted Report for Teachers

M. Suzanne Donovan and John D. Bransford, *Editors*

Division of Behavioral and Social Sciences and Education

NATIONAL RESEARCH COUNCIL
OF THE NATIONAL ACADEMIES

THE NATIONAL ACADEMIES PRESS
Washington, D.C.
www.nap.edu

THE NATIONAL ACADEMIES PRESS • 500 Fifth Street, N.W. • Washington, D.C. 20001

NOTICE: The project that is the subject of this report was approved by the Governing Board of the National Research Council, whose members are drawn from the councils of the National Academy of Sciences, the National Academy of Engineering, and the Institute of Medicine. The members of the committee responsible for the report were chosen for their special competences and with regard for appropriate balance.

This study was supported by Award No. R215U990024 between the National Academy of Sciences and the U.S. Department of Education. Any opinions, findings, conclusions, or recommendations expressed in this publication are those of the author(s) and do not necessarily reflect the views of the organizations or agencies that provided support for the project.

Library of Congress Cataloging-in-Publication Data

National Research Council (U.S.). Committee on How People Learn, A Targeted Report for Teachers.
  How students learn : history, mathematics, and science in the classroom / Committee on How People Learn, A Targeted Report for Teachers ; M. Suzanne Donovan and John D. Bransford, editors.
     p. cm.
  "Division of Behavioral and Social Sciences and Education."
  Includes bibliographical references and index.
  ISBN 0-309-07433-9 (hardcover) — ISBN 0-309-08948-4 (pbk.) — ISBN 0-309-08949-2 (pbk.) — ISBN 0-309-08950-6 (pbk.) 1. Learning. 2. Classroom management. 3. Curriculum planning. I. Donovan, Suzanne. II. Bransford, John. III. Title.
  LB1060.N38 2005
  370.15′23—dc22

                    2004026246

Additional copies of this report are available from the National Academies Press, 500 Fifth Street, N.W., Lockbox 285, Washington, DC 20055; (800) 624-6242 or (202) 334-3313 (in the Washington metropolitan area); Internet, http://www.nap.edu

Printed in the United States of America.

First Printing, December 2004
Second Printing, October 2005
Third Printing, April 2006

Suggested citation: National Research Council. (2005). *How Students Learn: Mathematics in the Classroom*. Committee on *How People Learn*, A Targeted Report for Teachers, M.S. Donovan and J.D. Bransford, Editors. Division of Behavioral and Social Sciences and Education. Washington, DC: The National Academies Press.

THE NATIONAL ACADEMIES
Advisers to the Nation on Science, Engineering, and Medicine

The **National Academy of Sciences** is a private, nonprofit, self-perpetuating society of distinguished scholars engaged in scientific and engineering research, dedicated to the furtherance of science and technology and to their use for the general welfare. Upon the authority of the charter granted to it by the Congress in 1863, the Academy has a mandate that requires it to advise the federal government on scientific and technical matters. Dr. Bruce M. Alberts is president of the National Academy of Sciences.

The **National Academy of Engineering** was established in 1964, under the charter of the National Academy of Sciences, as a parallel organization of outstanding engineers. It is autonomous in its administration and in the selection of its members, sharing with the National Academy of Sciences the responsibility for advising the federal government. The National Academy of Engineering also sponsors engineering programs aimed at meeting national needs, encourages education and research, and recognizes the superior achievements of engineers. Dr. Wm. A. Wulf is president of the National Academy of Engineering.

The **Institute of Medicine** was established in 1970 by the National Academy of Sciences to secure the services of eminent members of appropriate professions in the examination of policy matters pertaining to the health of the public. The Institute acts under the responsibility given to the National Academy of Sciences by its congressional charter to be an adviser to the federal government and, upon its own initiative, to identify issues of medical care, research, and education. Dr. Harvey V. Fineberg is president of the Institute of Medicine.

The **National Research Council** was organized by the National Academy of Sciences in 1916 to associate the broad community of science and technology with the Academy's purposes of furthering knowledge and advising the federal government. Functioning in accordance with general policies determined by the Academy, the Council has become the principal operating agency of both the National Academy of Sciences and the National Academy of Engineering in providing services to the government, the public, and the scientific and engineering communities. The Council is administered jointly by both Academies and the Institute of Medicine. Dr. Bruce M. Alberts and Dr. Wm. A. Wulf are chair and vice chair, respectively, of the National Research Council.

www.national-academies.org

COMMITTEE ON *HOW PEOPLE LEARN*: A TARGETED REPORT FOR TEACHERS

JOHN D. BRANSFORD (*Chair*), College of Education, University of Washington
SUSAN CAREY, Department of Psychology, Harvard University
KIERAN EGAN, Department of Education, Simon Fraser University, Burnaby, Canada
SUZANNE WILSON, School of Education, Michigan State University
SAMUEL S. WINEBURG, Department of Education, Stanford University

M. SUZANNE DONOVAN, *Study Director*
SUSAN R. MCCUTCHEN, *Research Associate*
ALLISON E. SHOUP, *Senior Project Assistant*
ELIZABETH B. TOWNSEND, *Senior Project Assistant*

Preface

This book has its roots in the report of the Committee on Developments in the Science of Learning, *How People Learn: Brain, Mind, Experience and School* (National Research Council, 1999, National Academy Press). That report presented an illuminating review of research in a variety of fields that has advanced understanding of human learning. The report also made an important attempt to draw from that body of knowledge implications for teaching. A follow-on study by a second committee explored what research and development would need to be done, and how it would need to be communicated, to be especially useful to teachers, principals, superintendents, and policy makers: *How People Learn: Bridging Research and Practice* (National Research Council, 1999). These two individual reports were combined to produce an expanded edition of *How People Learn* (National Research Council, 2000). We refer to this volume as *HPL*.

The next step in the work on how people learn was to provide examples of how the principles and findings on learning can be used to guide the teaching of a set of topics that commonly appear in the K-12 curriculum. The work focused on three subject areas— history, mathematics, and science—and resulted in the book *How Students Learn: History, Mathematics, and Science in the Classroom.* Each area was treated at three levels: elementary, middle, and high school.

This volume includes the subset of chapters from that book focused on mathematics, along with the introduction and concluding chapter of the larger volume. The full set of chapters can be found on the enclosed CD.

Distinguished researchers who have extensive experience in teaching or in partnering with teachers were invited to contribute the chapters. The committee shaped the goals for the volume, and commented—sometimes extensively—on the draft chapters as they were written and revised. The principles of *HPL* are embedded in each chapter, though there are differences from one chapter to the next in how explicitly they are discussed.

Taking this next step to elaborate the *HPL* principles in context poses a potential problem that we wish to address at the outset. The meaning and relevance of the principles for classroom teaching can be made clearer with specific examples. At the same time, however, many of the specifics of a particular example could be replaced with others that are also consistent with the *HPL* principles. In looking at a single example, it can be difficult to distinguish what is necessary to effective teaching from what is effective but easily replaced. With this in mind, it is critical that the teaching and learning examples in each chapter be seen as illustrative, not as blueprints for the "right" way to teach.

We can imagine, by analogy, that engineering students will better grasp the relationship between the laws of physics and the construction of effective supports for a bridge if they see some examples of well-designed bridges, accompanied by explanations for the choices of the critical design features. The challenging engineering task of crossing the entrance of the San Francisco Bay, for example, may bring the relationship between physical laws, physical constraints, and engineering solutions into clear and meaningful focus. But there are some design elements of the Golden Gate Bridge that could be replaced with others that serve the same end, and people may well differ on which among a set of good designs creates the most appealing bridge.

To say that the Golden Gate Bridge is a good example of a suspension bridge does not mean it is the only, or the best possible, design for a suspension bridge. If one has many successful suspension bridges to compare, the design features that are required for success, and those that are replaceable, become more apparent. And the requirements that are uniform across contexts, and the requirements that change with context, are more easily revealed.

The chapters in this volume highlight different approaches to addressing the same fundamental principles of learning. It would be ideal to be able to provide two or more "*HPL* compatible" approaches to teaching the same topic. However, we cannot provide that level of specific variability in this volume. We encourage readers to look at chapters in other disciplines as well in order to see more clearly the common features across chapters, and the variation in approach among the chapters.

This volume could not have come to life without the help and dedication of many people, and we are grateful to them. First and foremost, the committee acknowledges the contributions of Robbie Case, who was to have contributed to the mathematics chapters in this volume. Robbie was at the height of a very productive career when his life came to an unexpected end in May 2000. Robbie combined the very best in disciplinary research and attention to the incorporation of research findings into classroom tools to support teaching and learning. In this respect, he was a model for researchers interested in supporting improved educational practice. The mathematics chapters in this volume are marked by Robbie Case's influence.

The financial support of our sponsors, the U.S. Department of Education and the President's Circle of the National Academy of Sciences, was essential. We appreciate both their support and their patience during the unexpectedly long period required to shape and produce so extensive a volume with so many different contributors. Our thanks to C. Kent McGuire, former assistant secretary of the Office of Education Research and Improvement for providing the initial grant for this project, and to his successor and now director of the National Institute for Education Sciences, Grover J. Whitehurst; thanks are due as well to Patricia O'Connell Ross, Jill Edwards Staton, Michael Kestner, and Linda Jones at the Department of Education for working with us throughout, and providing the time required to produce a quality product.

This report is a somewhat unusual undertaking for the National Research Council in that the committee members did not author the report chapters, but served as advisers to the chapter authors. The contributions of committee members were extraordinary. In a first meeting the committee and chapter authors worked together to plan the volume. The committee then read each draft chapter, and provided extensive, and remarkably productive, feedback to chapter authors. As drafts were revised, committee members reviewed them again, pointing out concerns and proposing potential solutions. Their generosity and their commitment to the goal of this project are noteworthy.

Alexandra Wigdor, director of the Division on Education, Labor, and Human Performance when this project was begun, provided ongoing guidance and experienced assistance with revisions. Rona Brière brought her special skills in editing the entire volume. Our thanks go to Allison E. Shoup, who was senior project assistant, supporting the project through much of its life; to Susan R. McCutchen, who prepared the manuscript for review; to Claudia Sauls and Candice Crawford, who prepared the final manuscript; and to Deborah Johnson, Sandra Smotherman, and Elizabeth B. Townsend, who willingly provided additional support when needed. Kirsten Sampson Snyder handled the report review process, and Yvonne Wise handled report production—both challenging tasks for a report of this size and complexity. We are grateful for their help.

This report has been reviewed in draft form by individuals chosen for their diverse perspectives and technical expertise, in accordance with procedures approved by the National Research Council's Report Review Committee. The purpose of this independent review is to provide candid and critical comments that will assist the institution in making its published report as sound as possible and to ensure that the report meets institutional standards for objectivity, evidence, and responsiveness to the study charge. The review comments and draft manuscript remain confidential to protect the integrity of the deliberative process. We thank the following individuals for their review of this report: Jo Boaler, Mathematics Education, School of Education, Stanford University; Miriam L. Clifford, Mathematics Department, Carroll College, Waukesha, Wisconsin; O.L. Davis, Curriculum and Instruction, The University of Texas at Austin; Patricia B. Dodge, Science Teacher, Essex Middle School, Essex Junction, Vermont; Carol T. Hines, History Teacher, Darrel C. Swope Middle School, Reno, Nevada; Janis Lariviere, UTeach—Science and Mathematics Teacher Preparation, The University of Texas at Austin; Gaea Leinhardt, Learning Research and Development Center and School of Education, University of Pittsburgh; Alan M. Lesgold, Office of the Provost, University of Pittsburgh; Marcia C. Linn, Education in Mathematics, Science, and Technology, University of California, Berkeley; Kathleen Metz, Cognition and Development, Graduate School of Education, University of California, Berkeley; Thomas Romberg, National Center for Research in Mathematics and Science Education, University of Wisconsin–Madison; and Peter Seixas, Centre for the Study of Historical Consciousness, University of British Columbia.

Although the reviewers listed above have provided many constructive comments and suggestions, they did not see the final draft of the report before its release. The review of this report was overseen by Alan M. Lesgold, University of Pittsburgh. Appointed by the National Research Council, he was responsible for making certain that an independent examination of this report was carried out in accordance with institutional procedures and that all review comments were carefully considered. Responsibility for the final content of this report rests entirely with the authors, the committee, and the institution.

John D. Bransford, *Chair*
M. Suzanne Donovan, *Study Director*

Contents

Part I History
(on enclosed CD; not printed in this volume)

Part II Mathematics

Part III Science
(on enclosed CD; not printed in this volume)

A Final Synthesis:
Revisiting the Three Learning Principles

How Students Learn

MATHEMATICS IN THE CLASSROOM

1

Introduction

M. Suzanne Donovan and John D. Bransford

More than any other species, people are designed to be flexible learners and, from infancy, are active agents in acquiring knowledge and skills. People can invent, record, accumulate, and pass on organized bodies of knowledge that help them understand, shape, exploit, and ornament their environment. Much that each human being knows about the world is acquired informally, but mastery of the accumulated knowledge of generations requires intentional learning, often accomplished in a formal educational setting.

Decades of work in the cognitive and developmental sciences has provided the foundation for an emerging science of learning. This foundation offers conceptions of learning processes and the development of competent performance that can help teachers support their students in the acquisition of knowledge that is the province of formal education. The research literature was synthesized in the National Research Council report *How People Learn: Brain, Mind, Experience, and School*.[1] In this volume, we focus on three fundamental and well-established principles of learning that are highlighted in *How People Learn* and are particularly important for teachers to understand and be able to incorporate in their teaching:

1. Students come to the classroom with preconceptions about how the world works. If their initial understanding is not engaged, they may fail to grasp the new concepts and information, or they may learn them for purposes of a test but revert to their preconceptions outside the classroom.

2. To develop competence in an area of inquiry, students must (a) have a deep foundation of factual knowledge, (b) understand facts and ideas in the context of a conceptual framework, and (c) organize knowledge in ways that facilitate retrieval and application.

3. A "metacognitive" approach to instruction can help students learn to take control of their own learning by defining learning goals and monitoring their progress in achieving them.

A FISH STORY

The images from a children's story, *Fish Is Fish*,[2] help convey the essence of the above principles. In the story, a young fish is very curious about the world outside the water. His good friend the frog, on returning from the land, tells the fish about it excitedly:

> *"I have been about the world—hopping here and there,"*
> *said the frog, "and I have seen extraordinary things."*
> *"Like what?" asked the fish.*
> *"Birds," said the frog mysteriously. "Birds!" And he told the*
> *fish about the birds, who had wings, and two legs, and*
> *many, many colors. As the frog talked, his friend saw the*
> *birds fly through his mind like large feathered fish.*

The frog continues with descriptions of cows, which the fish imagines as black-and-white spotted fish with horns and udders, and humans, which the fish imagines as fish walking upright and dressed in clothing. Illustrations below from Leo Lionni's *Fish Is Fish* © 1970. Copyright renewed 1998 by Leo Lionni. Used by permission of Random House Children's Books, a division of Random House, Inc.

Principle #1: Engaging Prior Understandings

What Lionni's story captures so effectively is a fundamental insight about learning: *new understandings are constructed on a foundation of existing understandings and experiences.* With research techniques that permit the study of learning in infancy and tools that allow for observation of activity in the brain, we understand as never before how actively humans engage in learning from the earliest days of life (see Box 1-1). The understandings children carry with them into the classroom, even before the start of formal schooling, will shape significantly how they make sense of what they are

BOX 1-1 The Development of Physical Concepts in Infancy

Research studies have demonstrated that infants as young as 3 to 4 months of age develop understandings and expectations about the physical world. For example, they understand that objects need support to prevent them from falling to the ground, that stationary objects may be displaced when they come into contact with moving objects, and that objects at rest must be propelled into motion.[3]

In research by Needham and Baillargeon,[4] infants were shown a table on which a box rested. A gloved hand reached out from a window beside the table and placed another box in one of two locations: on top of the first box (the possible event), and beyond the box—creating the impression that the box was suspended in midair. In this and similar studies, infants look reliably longer at the impossible events, suggesting an awareness and a set of expectations regarding what is and is not physically possible.

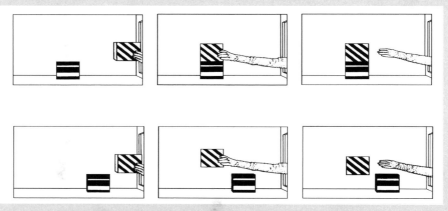

SOURCE: Needham and Baillargeon (1993). Reprinted with permission from Elsevier.

BOX 1-2 **Misconceptions About Momentum**

Andrea DiSessa[5] conducted a study in which he compared the performance of college physics students at a top technological university with that of elementary schoolchildren on a task involving momentum. He instructed both sets of students to play a computerized game that required them to direct a simulated object (a dynaturtle) so that it would hit a target, and to do so with minimum speed at impact. Participants were introduced to the game and given a hands-on trial that allowed them to apply a few taps with a wooden mallet to a ball on a table before they began.

DiSessa found that both groups of students failed miserably at the task. Despite their training, college physics majors—just like the elementary school children—applied the force when the object was just below the target, failing to take momentum into account. Further investigation with one college student revealed that she knew the relevant physical properties and formulas and would have performed well on a written exam. Yet in the context of the game, she fell back on her untrained conceptions of how the physical world works.

taught. Just as the fish constructed an image of a human as a modified fish, children use what they know to shape their new understandings.

While prior learning is a powerful support for further learning, it can also lead to the development of conceptions that can act as barriers to learning. For example, when told that the earth is round, children may look to reconcile this information with their experience with balls. It seems obvious that one would fall off a round object. Researchers have found that some children solve the paradox by envisioning the earth as a pancake, a "round" shape with a surface on which people could walk without falling off.[6]

How People Learn summarizes a number of studies demonstrating the active, preconception-driven learning that is evident in humans from infancy through adulthood.[7] Preconceptions developed from everyday experiences are often difficult for teachers to change because they generally work well enough in day-to-day contexts. But they can impose serious constraints on understanding formal disciplines. College physics students who do well on classroom exams on the laws of motion, for example, often revert to their untrained, erroneous models outside the classroom. When they are confronted with tasks that require putting their knowledge to use, they fail to take momentum into account, just as do elementary students who have had no physics training (see Box 1-2). If students' preconceptions are not addressed directly, they often memorize content (e.g., formulas in physics), yet still use their experience-based preconceptions to act in the world.

Principle #2: The Essential Role of Factual Knowledge and Conceptual Frameworks in Understanding

The *Fish Is Fish* story also draws attention to the kinds of knowledge, factual and conceptual, needed to support learning with understanding. The frog in the story provides information to the fish about humans, birds, and cows that is accurate and relevant, yet clearly insufficient. Feathers, legs, udders, and sport coats are surface features that distinguish each species. But if the fish (endowed now with human thinking capacity) is to understand how the land species are different from fish and different from each other, these surface features will not be of much help. Some additional, critical concepts are needed—for example, the concept of adaptation. Species that move through the medium of air rather than water have a different mobility challenge. And species that are warm-blooded, unlike those that are cold-blooded, must maintain their body temperature. It will take more explaining of course, but if the fish is to see a bird as something other than a fish with feathers and wings and a human as something other than an upright fish with clothing, then feathers and clothing must be seen as adaptations that help solve the problem of maintaining body temperature, and upright posture and wings must be seen as different solutions to the problem of mobility outside water.

Conceptual information such as a theory of adaptation represents a kind of knowledge that is unlikely to be induced from everyday experiences. It typically takes generations of inquiry to develop this sort of knowledge, and people usually need some help (e.g., interactions with "knowledgeable others") to grasp such organizing concepts.[8]

Lionni's fish, not understanding the described features of the land animals as adaptations to a terrestrial environment, leaps from the water to experience life on land for himself. Since he can neither breathe nor maneuver on land, the fish must be saved by the amphibious frog. The point is well illustrated: learning with understanding affects our ability to apply what is learned (see Box 1-3).

This concept of learning with understanding has two parts: (1) factual knowledge (e.g., about characteristics of different species) must be placed in a conceptual framework (about adaptation) to be well understood; and (2) concepts are given meaning by multiple representations that are rich in factual detail. Competent performance is built on neither factual nor conceptual understanding alone; the concepts take on meaning in the knowledge-rich contexts in which they are applied. In the context of Lionni's story, the general concept of adaptation can be clarified when placed in the context of the specific features of humans, cows, and birds that make the abstract concept of adaptation meaningful.

BOX 1-3 Learning with Understanding Supports Knowledge Use in New Situations

In one of the most famous early studies comparing the effects of "learning a procedure" with "learning with understanding," two groups of children practiced throwing darts at a target underwater.[9] One group received an explanation of refraction of light, which causes the apparent location of the target to be deceptive. The other group only practiced dart throwing, without the explanation. Both groups did equally well on the practice task, which involved a target 12 inches under water. But the group that had been instructed about the abstract principle did much better when they had to transfer to a situation in which the target was under only 4 inches of water. Because they understood what they were doing, the group that had received instruction about the refraction of light could adjust their behavior to the new task.

This essential link between the factual knowledge base and a conceptual framework can help illuminate a persistent debate in education: whether we need to emphasize "big ideas" more and facts less, or are producing graduates with a factual knowledge base that is unacceptably thin. While these concerns appear to be at odds, knowledge of facts and knowledge of important organizing ideas are mutually supportive. Studies of experts and novices—in chess, engineering, and many other domains—demonstrate that experts know considerably more relevant detail than novices in tasks within their domain and have better memory for these details (see Box 1-4). But the reason they remember more is that what novices see as separate pieces of information, experts see as organized sets of ideas.

Engineering experts, for example, can look briefly at a complex mass of circuitry and recognize it as an amplifier, and so can reproduce many of its circuits from memory using that one idea. Novices see each circuit separately, and thus remember far fewer in total. Important concepts, such as that of an amplifier, structure both what experts notice and what they are able to store in memory. Using concepts to organize information stored in memory allows for much more effective retrieval and application. Thus, the issue is not whether to emphasize facts or "big ideas" (conceptual knowledge); both are needed. Memory of factual knowledge is enhanced by conceptual knowledge, and conceptual knowledge is clarified as it is used to help organize constellations of important details. Teaching for understanding, then, requires that the core concepts such as adaptation that organize the knowledge of experts also organize instruction. This does not mean that that factual knowledge now typically taught, such as the characteristics of fish, birds, and mammals, must be replaced. Rather, that factual information is given new meaning and a new organization in memory because those features are seen as adaptive characteristics.

BOX 1-4   **Experts Remember Considerably More Relevant Detail Than Novices in Tasks Within Their Domain**

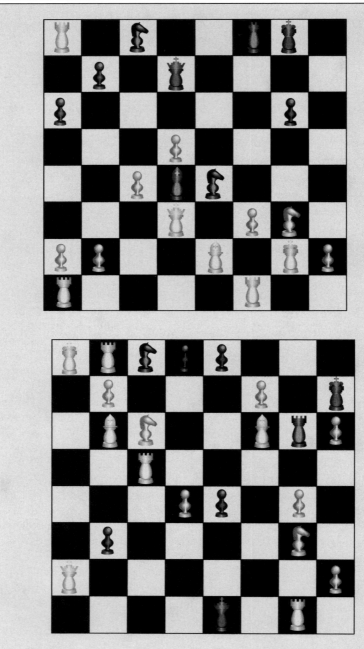

In one study, a chess master, a Class A player (good but not a master), and a novice were given 5 seconds to view a chess board position from the middle of a chess game (see below).

After 5 seconds the board was covered, and each participant attempted to reconstruct the board position on another board. This procedure was repeated for multiple trials until everyone received a perfect score. On the first trial, the master player correctly placed many more pieces than the Class A player, who in turn placed more than the novice: 16, 8, and 4, respectively. (See data graphed below.)

However, these results occurred only when the chess pieces were arranged in configurations that conformed to meaningful games of chess. When chess pieces were randomized and presented for 5 seconds, the recall of the chess master and Class A player was the same as that of the novice—they all placed 2 to 3 positions correctly. The apparent difference in memory capacity is due to a difference in pattern recognition. What the expert can remember as a single meaningful pattern, novices must remember as separate, unrelated items.

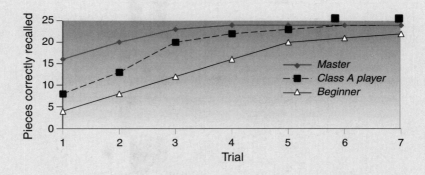

SOURCE: Chase and Simon (1973). Reprinted with permission from Elsevier.

Principle #3: The Importance of Self-Monitoring

Hero though he is for saving the fish's life, the frog in Lionni's story gets poor marks as a teacher. But the burden of learning does not fall on the teacher alone. Even the best instructional efforts can be successful only if the student can make use of the opportunity to learn. Helping students become effective learners is at the heart of the third key principle: a "metacognitive" or self-monitoring approach can help students develop the ability to take control of their own learning, consciously define learning goals, and monitor their progress in achieving them. Some teachers introduce the idea of metacognition to their students by saying, "You are the owners and operators of your own brain, but it came without an instruction book. We need to learn how we learn."

"Meta" is a prefix that can mean after, along with, or beyond. In the psychological literature, "metacognition" is used to refer to people's knowledge about themselves as information processors. This includes knowledge about what we need to do in order to learn and remember information (e.g., most adults know that they need to rehearse an unfamiliar phone number to keep it active in short-term memory while they walk across the room to dial the phone). And it includes the ability to monitor our current understanding to make sure we understand (see Box 1-5). Other examples include monitoring the degree to which we have been helpful to a group working on a project.[10]

BOX 1-5 Metacognitive Monitoring: An Example

Read the following passage from a literary critic, and pay attention to the strategies you use to comprehend:

> If a serious literary critic were to write a favorable, full-length review of How Could I Tell Mother She Frightened My Boyfriends Away, Grace Plumbuster's new story, his startled readers would assume that he had gone mad, or that Grace Plumbuster was his editor's wife.

Most good readers have to back up several times in order to grasp the meaning of this passage. In contrast, poor readers tend to simply read it all the way through without pausing and asking if the passage makes sense. Needless to say, when asked to paraphrase the passage they fall short.

SOURCE: Whimbey and Whimbey (1975, p. 42).

In Lionni's story, the fish accepted the information about life on land rather passively. Had he been monitoring his understanding and actively comparing it with what he already knew, he might have noted that putting on a hat and jacket would be rather uncomfortable for a fish and would slow his swimming in the worst way. Had he been more engaged in figuring out what the frog meant, he might have asked why humans would make themselves uncomfortable and compromise their mobility. A good answer to his questions might have set the stage for learning about differences between humans and fish, and ultimately about the notion of adaptation. The concept of metacognition includes an awareness of the need to ask how new knowledge relates to or challenges what one already knows—questions that stimulate additional inquiry that helps guide further learning.[11]

The early work on metacognition was conducted with young children in laboratory contexts.[12] In studies of "metamemory," for example, young children might be shown a series of pictures (e.g., drum, tree, cup) and asked to remember them after 15 seconds of delay (with the pictures no longer visible). Adults who receive this task spontaneously rehearse during the 15-second interval. Many of the children did not. When they were explicitly told to rehearse, they would do so, and their memory was very good. But when the children took part in subsequent trials and were not reminded to rehearse, many failed to rehearse even though they were highly motivated to perform well in the memory test. These findings suggest that the children had not made the "metamemory" connection between their rehearsal strategies and their short-term memory abilities.[13]

Over time, research on metacognition (of which metamemory is considered a subset) moved from laboratory settings to the classroom. One of the most striking applications of a metacognitive approach to instruction was pioneered by Palincsar and Brown in the context of "reciprocal teaching."[14] Middle school students worked in groups (guided by a teacher) to help one another learn to read with understanding. A key to achieving this goal involves the ability to monitor one's ongoing comprehension and to initiate strategies such as rereading or asking questions when one's comprehension falters. (Box 1-5 illustrates this point.) When implemented appropriately, reciprocal teaching has been shown to have strong effects on improving students' abilities to read with understanding in order to learn.

Appropriate kinds of self-monitoring and reflection have been demonstrated to support learning with understanding in a variety of areas. In one study,[15] for example, students who were directed to engage in self-explanation as they solved mathematics problems developed deeper conceptual understanding than did students who solved those same problems but did not engage in self-explanation. This was true even though the common time limitation on both groups meant that the self-explaining students solved fewer problems in total.

Helping students become more metacognitive about their own thinking and learning is closely tied to teaching practices that emphasize self-assessment. The early work of Thorndike[16] demonstrated that feedback is important for learning. However, there is a difference between responding to feedback that someone else provides and actively seeking feedback in order to assess one's current levels of thinking and understanding. Providing support for self-assessment is an important component of effective teaching. This can include giving students opportunities to test their ideas by building things and seeing whether they work, performing experiments that seek to falsify hypotheses, and so forth. Support for self-assessment is also provided by opportunities for discussion where teachers and students can express different views and explore which ones appear to make the most sense. Such questioning models the kind of dialogue that effective learners internalize. Helping students explicitly understand that a major purpose of these activities is to support metacognitive learning is an important component of successful teaching strategies.[17]

Supporting students to become aware of and engaged in their own learning will serve them well in all learning endeavors. To be optimally effective, however, some metacognitive strategies need to be taught in the context of individual subject areas. For example, guiding one's learning in a particular subject area requires awareness of the disciplinary standards for knowing. To illustrate, asking the question "What is the evidence for this claim?" is relevant whether one is studying history, science, or mathematics. However, what counts as evidence often differs. In mathematics, for example, formal proof is very important. In science, formal proofs are used when possible, but empirical observations and experimental data also play a major role. In history, multiple sources of evidence are sought and attention to the perspective from which an author writes and to the purpose of the writing is particularly important. Overall, knowledge of the discipline one is studying affects people's abilities to monitor their own understanding and evaluate others' claims effectively.

LEARNING ENVIRONMENTS AND THE DESIGN OF INSTRUCTION

The key principles of learning discussed above can be organized into a framework for thinking about teaching, learning, and the design of classroom and school environments. In *How People Learn*, four design characteristics are described that can be used as lenses to evaluate the effectiveness of teaching and learning environments. These lenses are not themselves research findings; rather, they are implications drawn from the research base:

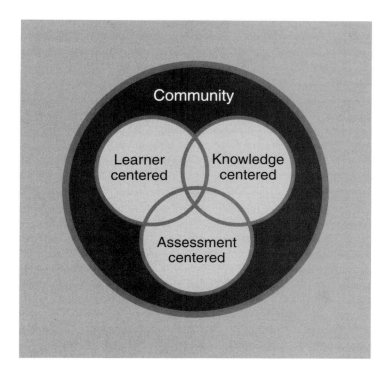

FIGURE 1-1 Perspectives on learning environments.

- The *learner-centered lens* encourages attention to preconceptions, and begins instruction with what students think and know.
- The *knowledge-centered lens* focuses on what is to be taught, why it is taught, and what mastery looks like.
- The *assessment-centered lens* emphasizes the need to provide frequent opportunities to make students' thinking and learning visible as a guide for both the teacher and the student in learning and instruction.
- The *community-centered lens* encourages a culture of questioning, respect, and risk taking.

These aspects of the classroom environment are illustrated in Figure 1-1 and are discussed below.

Learner-Centered Classroom Environments

Instruction must begin with close attention to students' ideas, knowledge, skills, and attitudes, which provide the foundation on which new learning builds. Sometimes, as in the case of Lionni's fish, learners' existing ideas lead to misconceptions. More important, however, those existing conceptions can also provide a path to new understandings. Lionni's fish mistakenly projects the model of a fish onto humans, birds, and cows. But the fish does know a lot about being a fish, and that experience can provide a starting point for understanding adaptation. How do the scales and fins of a fish help it survive? How would clothing and feathers affect a fish? The fish's existing knowledge and experience provide a route to understanding adaptation in other species. Similarly, the ideas and experiences of students provide a route to new understandings both about and beyond their experience.

Sometimes the experiences relevant to teaching would appear to be similar for all students: the ways in which forces act on a falling ball or feather, for example. But students in any classroom are likely to differ in how much they have been encouraged to observe, think about, or talk about a falling ball or feather. Differences may be larger still when the subject is a social rather than a natural phenomenon because the experiences themselves, as well as norms regarding reflection, expression, and interaction, differ for children from different families, communities, and cultures. Finally, students' expectations regarding their own performances, including what it means to be intelligent, can differ in ways that affect their persistence in and engagement with learning.

Being learner-centered, then, involves paying attention to students' backgrounds and cultural values, as well as to their abilities. To build effectively on what learners bring to the classroom, teachers must pay close attention to individual students' starting points and to their progress on learning tasks. They must present students with "just-manageable difficulties"—challenging enough to maintain engagement and yet not so challenging as to lead to discouragement. They must find the strengths that will help students connect with the information being taught. Unless these connections are made explicitly, they often remain inert and so do not support subsequent learning.

Knowledge-Centered Classroom Environments

While the learner-centered aspects of the classroom environment focus on the student as the starting point, the knowledge-centered aspects focus on what is taught (subject matter), why it is taught (understanding), how the knowledge should be organized to support the development of expertise (curriculum), and what competence or mastery looks like (learning goals). Several important questions arise when one adopts the knowledge-centered lens:

- What is it important for students to know and be able to do?
- What are the core concepts that organize our understanding of this subject matter, and what concrete cases and detailed knowledge will allow students to master those concepts effectively?
- [The knowledge-centered lens overlaps with the assessment-centered lens (discussed below) when we ask], How will we know when students achieve mastery?[18] This question overlaps the knowledge-centered and assessment-centered lenses.

An important point that emerges from the expert–novice literature is the need to emphasize *connected* knowledge that is organized around the foundational ideas of a discipline. Research on expertise shows that it is the organization of knowledge that underlies experts' abilities to understand and solve problems.[19] Bruner, one of the founding fathers of the new science of learning, has long argued the importance of this insight to education:[20]

> The curriculum of a subject should be determined by the most fundamental understanding that can be achieved of the underlying principles that give structure to a subject. Teaching specific topics or skills without making clear their context in the broader fundamental structure of a field of knowledge is uneconomical. . . . An understanding of fundamental principles and ideas appears to be the main road to adequate transfer of training. To understand something as a specific instance of a more general case—which is what understanding a more fundamental structure means—is to have learned not only a specific thing but also a model for understanding other things like it that one may encounter.

Knowledge-centered and learner-centered environments intersect when educators take seriously the idea that students must be supported to develop expertise over time; it is not sufficient to simply provide them with expert models and expect them to learn. For example, intentionally organizing subject matter to allow students to follow a path of "progressive differentiation" (e.g., from qualitative understanding to more precise quantitative understanding of a particular phenomenon) involves a simultaneous focus on the structure of the knowledge to be mastered and the learning process of students.[21]

In a comparative study of the teaching of mathematics in China and the United States, Ma sought to understand why Chinese students outperform students from the United States in elementary mathematics, even though teachers in China often have less formal education. What she documents is that Chinese teachers are far more likely to identify core mathematical concepts (such as decomposing a number in subtraction with regrouping), to plan instruction to support mastery of the skills and knowledge required for conceptual understanding, and to use those concepts to develop clear connections across topics (see Box 1-6).

If identifying a set of "enduring connected ideas" is critical to effective educational design, it is a task not just for teachers, but also for the developers of curricula, text books, and other instructional materials; universities and other teacher preparation institutions; and the public and private groups involved in developing subject matter standards for students and their teachers. There is some good work already in place, but much more needs to be done. Indeed, an American Association for the Advancement of Science review of middle school and high school science textbooks found that although a great deal of detailed and sophisticated material was presented, very little attention was given to the concepts that support an understanding of the discipline.[22]

The four mathematics chapters in this volume describe core ideas in teaching about whole number, rational number, and functions that support conceptual understanding and that connect the particular topic to the larger discipline. Because textbooks sometimes focus primarily on methods of problem solving and neglect organizing principles, creating a knowledge-centered classroom will often require that a teacher go beyond the textbook to help students see a structure to the knowledge, mainly by introducing them to essential concepts. These chapters provide examples of how this might be done.

Assessment-Centered Classroom Environments

Formative assessments—ongoing assessments designed to make students' thinking visible to both teachers and students—are essential. Assessments are a central feature of both a learner-centered and a knowledge-centered classroom. They permit the teacher to grasp students' preconceptions, which is critical to working with and building on those notions. Once the knowledge to be learned is well defined, assessment is required to monitor student progress (in mastering concepts as well as factual information), to understand where students are in the developmental path from informal to formal thinking, and to design instruction that is responsive to student progress.

An important feature of the assessment-centered classroom is assessment that supports learning by providing students with opportunities to revise and improve their thinking.[23] Such assessments help students see their own progress over time and point to problems that need to be addressed in instruction. They may be quite informal. A physics teacher, for example, reports showing students who are about to study structure a video clip of a bridge collapsing. He asks his students why they think the bridge collapsed. In giving their answers, the students reveal their preconceptions about structure. Differences in their answers provide puzzles that engage the students in self-questioning. As the students study structure, they can mark their changing understanding against their initial beliefs. Assessment in this sense provides a starting point for additional instruction rather than a summative ending. Formative assessments are often referred to as "classroom-based assessments" because, as compared with standardized assessments, they are most likely to occur in the context of the classrooms. However, many classroom-based assessments are summative rather than formative (they are used to provide grades at the end of a unit with no opportunities to revise). In addition, one can use standardized assessments in a formative manner (e.g., to help teachers identify areas where students need special help).

Ultimately, students need to develop metacognitive abilities—the habits of mind necessary to assess their own progress—rather than relying solely on external indicators. A number of studies show that achievement improves when students are encouraged to assess their own contributions and work.[24] It is also important to help students assess the kinds of strategies they are using to learn and solve problems. For example, in quantitative courses such as physics, many students simply focus on formulas and fail to think first about the problem to be solved and its relation to key ideas in the discipline (e.g., Newton's second law). When students are helped to do the latter, their performance on new problems greatly improves.[25]

The classroom interactions described in the following chapters provide many examples of formative assessment in action, though these interactions are often not referred to as assessments. Early activities or problems given to students are designed to make student thinking public and, therefore, observable by teachers. Work in groups and class discussions provide students with the opportunity to ask each other questions and revise their own thinking. In some cases, the formative assessments are formal, but even when informal the teaching described in the chapters involves frequent opportunities for both teachers and students to assess understanding and its progress over time.

Community-Centered Classroom Environments

A community-centered approach requires the development of norms for the classroom and school, as well as connections to the outside world, that support core learning values. Learning is influenced in fundamental ways by the context in which it takes place. Every community, including classrooms and schools, operates with a set of norms, a culture—explicit or implicit—that influences interactions among individuals. This culture, in turn,

BOX 1-6 Organizing Knowledge Around Core Concepts: Subtraction with Regrouping[26]

A study by Ma[27] compares the knowledge of elementary mathematics of teachers in the United States and in China. She gives the teachers the following scenario (p. 1):

> Look at these questions (52 – 25; 91 – 79 etc.). How would you approach these problems if you were teaching second grade? What would you say pupils would need to understand or be able to do before they could start learning subtraction with regrouping?

The responses of teachers were wide-ranging, reflecting very different levels of understanding of the core mathematical concepts. Some teachers focused on the need for students to learn the *procedure* for subtraction with regrouping (p. 2):

> Whereas there is a number like 21 – 9, they would need to know that you cannot subtract 9 from 1, then in turn you have to borrow a 10 from the tens space, and when you borrow that 1, it equals 10, you cross out the 2 that you had, you turn it into a 10, you now have 11 – 9, you do that subtraction problem then you have the 1 left and you bring it down.

Some teachers in both the United States and China saw the knowledge to be mastered as procedural, though the proportion who held this view was considerably higher in the United States. Many teachers in both countries believed students needed a conceptual understanding, but within this group there were considerable differences. Some teachers wanted children to think through what they were doing, while others wanted them to understand core mathematical concepts. The difference can be seen in the two explanations below.

> They have to understand what the number 64 means. . . . I would show that the number 64, and the number 5 tens and 14 ones, equal the 64. I would try to draw the comparison between that because when you are doing regrouping it is not so much knowing the facts, it is the regrouping part that has to be understood. The regrouping right from the beginning.

This explanation is more conceptual than the first and helps students think more deeply about the subtraction problem. But it does not make clear to students the more fundamental concept of the place value system that allows the subtraction problems to be connected to other areas of mathematics. In the place value system, numbers are "composed" of tens. Students already have been taught to compose tens as 10 ones, and hundreds as 10 tens. A Chinese teacher explains as follows (p. 11):

> What is the rate for composing a higher value unit? The answer is simple: 10. Ask students how many ones there are in a 10, or ask them what the rate for composing a higher value unit is, their answers will be the same: 10. However, the effect of the two questions on their learning is not the

same. When you remind students that 1 ten equals 10 ones, you tell them the fact that is used in the procedure. And, this somehow confines them to the fact. When you require them to think about the rate for composing a higher value unit, you lead them to a theory that explains the fact as well as the procedure. Such an understanding is more powerful than a specific fact. It can be applied to more situations. Once they realize that the rate of composing a higher value unit, 10 is the reason why we decompose a ten into 10 ones, they will apply it to other situations. You don't need to remind them again that 1 hundred equals 10 tens when in the future they learn subtraction with three-digit numbers. They will be able to figure it out on their own.

Emphasizing core concepts does not imply less of an emphasis on mastery of procedures or algorithms. Rather, it suggests that procedural knowledge and skills be *organized around core concepts.* Ma describes those Chinese teachers who emphasize core concepts as seeing the knowledge in "packages" in which the concepts and skills are related. While the packages differed somewhat from teacher to teacher, the knowledge "pieces" to be included were the same. She illustrates a knowledge package for subtraction with regrouping, which is reproduced below (p. 19).

The two shaded elements in the knowledge package are considered critical. "Addition and subtraction within 20" is seen as the ability that anchors more complex problem solving with larger numbers. That ability is viewed as both conceptual and procedural. "Composing and decomposing a higher value unit" is the core concept that ties this set of problems to the mathematics students have done in the past and to all other areas of mathematics they will learn in the future.

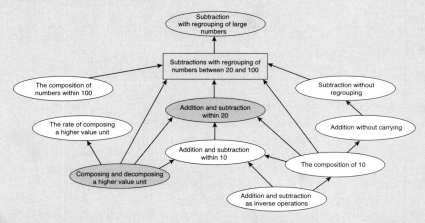

SOURCE: Ma (1999). Illustration reprinted with permission of Lawrence Erlbaum Associates.

mediates learning. The principles of *How People Learn* have important implications for classroom culture. Consider the finding that new learning builds on existing conceptions, for example. If classroom norms encourage and reward students only for being "right," we would expect students to hesitate when asked to reveal their unschooled thinking. And yet revealing preconceptions and changing ideas in the course of instruction is a critical component of effective learning and responsive teaching. A focus on student thinking requires classroom norms that encourage the expression of ideas (tentative and certain, partially and fully formed), as well as risk taking. It requires that mistakes be viewed not as revelations of inadequacy, but as helpful contributions in the search for understanding.[28]

Similarly, effective approaches to teaching metacognitive strategies rely on initial teacher modeling of the monitoring process, with a gradual shift to students. Through asking questions of other students, skills at monitoring understanding are honed, and through answering the questions of fellow students, understanding of what one has communicated effectively is strengthened. To those ends, classroom norms that encourage questioning and allow students to try the role of the questioner (sometimes reserved for teachers) are important.

While the chapters in this volume make few direct references to learning communities, they are filled with descriptions of interactions revealing classroom cultures that support learning with understanding. In these classrooms, students are encouraged to question; there is much discussion among students who work to solve problems in groups. Teachers ask many probing questions, and incorrect or naïve answers to questions are explored with interest, as are different strategies for analyzing a problem and reaching a solution.

PUTTING THE PRINCIPLES TO WORK IN THE CLASSROOM

Although the key findings from the research literature reviewed above have clear implications for practice, they are not at a level of specificity that would allow them to be immediately useful to teachers. While teachers may fully grasp the importance of working with students' prior conceptions, they need to know the typical conceptions of students with respect to the topic about to be taught. For example, it may help mathematics teachers to know that students harbor misconceptions that can be problematic, but those teachers will be in a much better position to teach a unit on rational number if they know specifically what misconceptions students typically exhibit.

Moreover, while teachers may be fully convinced that knowledge should be organized around important concepts, the concepts that help organize their particular topic may not be at all clear. History teachers may know that they are to teach certain eras, for example, but they often have little support in identifying core concepts that will allow students to understand the era more deeply than would be required to reproduce a set of facts. To make this observation is in no way to fault teachers. Indeed, as the group involved in this project engaged in the discussion, drafting, and review of various chapters of this volume, it became clear that the relevant core concepts in specific areas are not always obvious, transparent, or uncontested.

Finally, approaches to supporting metacognition can be quite difficult to carry out in classroom contexts. Some approaches to instruction reduce metacognition to its simplest form, such as making note of the subtitles in a text and what they signal about what is to come, or rereading for meaning. The more challenging tasks of metacognition are difficult to reduce to an instructional recipe: to help students develop the habits of mind to reflect spontaneously on their own thinking and problem solving, to encourage them to activate relevant background knowledge and monitor their under-standing, and to support them in trying the lens through which those in a particular discipline view the world. The teacher–student interactions de-scribed in the chapters of this volume and the discipline-specific examples of supporting students in monitoring their thinking give texture to the in-structional challenge that a list of metacognitive strategies could not.

INTENT AND ORGANIZATION OF THIS VOLUME

In the preface, we note that this volume is intended to take the work of *How People Learn* a next step in specificity: to provide examples of how its principles and findings might be incorporated in the teaching of a set of topics that frequently appear in the K–12 curriculum. The goal is to provide for teachers what we have argued above is critical to effective learning—the application of concepts (about learning) in enough different, concrete con-texts to give them deeper meaning.

To this end, we invited contributions from researchers with extensive experience in teaching or partnering with teachers, whose work incorpo-rates the ideas highlighted in *How People Learn*. The chapter authors were given leeway in the extent to which the three learning principles and the four classroom characteristics described above were treated explicitly or implicitly. Most of the authors chose to emphasize the three learning prin-ciples explicitly as they described their lessons and findings. The four design characteristics of the *How People Learn* framework (Figure 1-2) are implicitly represented in the activities sketched in each of the chapters but often not discussed explicitly. Interested readers can map these discussions to the *How People Learn* framework if they desire.

While we began with a common description of our goal, we had no common model from which to work. One can point to excellent research papers on principles of learning, but the chapters in this volume are far more focused on teaching a particular topic. There are also examples of excellent curricula, but the goal of these chapters is to give far more attention to the principles of learning and their incorporation into teaching than is typical of curriculum materials. Thus the authors were charting new territory as they undertook this task, and each found a somewhat different path.

This volume includes four mathematics chapters. Chapter 2 presents an introduction to the principles as they apply to mathematics. It focuses on the changes in expectations for mathematics performance as we move into the twenty-first century and what those changes mean for instruction—particularly at the elementary level. This chapter, then, is part introduction and part elementary mathematics. The three chapters that follow treat important topics at the three different grade levels: whole number in elementary school (Chapter 3), rational number in middle school (Chapter 4), and functions in high school (Chapter 5).

The major focus of the volume is student learning. It is clear that successful and sustainable changes in educational practice also require learning by others, including teachers, principals, superintendents, parents, and community members. For the present volume, however, student learning is the focus, and issues of adult learning are left for others to take up.

The willingness of the chapter authors to accept this task represents an outstanding contribution to the field. First, all the authors devoted considerable time to this effort—more than any of them had anticipated initially. Second, they did so knowing that some readers will disagree with virtually every teaching decision discussed in these chapters. But by making their thinking visible and inviting discussion, they are helping the field progress as a whole. The examples discussed in this volume are not offered as "the" way to teach, but as approaches to instruction that in some important respects are designed to incorporate the principles of learning highlighted in *How People Learn* and that can serve as valuable examples for further discussion.

In 1960, Nobel laureate Richard Feynman, who was well known as an extraordinary teacher, delivered a series of lectures in introductory physics that were recorded and preserved. Feynman's focus was on the fundamental principles of physics, not the fundamental principles of learning. But his lessons apply nonetheless. He emphasized how little the fundamental principles of physics "as we now understand them" tell us about the complexity of the world despite the enormous importance of the insights they offer. Feynman offered an effective analogy for the relationship between understanding general principles identified through scientific efforts and understanding the far more complex set of behaviors for which those principles provide only a broad set of constraints:[29]

We can imagine that this complicated array of moving things which constitutes "the world" is something like a great chess game being played by the gods, and we are observers of the game. We do not know what the rules of the game are; all we are allowed to do is to *watch* the playing. Of course, if we watch long enough, we may eventually catch on to a few of the rules. *The rules of the game* are what we mean by *fundamental physics*. Even if we knew every rule, however, we might not be able to understand why a particular move is made in the game, merely because it is too complicated and our minds are limited. If you play chess you must know that it is easy to learn all the rules, and yet it is often very hard to select the best move or to understand why a player moves as he does. . . . Aside from not knowing all of the rules, what we really can explain in terms of those rules is very limited, because almost all situations are so enormously complicated that we cannot follow the plays of the game using the rules, much less tell what is going to happen next. (p. 24)

The individual chapters in this volume might be viewed as presentations of the strategies taken by individuals (or teams) who understand the rules of the teaching and learning "game" *as we now understand them.* Feynman's metaphor is helpful in two respects. First, what each chapter offers goes well beyond the science of learning and relies on creativity in strategy development. And yet what we know from research thus far is critical in defining the constraints on strategy development. Second, what we expect to learn from a well-played game (in this case, what we expect to learn from well-conceptualized instruction) is not how to reproduce it. Rather, we look for insights about playing/teaching well that can be brought to one's own game. Even if we could replicate every move, this would be of little help. In an actual game, the best move must be identified in response to another party's move. In just such a fashion, a teacher's "game" must respond to the rather unpredictable "moves" of the students in the classroom whose learning is the target.

This, then, is not a "how to" book, but a discussion of strategies that incorporate the rules of the game as we currently understand them. The science of learning is a young, emerging one. We expect our understanding to evolve as we design new learning opportunities and observe the outcomes, as we study learning among children in different contexts and from different backgrounds, and as emerging research techniques and opportunities provide new insights. These chapters, then, might best be viewed as part of a conversation begun some years ago with the first *How People Learn* volume. By clarifying ideas through a set of rich examples, we hope to encourage the continuation of a productive dialogue well into the future.

NOTES

1. National Research Council, 2000.
2. Lionni, 1970.
3. National Research Council, 2000, p. 84.
4. Needham and Baillargeon, 1993.
5. diSessa, 1982.
6. Vosniadou and Brewer, 1989.
7. Carey and Gelman, 1991; Driver et al., 1994.
8. Hanson, 1970.
9. Judd, 1908; see a conceptual replication by Hendrickson and Schroeder, 1941.
10. White and Fredrickson, 1998.
11. Bransford and Schwartz, 1999.
12. Brown, 1975; Flavell, 1973.
13. Keeney et al., 1967.
14. Palincsar and Brown, 1984.
15. Aleven and Koedinger, 2002.
16. Thorndike, 1913.
17. Brown et al., 1983.
18. Wood and Sellers, 1997.
19. National Research Council, 2000, Chapter 2.
20. Bruner, 1960, pp. 6, 25, 31.
21. National Research Council, 2000.
22. American Association for the Advancement of Science Project 2061 Website. http://www.project2061.org/curriculum.html.
23. Barron et al., 1998; Black and William, 1989; Hunt and Minstrell, 1994; Vye et al., 1998.
24. Lin and Lehman, 1999; National Research Council, 2000; White and Fredrickson, 1998.
25. Leonard et al., 1996.
26. National Research Council, 2003, pp. 78-79.
27. Ma, 1999.
28. Brown and Campione, 1994; Cobb et al., 1992.
29. Feynman, 1995, p. 24.

REFERENCES

Aleven, V., and Koedinger, K. (2002). An effective metacognitive strategy—Learning by doing and explaining with a computer-based cognitive tutor. *Cognitive Science, 26*, 147-179.

American Association for the Advancement of Science. (2004). About *Project 2061.* Available: http://www.project2061.org/about/default/htm. [August 11, 2004].

Barron, B.J., Schwartz, D.L., Vye, N.J., Moore, A., Petrosino, A., Zech, L., Bransford, J.D., and Cognition and Technology Group at Vanderbilt. (1998). Doing with understanding: Lessons from research on problem and project-based learning. *Journal of Learning Sciences, 7*(3 and 4), 271-312.

Black, P., and William, D. (1989). Assessment and classroom learning. *Special Issue of Assessment in Education: Principles, Policy and Practice, 5*(1), 7-75.

Bransford, J.D., and Schwartz, D.L. (1999). Rethinking transfer: A simple proposal with multiple implications. *Review of Research in Education, 24*(40), 61-100.

Brown, A.L. (1975). The development of memory: Knowing about knowing and knowing how to know. In H.W. Reese (Ed.), *Advances in child development and behavior* (p. 10). New York: Academic Press.

Brown, A.L., and Campione, J.C. (1994). Guided discovery in a community of learners. In K. McGilly (Ed.), *Classroom lessons: Integrating cognitive theory and classroom practices*. Cambridge, MA: MIT Press.

Brown, A.L., Bransford, J.D., Ferrara, R.A., and Campione J.C. (1983). Learning, remembering, and understanding. In J.H. Flavell and E.M Markman (Eds.), *Handbook of child psychology: Cognitive development volume 3* (pp. 78-166). New York: Wiley.

Bruner, J. (1960). *The process of education*. Cambridge, MA: Harvard University Press.

Carey, S., and Gelman, R. (1991). *The epigenesis of mind: Essays on biology and cognition*. Mahwah, NJ: Lawrence Erlbaum Associates.

Chase, W.G., and Simon, H.A. (1973). Perception in chess. *Cognitive Psychology, 4*(1), 55-81.

Cobb P., Yackel, E., and Wood, T. (1992). A constructivist alternative to the representational view of mind in mathematics education. *Journal for Research in Mathematics Education, 19*, 99-114.

Cognition and Technology Group at Vanderbilt. (1996). Looking at technology in context: A framework for understanding technology and education research. In D.C. Berliner and R.C. Calfee (Eds.), *The handbook of educational psychology* (pp. 807-840). New York: Simon and Schuster-MacMillan.

diSessa, A. (1982). Unlearning Aristotelian physics: A study of knowledge-based learning. *Cognitive Science, 6*(2), 37-75.

Driver, R., Squires, A., Rushworth, P., and Wood-Robinson, V. (1994). *Making sense out of secondary science*. London, England: Routledge Press.

Feynman, R.P. (1995). *Six easy pieces: Essentials of physics explained by its most brilliant teacher*. Reading, MA: Perseus Books.

Flavell, J.H. (1973). Metacognitive aspects of problem-solving. In L.B. Resnick (Ed.), *The nature of intelligence*. Mahwah, NJ: Lawrence Erlbaum Associates.

Hanson, N.R. (1970). A picture theory of theory meaning. In R.G. Colodny (Ed.), *The nature and function of scientific theories* (pp. 233-274). Pittsburgh, PA: University of Pittsburgh Press.

Hendrickson, G., and Schroeder, W.H. (1941). Transfer training in learning to hit a submerged target. *Journal of Educational Psychology, 32*, 205-213.

Hunt, E., and Minstrell, J. (1994). A cognitive approach to the teaching of physics. In K. McGilly (Ed.), *Classroom lessons: Integrating cognitive theory and classroom practice* (pp. 51-74). Cambridge, MA: MIT Press.

Judd, C.H. (1908). The relation of special training to general intelligence. *Educational Review, 36*, 28-42.

Keeney, T.J., Cannizzo, S.R., and Flavell, J.H. (1967). Spontaneous and induced verbal rehearsal in a recall task. *Child Development, 38*, 953-966.

Leonard, W.J., Dufresne, R.J., and Mestre, J.P. (1996). Using qualitative problem solving strategies to highlight the role of conceptual knowledge in solving problems. *American Journal of Physics, 64*, 1495-1503.

Lin, X.D., and Lehman, J. (1999). Supporting learning of variable control in a computer-based biology environment: Effects of prompting college students to reflect on their own thinking. *Journal of Research in Science Teaching, 36*(7), 837-858.

Lionni, L. (1970). *Fish is fish.* New York: Scholastic Press.

Ma, L. (1999). *Knowing and teaching elementary mathematics.* Mahwah, NJ: Lawrence Erlbaum Associates.

National Research Council. (1999). *How people learn: Brain, mind, experience, and school.* Committee on Developments in the Science of Learning. J. D. Bransford, A.L. Brown, and R.R. Cocking (Eds.). Commission on Behavioral and Social Sciences and Education. Washington, DC: National Academy Press.

National Research Council. (2000). *How people learn: Brain, mind, experience, and school, Expanded edition.* Committee on Developments in the Science of Learning and Committee on Learning Research and Educational Practice. J.D. Bransford, A. Brown, and R.R. Cocking (Eds.). Commission on Behavioral and Social Sciences and Education. Washington, DC: National Academy Press.

National Research Council. (2003). *Learning and instruction: A SERP research agenda.* Panel on Learning and Instruction, Strategic Education Research Partnership. M.S. Donovan and J.W. Pellegrino (Eds.). Division of Behavioral and Social Sciences and Education. Washington, DC: The National Academies Press.

Needham, A., and Baillargeon, R. (1993). Intuitions about support in 4 1/2 month-old-infants. *Cognition, 47*(2), 121-148.

Palincsar, A.S., and Brown, A.L. (1984). Reciprocal teaching of comprehension monitoring activities. *Cognition and Instruction, 1*, 117-175.

Thorndike, E.L. (1913). *Educational psychology* (Vols. 1 and 2). New York: Columbia University Press.

Vosniadou, S., and Brewer, W.F. (1989). *The concept of the Earth's shape: A study of conceptual change in childhood.* Unpublished manuscript. Champaign, IL: Center for the Study of Reading, University of Illinois.

Vye, N.J., Schwartz, D.L., Bransford, J.D., Barron, B.J., Zech, L., and Cognitive and Technology Group at Vanderbilt. (1998). SMART environments that support monitoring, reflection, and revision. In D. Hacker, J. Dunlosky, and A. Graessner (Eds.), *Metacognition in educational theory and practice.* Mahwah, NJ: Lawrence Erlbaum Associates.

Whimbey, A., and Whimbey, L.S. (1975). *Intelligence can be taught.* New York: Dutton.

White, B.Y., and Fredrickson, J.R. (1998). Inquiry, modeling, and metacognition: Making science accessible to all students. *Cognition and Instruction, 16*(1), 3-118.

Wood, T., and Sellers, P. (1997). Deepening the analysis: Longitudinal assessment of a problem-centered mathematics program. *Journal for Research in Mathematics Education, 28*, 163-186.

Part II

MATHEMATICS

Pages 27-214 are not printed in this volume.
They are on the CD attached to the back cover.

5

Mathematical Understanding:
An Introduction

Karen C. Fuson, Mindy Kalchman, and John D. Bransford

For many people, free association with the word "mathematics" would produce strong, negative images. Gary Larson published a cartoon entitled "Hell's Library" that consisted of nothing but book after book of math word problems. Many students—and teachers—resonate strongly with this cartoon's message. It is not just funny to them; it is true.

Why are associations with mathematics so negative for so many people? If we look through the lens of *How People Learn,* we see a subject that is rarely taught in a way that makes use of the three principles that are the focus of this volume. Instead of connecting with, building on, and refining the mathematical understandings, intuitions, and resourcefulness that students bring to the classroom (Principle 1), mathematics instruction often overrides students' reasoning processes, replacing them with a set of rules and procedures that disconnects problem solving from meaning making. Instead of organizing the skills and competences required to do mathematics fluently around a set of core mathematical concepts (Principle 2), those skills and competencies are often themselves the center, and sometimes the whole, of instruction. And precisely because the acquisition of procedural knowledge is often divorced from meaning making, students do not use metacognitive strategies (Principle 3) when they engage in solving mathematics problems. Box 5-1 provides a vignette involving a student who gives an answer to a problem that is quite obviously impossible. When quizzed, he can see that his answer does not make sense, but he does not consider it wrong because he believes he followed the rule. Not only did he neglect to use metacognitive strategies to monitor whether his answer made sense, but he believes that sense making is irrelevant.

BOX 5-1 Computation Without Comprehension: An Observation by John Holt

One boy, quite a good student, was working on the problem, "If you have 6 jugs, and you want to put 2/3 of a pint of lemonade into each jug, how much lemonade will you need?" His answer was 18 pints. I said, "How much in each jug?" "Two-thirds of a pint." I said, "Is that more or less that a pint?" "Less." I said, "How many jugs are there?" "Six." I said, "But that [the answer of 18 pints] doesn't make any sense." He shrugged his shoulders and said, "Well, that's the way the system worked out." Holt argues: "He has long since quit expecting school to make sense. They tell you these facts and rules, and your job is to put them down on paper the way they tell you. Never mind whether they mean anything or not."[1]

A recent report of the National Research Council,[2] *Adding It Up*, reviews a broad research base on the teaching and learning of elementary school mathematics. The report argues for an instructional goal of "mathematical proficiency," a much broader outcome than mastery of procedures. The report argues that five intertwining strands constitute mathematical proficiency:

1. *Conceptual understanding*—comprehension of mathematical concepts, operations, and relations
2. *Procedural fluency*—skill in carrying out procedures flexibly, accurately, efficiently, and appropriately
3. *Strategic competence*—ability to formulate, represent, and solve mathematical problems
4. *Adaptive reasoning*—capacity for logical thought, reflection, explanation, and justification
5. *Productive disposition*—habitual inclination to see mathematics as sensible, useful, and worthwhile, coupled with a belief in diligence and one's own efficacy

These strands map directly to the principles of *How People Learn*. Principle 2 argues for a foundation of factual knowledge (procedural fluency), tied to a conceptual framework (conceptual understanding), and organized in a way to facilitate retrieval and problem solving (strategic competence). Metacognition and adaptive reasoning both describe the phenomenon of ongoing sense making, reflection, and explanation to oneself and others. And, as we argue below, the preconceptions students bring to the study of mathematics affect more than their understanding and problem solving; those preconceptions also play a major role in whether students have a productive disposition toward mathematics, as do, of course, their experiences in learning mathematics.

The chapters that follow on whole number, rational number, and functions look at the principles of *How People Learn* as they apply to those specific domains. In this introduction, we explore how those principles apply to the subject of mathematics more generally. We draw on examples from the Children's Math World project, a decade-long research project in urban and suburban English-speaking and Spanish-speaking classrooms.[3]

PRINCIPLE #1: TEACHERS MUST ENGAGE STUDENTS' PRECONCEPTIONS

At a very early age, children begin to demonstrate an awareness of number.[4] As with language, that awareness appears to be universal in normally developing children, though the rate of development varies at least in part because of environmental influences.[5]

But it is not only the awareness of quantity that develops without formal training. Both children and adults engage in mathematical problem solving, developing untrained strategies to do so successfully when formal experiences are not provided. For example, it was found that Brazilian street children could perform mathematics when making sales in the street, but were unable to answer similar problems presented in a school context.[6] Likewise, a study of housewives in California uncovered an ability to solve mathematical problems when comparison shopping, even though the women could not solve problems presented abstractly in a classroom that required the same mathematics.[7] A similar result was found in a study of a group of Weight Watchers, who used strategies for solving mathematical measurement problems related to dieting that they could not solve when the problems were presented more abstractly.[8] And men who successfully handicapped horse races could not apply the same skill to securities in the stock market.[9]

These examples suggest that people possess resources in the form of informal strategy development and mathematical reasoning that can serve as a foundation for learning more abstract mathematics. But they also suggest that the link is not automatic. If there is no bridge between informal and formal mathematics, the two often remain disconnected.

The first principle of *How People Learn* emphasizes both the need to build on existing knowledge and the need to engage students' preconceptions—particularly when they interfere with learning. In mathematics, certain preconceptions that are often fostered early on in school settings are in fact counterproductive. Students who believe them can easily conclude that the study of mathematics is "not for them" and should be avoided if at all possible. We discuss these preconceptions below.

Some Common Preconceptions About Mathematics

Preconception #1: Mathematics is about learning to compute.

Many of us who attended school in the United States had mathematics instruction that focused primarily on computation, with little attention to learning with understanding. To illustrate, try to answer the following question:

What, approximately, is the sum of 8/9 plus 12/13?

Many people immediately try to find the lowest common denominator for the two sets of fractions and then add them because that is the procedure they learned in school. Finding the lowest common denominator is not easy in this instance, and the problem seems difficult. A few people take a conceptual rather than a procedural (computational) approach and realize that 8/9 is almost 1, and so is 12/13, so the approximate answer is a little less than 2.

The point of this example is not that computation should not be taught or is unimportant; indeed, it is very often critical to efficient problem solving. But if one believes that mathematics is about problem solving and that computation is a tool for use to that end when it is helpful, then the above problem is viewed not as a "request for a computation," but as a problem to be solved that may or may not require computation—and in this case, it does not.

If one needs to find the exact answer to the above problem, computation is the way to go. But even in this case, conceptual understanding of the nature of the problem remains central, providing a way to estimate the correctness of a computation. If an answer is computed that is more than 2 or less than 1, it is obvious that some aspect of problem solving has gone awry. If one believes that mathematics is about computation, however, then sense making may never take place.

Preconception #2: Mathematics is about "following rules" to guarantee correct answers.

Related to the conception of mathematics as computation is that of mathematics as a cut-and-dried discipline that specifies rules for finding the right answers. Rule following is more general than performing specific computations. When students learn procedures for keeping track of and canceling units, for example, or learn algebraic procedures for solving equations, many view use of these procedures only as following the rules. But the "rules" should not be confused with the game itself.

The authors of the chapters in this part of the book provide important suggestions about the much broader nature of mathematical proficiency and about ways to make the involving nature of mathematical inquiry visible to students. Groups such as the National Council of Teachers of Mathematics[10] and the National Research Council[11] have provided important guidelines for the kinds of mathematics instruction that accord with what is currently known about the principles of *How People Learn*. The authors of the following chapters have paid careful attention to this work and illustrate some of its important aspects.

In reality, mathematics is a constantly evolving field that is far from cut and dried. It involves systematic pattern finding and continuing invention. As a simple example, consider the selection of units that are relevant to quantify an idea such as the fuel efficiency of a vehicle. If we choose miles per gallon, a two-seater sports car will be more efficient than a large bus. If we choose passenger miles per gallon, the bus will be more fuel efficient (assuming it carries large numbers of passengers). Many disciplines make progress by inventing new units and metrics that provide insights into previously invisible relationships.

Attention to the history of mathematics illustrates that what is taught at one point in time as a set of procedures really was a set of clever inventions designed to solve pervasive problems of everyday life. In Europe in the Middle Ages, for example, people used calculating cloths marked with vertical columns and carried out procedures with counters to perform calculations. Other cultures fastened their counters on a rod to make an abacus. Both of these physical means were at least partially replaced by written methods of calculating with numerals and more recently by methods that involve pushing buttons on a calculator. If mathematics procedures are understood as inventions designed to make common problems more easily solvable, and to facilitate communications involving quantity, those procedures take on a new meaning. Different procedures can be compared for their advantages and disadvantages. Such discussions in the classroom can deepen students' understanding and skill.

Preconception #3: Some people have the ability to "do math" and some don't.

This is a serious preconception that is widespread in the United States, but not necessarily in other countries. It can easily become a self-fulfilling prophesy. In many countries, the ability to "do math" is assumed to be attributable to the amount of effort people put into learning it.[12] Of course, some people in these countries do progress further than others, and some appear to have an easier time learning mathematics than others. But effort is still considered to be the key variable in success. In contrast, in the United States we are more likely to assume that ability is much more important than effort, and it is socially acceptable, and often even desirable, not to put forth effort in learning mathematics. This difference is also related to cultural differences in the value attributed to struggle. Teachers in some countries believe it is desirable for students to struggle for a while with problems, whereas teachers in the United States simplify things so that students need not struggle at all.[13]

This preconception likely shares a common root with the others. If mathematics learning is not grounded in an understanding of the nature of the problem to be solved and does not build on a student's own reasoning and strategy development, then solving problems successfully will depend on the ability to recall memorized rules. If a student has not reviewed those rules recently (as is the case when a summer has passed), they can easily be forgotten. Without a conceptual understanding of the nature of problems and strategies for solving them, failure to retrieve learned procedures can leave a student completely at a loss.

Yet students can feel lost not only when they have forgotten, but also when they fail to "get it" from the start. Many of the conventions of mathematics have been adopted for the convenience of communicating efficiently in a shared language. If students learn to memorize procedures but do not understand that the procedures are full of such conventions adopted for efficiency, they can be baffled by things that are left unexplained. If students never understand that x and y have no intrinsic meaning, but are conventional notations for labeling unknowns, they will be baffled when a z appears. When an m precedes an x in the equation of a line, students may wonder, Why m? Why not s for slope? If there is no m, then is there no slope? To someone with a secure mathematics understanding, the missing m is simply an unstated $m = 1$. But to a student who does not understand that the point is to write the equation efficiently, the missing m can be baffling. Unlike language learning, in which new expressions can often be figured out because they are couched in meaningful contexts, there are few clues to help a student who is lost in mathematics. Providing a secure conceptual understanding of the mathematics enterprise that is linked to students' sense-making capacities is critical so that students can puzzle productively over new material, identify the source of their confusion, and ask questions when they do not understand.

Engaging Students' Preconceptions and Building on Existing Knowledge

Engaging and building on student preconceptions, then, poses two instructional challenges. First, how can we teach mathematics so students come to appreciate that it is not about computation and following rules, but about solving important and relevant quantitative problems? This perspective includes an understanding that the rules for computation and solution are a set of clever human inventions that in many cases allow us to solve complex problems more easily, and to communicate about those problems with each other effectively and efficiently. Second, how can we link formal mathematics training with students' informal knowledge and problem-solving capacities?

Many recent research and curriculum development efforts, including those of the authors of the chapters that follow, have addressed these questions. While there is surely no single best instructional approach, it is possible to identify certain features of instruction that support the above goals:

- Allowing students to use their own informal problem-solving strategies, at least initially, and then guiding their mathematical thinking toward more effective strategies and advanced understandings.
- Encouraging math talk so that students can clarify their strategies to themselves and others, and compare the benefits and limitations of alternate approaches.
- Designing instructional activities that can effectively bridge commonly held conceptions and targeted mathematical understandings.

Allowing Multiple Strategies

To illustrate how instruction can be connected to students' existing knowledge, consider three subtraction methods encountered frequently in urban second-grade classrooms involved in the Children's Math Worlds Project (see Box 5-2). Maria, Peter, and Manuel's teacher has invited them to share their methods for solving a problem, and each of them has displayed a different method. Two of the methods are correct, and one is mostly correct but has one error. What the teacher does depends on her conception of what mathematics is.

One approach is to show the students the "right" way to subtract and have them and everyone else practice that procedure. A very different approach is to help students explore their methods and see what is easy and difficult about each. If students are taught that for each kind of math situation or problem, there is one correct method that needs to be taught and learned, the seeds of the disconnection between their reasoning and strategy development and "doing math" are sown. An answer is either wrong or

BOX 5-2 Three Subtraction Methods

Maria's add-equal-quantities method	Peter's ungrouping method	Manuel's mixed method
$1\ 2\ ^1 4$ $-\ ^1 5\ \ 6$ ——— $6\ \ 8$	$+\ \overset{11}{2}\ \overset{14}{4}$ $-\ 5\ \ 6$ ——— $6\ \ 8$	$+\ \overset{11}{2}\ \ \overset{14}{4}$ $-\ ^1 5\ \ \ 6$ ——— $5\ \ \ 8$

right, and one does not need to look at wrong answers more deeply—one needs to look at how to get the right answer. The problem is not that students will fail to solve the problem accurately with this instructional approach; indeed, they may solve it more accurately. But when the nature of the problem changes slightly, or students have not used the taught approach for a while, they may feel completely lost when confronting a novel problem because the approach of developing strategies to grapple with a problem situation has been short-circuited.

If, on the other hand, students believe that for each kind of math situation or problem there can be several correct methods, their engagement in strategy development is kept alive. This does not mean that all strategies are equally good. But students can learn to evaluate different strategies for their advantages and disadvantages. What is more, a wrong answer is usually partially correct and reflects some understanding; finding the part that is wrong and understanding why it is wrong can be a powerful aid to understanding and promotes metacognitive competencies. A vignette of students engaged in the kind of mathematical reasoning that supports active strategy development and evaluation appears in Box 5-3.

It can be initially unsettling for a teacher to open up the classroom to calculation methods that are new to the teacher. But a teacher does not have to understand a new method immediately or alone, as indicated in the description in the vignette of how the class together figured out over time how Maria's method worked (this method is commonly taught in Latin America and Europe). Understanding a new method can be a worthwhile mathematical project for the class, and others can be involved in trying to figure out why a method works. This illustrates one way in which a classroom community can function. If one relates a calculation method to the quantities involved, one can usually puzzle out what the method is and why it works. This also demonstrates that not all mathematical issues are solved or understood immediately; sometimes sustained work is necessary.

BOX 5-3 Engaging Students' Problem-Solving Strategies

The following example of a classroom discussion shows how second-grade students can explain their methods rather than simply performing steps in a memorized procedure. It also shows how to make student thinking visible. After several months of teaching and learning, the students reached the point illustrated below. The students' methods are shown in Box 5-2.

Teacher	Maria, can you please explain to your friends in the class how you solved the problem?
Maria	Six is bigger than 4, so I can't subtract here [pointing] in the ones.
	So I have to get more ones. But I have to be fair when I get more ones, so I add ten to both my numbers. I add a ten here in the top of the ones place [pointing] to change the 4 to a 14, and I add a ten here in the bottom in the tens place, so I write another ten by my 5.
	So now I count up from 6 to 14, and I get 8 ones [demonstrating by counting "6, 7, 8, 9, 10, 11, 12, 13, 14" while raising a finger for each word from 7 to 14]. And I know my doubles, so 6 plus 6 is 12, so I have 6 tens left. [She thought, "1 + 5 = 6 tens and 6 + ? = 12 tens. Oh, I know 6 + 6 = 12, so my answer is 6 tens."]
Jorge	I don't see the other 6 in your tens. I only see one 6 in your answer.
Maria	The other 6 is from adding my 1 ten to the 5 tens to get 6 tens. I didn't write it down.
Andy	But you're changing the problem. How do you get the right answer?
Maria	If I make both numbers bigger by the same amount, the difference will stay the same. Remember we looked at that on drawings last week and on the meter stick.
Michelle	Why did you count up?
Maria	Counting down is too hard, and my mother taught me to count up to subtract in first grade.

BOX 5-3 **Continued**

Teacher	How many of you remember how confused we were when we first saw Maria's method last week? Some of us could not figure out what she was doing even though Elena and Juan and Elba did it the same way. What did we do?
Rafael	We made drawings with our ten-sticks and dots to see what those numbers meant. And we figured out they were both tens. Even though the 5 looked like a 15, it was really just 6. And we went home to see if any of our parents could explain it to us, but we had to figure it out ourselves and it took us 2 days.
Teacher	Yes, I was asking other teachers, too. We worked on other methods too, but we kept trying to understand what this method was and why it worked. And Elena and Juan decided it was clearer if they crossed out the 5 and wrote a 6, but Elba and Maria liked to do it the way they learned at home. Any other questions or comments for Maria? No? Ok, Peter, can you explain your method?
Peter	Yes, I like to ungroup my top number when I don't have enough to subtract everywhere. So here I ungrouped 1 ten and gave it to the 4 ones to make 14 ones, so I had 1 ten left here. So 6 up to 10 is 4 and 4 more up to 14 is 8, so 14 minus 6 is 8 ones. And 5 tens up to 11 tens is 6 tens. So my answer is 68.
Carmen	How did you know it was 11 tens?
Peter	Because it is 1 hundred and 1 ten and that is 11 tens.
Carmen	I don't get it.
Peter	Because 1 hundred is 10 tens.
Carmen	Oh, so why didn't you cross out the 1 hundred and put it with the tens to make 11 tens like Manuel?
Peter	I don't need to. I just know it is 11 tens by looking at it.
Teacher	Manuel, don't erase your problem. I know you think it is probably wrong because you got a different answer, but remember how making a mistake helps everyone learn—because other

	students make that same mistake and you helped us talk about it. Do you want to draw a picture and think about your method while we do the next problem, or do you want someone to help you?
Manuel	Can Rafael help me?
Teacher	Yes, but what kind of helping should Rafael do?
Manuel	He should just help me with what I need help on and not do it for me.
Teacher	Ok, Rafael, go up and help Manuel that way while we go on to the next problem. I think it would help you to draw quick-tens and ones to see what your numbers mean. [These drawings are explained later.] But leave your first solution so we can all see where the problem is. That helps us all get good at debugging— finding our mistakes. Do we all make mistakes?
Class	Yes.
Teacher	Can we all get help from each other?
Class	Yes.
Teacher	So mistakes are just a part of learning. We learn from our mistakes. Manuel is going to be brave and share his mistake with us so we can all learn from it.

Manuel's method combined Maria's add-equal-quantities method, which he had learned at home, and Peter's ungrouping method, which he had learned at school. It increases the ones once and decreases the tens twice by subtracting a ten from the top number and adding a ten to the bottom subtracted number. In the Children's Math Worlds Project, we rarely found children forming such a meaningless combination of methods if they understood tens and ones and had a method of drawing them so they could think about the quantities in a problem (a point discussed more later). Students who transferred into our classes did sometimes initially use Manuel's mixed approach. But students were eventually helped to understand both the strengths and weaknesses of their existing methods and to find ways of improving their approaches.

SOURCE: Karen Fuson, Children's Math Worlds Project.

Encouraging Math Talk

One important way to make students' thinking visible is through math talk—talking about mathematical thinking. This technique may appear obvious, but it is quite different from simply giving lectures or assigning textbook readings and then having students work in isolation on problem sets or homework problems. Instead, students and teachers actively discuss how they approached various problems and why. Such communication about mathematical thinking can help everyone in the classroom understand a given concept or method because it elucidates contrasting approaches, some of which are wrong—but often for interesting reasons. Furthermore, communicating about one's thinking is an important goal in itself that also facilitates other sorts of learning. In the lower grades, for example, such math talk can provide initial experiences with mathematical justification that culminate in later grades with more formal kinds of mathematical proof.

An emphasis on math talk is also important for helping teachers become more learner focused and make stronger connections with each of their students. When teachers adopt the role of learners who try to understand their students' methods (rather than just marking the students' procedures and answers as correct or incorrect), they frequently discover thinking that can provide a springboard for further instruction, enabling them to extend thinking more deeply or understand and correct errors. Note that, when beginning to make student thinking visible, teachers must focus on the community-centered aspects of their instruction. Students need to feel comfortable expressing their ideas and revising their thinking when feedback suggests the need to do so.

Math talk allows teachers to draw out and work with the preconceptions students bring with them to the classroom and then helps students learn how to do this sort of work for themselves and for others. We have found that it is also helpful for students to make math drawings of their thinking to help themselves in problem solving and to make their thinking more visible (see Figure 5-1). Such drawings also support the classroom math talk because they are a common visual referent for all participants. Students need an effective bridge between their developing understandings and formal mathematics. Teachers need to use carefully designed visual, linguistic, and situational conceptual supports to help students connect their experiences to formal mathematical words, notations, and methods.

The idea of conceptual support for math talk can be further clarified by considering the language students used in the vignette in Box 5-3 when they explained their different multidigit methods. For these explanations to become meaningful in the classroom, it was crucially important that the students explain their multidigit adding or subtracting methods using the meaningful words in the middle pedagogical triangle of Figure 5-2 (e.g., "three

Drawings for Jackie's and
Juan's Addition Methods

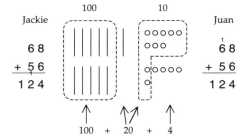

Drawing for "Show All Totals" Method

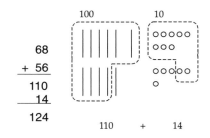

Peter's Ungrouping Method

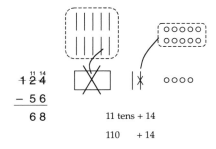

Maria's Add-Equal-Quantities Method

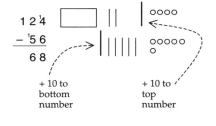

FIGURE 5-1

tens six ones"), as well as the usual math words (e.g., "thirty-six"). It is through such extended connected explanations and use of the quantity words "tens" and "ones" that the students in the Children's Math Worlds Project came to explain their methods. Their explanations did not begin that way, and the students did not spontaneously use the meaningful language when describing their methods. The teacher needed to model the language and help students use it in their descriptions. More-advanced students also helped less-advanced students learn by modeling, asking questions, and helping others form more complete descriptions.

Initially in the Children's Math Worlds Project, all students made conceptual support drawings such as those in Figure 5-1. They explicitly linked these drawings to their written methods during explanations. Such drawings linked to the numerical methods facilitated understanding, accuracy, communication, and helping. Students stopped making drawings when they were no longer needed (this varied across students by months). Eventually, most students applied numerical methods without drawings, but these numerical

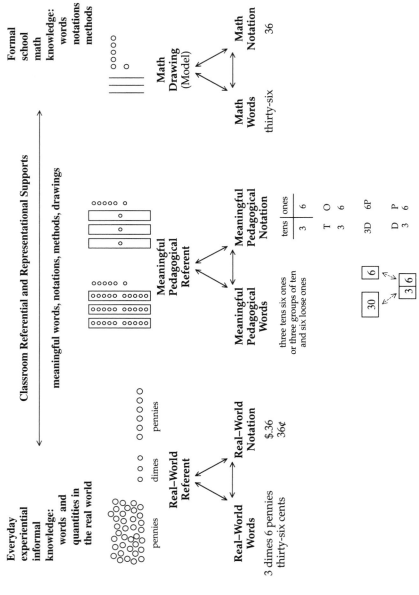

FIGURE 5-2

methods then carried for the members of the classroom the meanings from the conceptual support drawings. If errors crept in, students were asked to think about (or make) a drawing and most errors were then self-corrected.

Designing Bridging Instructional Activities

The first two features of instruction discussed above provide opportunities for students to use their own strategies and to make their thinking visible so it can be built on, revised, and made more formal. This third strategy is more proactive. Research has uncovered common student preconceptions and points of difficulty with learning new mathematical concepts that can be addressed preemptively with carefully designed instructional activities.

This kind of bridging activity is used in the Children's Math Worlds curriculum to help students relate their everyday, experiential, informal understanding of money to the formal school concepts of multidigit numbers. Real-world money is confusing for many students (e.g., dimes are smaller than pennies but are worth 10 times as much). Also, the formal school math number words and notations are abstract and potentially misleading (e.g., 36 looks like a 3 and a 6, not like 30 and 6) and need to be linked to visual quantities of tens and ones to become meaningful. Fuson designed conceptual "supports" into the curriculum to bridge the two. The middle portion of Figure 5-2 shows an example of the supports that were used to help students build meaning. A teacher or curriculum designer can make a framework like that of Figure 5-2 for any math domain by selecting those conceptual supports that will help students make links among the math words, written notations, and quantities in that domain.

Identifying real-world contexts whose features help direct students' attention and thinking in mathematically productive ways is particularly helpful in building conceptual bridges between students' informal experiences and the new formal mathematics they are learning. Examples of such bridging contexts are a key feature of each of the three chapters that follow.

PRINCIPLE #2: UNDERSTANDING REQUIRES FACTUAL KNOWLEDGE AND CONCEPTUAL FRAMEWORKS

The second principle of *How People Learn* suggests the importance of both conceptual understanding and procedural fluency, as well as an effective organization of knowledge—in this case one that facilitates strategy development and adaptive reasoning. It would be difficult to name a discipline in which the approach to achieving this goal is more hotly debated than mathematics. Recognition of the weakness in the conceptual understanding of students in the United States has resulted in increasing attention to the problems involved in teaching mathematics as a set of procedural competences.[14] At the same time, students with too little knowledge of procedures do not become competent and efficient problem solvers. When instruction places too little emphasis on factual and procedural knowledge, the problem is not solved; it is only changed. Both are clearly critical.

Equally important, procedural knowledge and conceptual understandings must be closely linked. As the mathematics confronted by students becomes more complex through the school years, new knowledge and competencies require that those already mastered be brought to bear. Box 1-6 in Chapter 1, for example, describes a set of links in procedural and conceptual knowledge required to support the ability to do multidigit subtraction with regrouping—a topic encountered relatively early in elementary school. By the time a student begins algebra years later, the network of knowledge must include many new concepts and procedures (including those for rational number) that must be effectively linked and available to support new algebraic understandings. The teacher's challenge, then, is to help students build and consolidate prerequisite competencies, understand new concepts in depth, and organize both concepts and competencies in a network of knowledge. Furthermore, teachers must provide sustained and then increasingly spaced opportunities to consolidate new understandings and procedures.

In mathematics, such networks of knowledge often are organized as learning paths from informal concrete methods to abbreviated, more general, and more abstract methods. Discussing multiple methods in the classroom—drawing attention to why different methods work and to the relative efficiency and reliability of each—can help provide a conceptual ladder that helps students move in a connected way from where they are to a more efficient and abstract approach. Students also can adopt or adapt an intermediate method with which they might feel more comfortable. Teachers can help students move at least to intermediate "good-enough" methods that can be understood and explained. Box 5-4 describes such a learning path for single-digit addition and subtraction that is seen worldwide. Teachers in some countries support students in moving through this learning path.

Developing Mathematical Proficiency

Developing mathematical proficiency requires that students master both the concepts and procedural skills needed to reason and solve problems effectively in a particular domain. Deciding which advanced methods all students should learn to attain proficiency is a policy matter involving judgments about how to use scarce instructional time. For example, the level 2 counting-on methods in Box 5-4 may be considered "good-enough" methods; they are general, rapid, and sufficiently accurate that valuable school time might better be spent on topics other than mastery of the whole network of knowledge required for carrying out the level 3 methods. Decisions about which methods to teach must also take into account that some methods are clearer conceptually and procedurally than the multidigit methods usually taught in the United States (see Box 5-5). The National Research Council's *Adding It Up* reviews these and other accessible algorithms in other domains.

This view of mathematics as involving different methods does not imply that a teacher or curriculum must teach multiple methods for every domain. However, alternative methods will frequently arise in a classroom, either because students bring them from home (e.g., Maria's add-equal-quantities subtraction method, widely taught in other countries) or because students think differently about many mathematical problems. Frequently there are viable alternative methods for solving a problem, and discussing the advantages and disadvantages of each can facilitate flexibility and deep understanding of the mathematics involved. In some countries, teachers emphasize multiple solution methods and purposely give students problems that are conducive to such solutions, and students solve a problem in more than one way.

However, the less-advanced students in a classroom also need to be considered. It can be helpful for either a curriculum or teacher or such less-advanced students to select an accessible method that can be understood and is efficient enough for the future, and for these students to concentrate on learning that method and being able to explain it. Teachers in some countries do this while also facilitating problem solving with alternative methods.

Overall, knowing about student learning paths and knowledge networks helps teachers direct math talk along productive lines toward valued knowledge networks. Research in mathematics learning has uncovered important information on a number of typical learning paths and knowledge networks involved in acquiring knowledge about a variety of concepts in mathematics (see the next three chapters for examples).

Instruction to Support Mathematical Proficiency

To teach in a way that supports both conceptual understanding and procedural fluency requires that the primary concepts underlying an area of mathematics be clear to the teacher or become clear during the process of teaching for mathematical proficiency. Because mathematics has traditionally been taught with an emphasis on procedure, adults who were taught this way may initially have difficulty identifying or using the core conceptual understandings in a mathematics domain.

BOX 5-4 A Learning Path from Children's Math Worlds for Single-Digit Addition and Subtraction

Children around the world pass through three levels of increasing sophistication in methods of single-digit addition and subtraction. The first level is direct modeling by counting all of the objects at each step (counting all or taking away). Students can be helped to move rapidly from this first level to counting on, in which counting begins with one addend. For example, 8 + 6 is not solved by counting from 1 to 14 (counting all), but by counting on 6 from 8: counting 8, 9, 10, 11, 12, 13, 14 while keeping track of the 6 counted on.

For subtraction, Children's Math Worlds does what is common in many countries: it helps students see subtraction as involving a mystery addend. Students then solve a subtraction problem by counting on from the known addend to the known total. Earlier we saw how Maria solved 14 - 6 by counting up from 6 to 14, raising 8 fingers while doing so to find that 6 plus 8 more is 14. Many students in the United States instead follow a learning path that moves from drawing little sticks or circles for all of the objects and crossing some out (e.g., drawing 14 sticks, crossing out 6, and counting the rest) to counting down (14, 13, 12, 11, 10, 9, 8, 7, 6). But counting down is difficult and error prone. When first or second graders are helped to move to a different learning path that solves subtraction problems by forward methods, such as counting on or adding on over 10 (see below), subtraction becomes as easy as addition. For many students, this is very empowering.

The third level of single-digit addition and subtraction is exemplified by Peter in the vignette in Box 5-2. At this level, students can chunk

The approaches in the three chapters that follow identify the central conceptual structures in several areas of mathematics. The areas of focus—whole number, rational number, and functions—were identified by Case and his colleagues as requiring major conceptual shifts. In the first, students are required to master the concept of *quantity*; in the second, the concept of *proportion* and relative number; and in the third, the concept of *dependence* in quantitative relationships. Each of these understandings requires that a supporting set of concepts and procedural abilities be put in place. The extensive research done by Griffin and Case on whole number, by Case and Moss on rational number, and by Case and Kalchman on functions provides a strong foundation for identifying the major conceptual challenges students

numbers and relate these chunks. The chunking enables them to carry out make-a-ten methods: they give part of one number to the other number to make a ten. These methods are taught in many countries. They are very helpful in multidigit addition and subtraction because a number found in this way is already thought of as 1 ten and some ones. For example, for 8 + 6, 6 gives 2 to 8 to make 10, leaving 4 in the 6, so 10 + 4 = 14. Solving 14 − 8 is done similarly: with 8, how many make 10 (2), plus the 4 in 14, so the answer is 6. These make-a-ten methods demonstrate the learning paths and network of knowledge required for advanced solution methods. Children may also use a "doubles" strategy for some problems— e.g., 7 + 6 = 6 + 6 + 1 = 12 + 1 = 13—because the doubles (for example, 6 + 6 or 8 + 8) are easy to learn.

The make-a-ten methods illustrate the importance of a network of knowledge. Students must master three kinds of knowledge to be able to carry out a make-a-ten method fluently: they must (1) for each number below 10, know how much more makes 10; (2) break up any number below 10 into all possible pairs of parts (because 9 + 6 requires knowing 6 = 1 + 5, but 8 + 6 requires knowing 6 = 2 + 4, etc.); and (3) know 10 + 1 = 11, 10 + 2 = 12, 10 + 3 = 13, etc., rapidly without counting.

Note that particular methods may be more or less easy for learners from different backgrounds. For example, the make-a-ten methods are easier for East Asian students, whose language says, "Ten plus one is ten one, ten plus two is ten two," than for English-speaking students, whose language says, "Ten plus one is eleven, ten plus two is twelve, etc."

face in mastering these areas. This research program traced developmental/ experiential changes in children's thinking as they engaged with innovative curriculum. In each area of focus, instructional approaches were developed that enable teachers to help children move through learning paths in productive ways. In doing so, teachers often find that they also build a more extensive knowledge network.

As teachers guide a class through learning paths, a balance must be maintained between learner-centered and knowledge-centered needs. The learning path of the class must also continually relate to individual learner knowledge. Box 5-6 outlines two frameworks that can facilitate such balance.

BOX 5-5 Accessible Algorithms

In over a decade of working with a range of urban and suburban classrooms in the Children's Math Worlds Project, we found that one multidigit addition method and one multidigit subtraction method were accessible to all students. The students easily learned, understood, and remembered these methods and learned to draw quantities for and explain them. Both methods are modifications of the usual U.S. methods. The addition method is the write-new-groups-below method, in which the new 1 ten or 1 hundred, etc., is written below the column on the line rather than above the column (see Jackie's method in Figure 5-1). In the subtraction fix-everything-first method, every column in the top number that needs ungrouping is ungrouped (in any order), and then the subtracting in every column is done (in any order). Because this method can be done from either direction and is only a minor modification of the common U.S. methods, learning-disabled and special-needs students find it especially accessible. Both of these methods stimulate productive discussions in class because they are easily related to the usual U.S. methods that are likely to be brought to class by other students.

PRINCIPLE #3: A METACOGNITIVE APPROACH ENABLES STUDENT SELF-MONITORING

Learning about oneself as a learner, thinker, and problem solver is an important aspect of metacognition (see Chapter 1). In the area of mathematics, as noted earlier, many people who take mathematics courses "learn" that "they are not mathematical." This is an unintended, highly unfortunate, consequence of some approaches to teaching mathematics. It is a consequence that can influence people for a lifetime because they continue to avoid anything mathematical, which in turn ensures that their belief about being "nonmathematical" is true.[15]

An article written in 1940 by Charles Gragg, entitled "Because Wisdom Can't be Told," is relevant to issues of metacognition and mathematics learning. Gragg begins with the following quotation from Balzac:

> So he had grown rich at last, and thought to transmit to his only son all the cut-and-dried experience which he himself had purchased at the price of his lost illusions; a noble last illusion of age.

Except for the part about growing rich, Balzac's ideas fit many peoples' experiences quite well. In our roles as parents, friends, supervisors, and professional educators, we frequently attempt to prepare people for the future by imparting the wisdom gleaned from our own experiences. Some-

BOX 5-6 **Supporting Student and Teacher Learning Through a Classroom Discourse Community**

Eliciting and then building on and using students' mathematical thinking can be challenging. Yet recent research indicates that teachers can move their students through increasingly productive levels of classroom discourse. Hufferd-Ackles and colleagues[16] describe four levels of a "math-talk learning community," beginning with a traditional, teacher-directed format in which the teacher asks short-answer questions, and student responses are directed to the teacher. At the next level, "getting started," the teacher begins to pursue and assess students' mathematical thinking, focusing less on answers alone. In response, students provide brief descriptions of their thinking. The third level is called "building." At this point the teacher elicits and students respond with fuller descriptions of their thinking, and multiple methods are volunteered. The teacher also facilitates student-to-student talk about mathematics. The final level is "math-talk." Here students share responsibility for discourse with the teacher, justifying their own ideas and asking questions of and helping other students.

Key shifts in teacher practice that support a class moving through these levels include asking questions that focus on mathematical thinking rather than just on answers, probing extensively for student thinking, modeling and expanding on explanations when necessary, fading physically from the center of the classroom discourse (e.g., moving to the back of the classroom), and coaching students in their participatory roles in the discourse ("Everyone have a thinker question ready.").

Related research indicates that when building a successful classroom discourse community, it is important to balance the *process* of discourse, that is, the ways in which student ideas are elicited, with the *content* of discourse, the substance of the ideas that are discussed. In other words, how does a teacher ensure both that class discussions provide sufficient space for students to share their ideas and that discussions are mathematically productive? Sherin[17] describes one model for doing so whereby class discussions begin with a focus on "idea generation," in which many student ideas are solicited. Next, discussion moves into a "comparison and evaluation" phase, in which the class looks more closely at the ideas that have been raised, but no new ideas are raised.

The teacher then "filters" ideas for the class, highlighting a subset of ideas for further pursuit. In this way, student ideas are valued throughout discussion, but the teacher also plays a role in determining the extent to which specific mathematical ideas are considered in detail. A class may proceed through several cycles of these three phases in a single discussion.

times our efforts are rewarded, but we are often less successful than we would like to be, and we need to understand why.

The idea that "wisdom can't be told" helps educators rethink the strategy of simply telling students that some topic (e.g., mathematics) is important, and they can master it if they try. There are important differences between simply being told something and being able to experience it for oneself. Students' experiences have strong effects on their beliefs about themselves, as well as their abilities to remember information and use it spontaneously to solve new problems.[18] If their experiences in mathematics classes involve primarily frustration and failure, simply telling them, "trust me, this will be relevant someday" or "believe me, you have the ability to understand this" is a weak intervention. On the other hand, helping students experience their own abilities to find patterns and problems, invent solutions (even if they are not quite as good as expert solutions), and contribute to and learn from discussions with others provides the kinds of experiences that can help them learn with understanding, as well as change their views about the subject matter and themselves.[19]

However, research on metacognition suggests that an additional instructional step is needed for optimal learning—one that involves helping students reflect on their experiences and begin to see their ideas as instances of larger categories of ideas. For example, students might begin to see their way of showing more ones when subtracting as one of several ways to demonstrate this same important mathematical idea.

One other aspect of metacognition that is nicely illustrated in the context of mathematics involves the claim made in Chapter 1 that metacognition is not simply a knowledge-free ability, but requires relevant knowledge of the topics at hand. At the beginning of this chapter, we noted that many students approach problems such as adding fractions as purely computational (e.g., "What is the approximate sum of 8/9 plus 11/13?"). Ideally, we also want students to monitor the accuracy of their problem solving, just as we want them to monitor their understanding when reading about science, history, or literature.

One way to monitor the accuracy of one's computation is to go back and recheck each of the steps. Another way is to estimate the answer and see whether there is a discrepancy between one's computations and the estimate. However, the ability to estimate requires the kind of knowledge that might be called "number sense." For the above fraction problem, for example, a person with number sense who computes an answer and sees that it is greater than 2 knows that the computation is obviously wrong. But it is "obvious" only if the person has learned ways to think about number that go beyond the ability merely to count and compute.

Instruction That Supports Metacognition

Much of what we have discussed with regard to making student thinking visible can be thought of as ongoing assessment of students. Such assessment can include students so they become involved in thinking about their own mathematical progress and that of their classmates. Such ongoing assessment can then become internalized as metacognitive self-monitoring. Classroom communication about students' mathematical thinking greatly facilitates both teacher and student assessment of learning. Teachers and students can see difficulties particular students are having and can help those students by providing explanations. Teachers can discern primitive solution methods that need to be advanced to more effective methods. They also can see how students are advancing in their helping and explaining abilities and plan how to foster continued learning in those areas.

Students can also learn some general problem-solving strategies, such as "make a drawing of the situation" or "ask yourself questions" that apply to many different kinds of problems. Drawings and questions are a means of self-monitoring. They also can offer teachers windows into students' thinking and thus provide information about how better to help students along a learning path to efficient problem-solving methods.

An Emphasis on Debugging

Metacognitive functioning is also facilitated by shifting from a focus on answers as just right or wrong to a more detailed focus on "debugging" a wrong answer, that is, finding where the error is, why it is an error, and correcting it. Of course, good teachers have always done this, but there are now two special reasons for doing so. One is the usefulness of this approach in complex problem solving, such as debugging computer programs. Technological advances mean that more adults will need to do more complex problem solving and error identification throughout their lives, so debugging—locating the source of an error—is a good general skill that can be learned in the math classroom.

The second reason is based on considerable amount of research in the past 30 years concerning student errors. Figure 5-3 illustrates two such typical kinds of errors in early and late school topics. The partial student knowledge reflected in each error is described in the figure. One can also see how a focus on understanding can help students debug their own errors. For example, asking how much the little "1's" really represent can help students start to see their error in the top example and thus modify the parts of the method that are wrong.

Early Partial Knowledge

268
+ 156
514

This error reflects a wrong generalization from 2-digit problems: where the little 1 is put above the left-most column. Left-most and next-left are confused in this solution. Trying to understand the meanings of the 1s as 1 ten and as 1 hundred can debug this error. The student does know to add ones, to add tens, and to add hundreds and does this correctly.

Later Partial Knowledge

1. What shape would the graph of the function $y = x^2 + 1$ have? Draw it below.

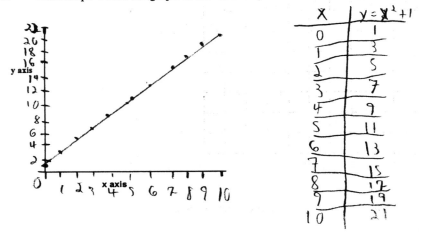

A common error among middle school students is to treat an exponent as a coefficient or multiplier. Here, Graham has generated a table of values for the function $y = 2x + 1$ rather than $y = x^2 + 1$. This type of error has broad implications. For example, it will be difficult for students to develop a good conceptual understanding for functions and the ways in which their representations are interconnected because the graph of $y = 2x + 1$ is a straight line rather than the parabolic curve of $y = x^2 + 1$. He does know, however, how to make a table of values and to graph resulting pairs of values. He also knows how to solve for y in an equation given x.

FIGURE 5-3

Internal and External Dialogue as Support for Metacognition

The research summarized in *How People Learn* and *Adding It Up* and the professional experience summarized in the standards of the National Council of Teachers of Mathematics all emphasize how important it is for students to communicate about mathematics and for teachers to help them learn to do so. Students can learn to reflect on and describe their mathematical thinking. They can learn to compare methods of solving a problem and identify the advantages and disadvantages of each. Peers can learn to ask thoughtful questions about other students' thinking or help edit such statements to clarify them. Students can learn to help each other, sometimes in informal, spontaneous ways and sometimes in more organized, coaching-partner situations. The vignette in Box 5-3 illustrates such communication about mathematical thinking after it has been developed in a classroom. Experience in the Children's Math Worlds Project indicates that students from all backgrounds can learn to think critically and ask thoughtful questions, reflect on and evaluate their own achievement, justify their points of view, and understand the perspectives of others. Even first-grade students can learn to interact in these ways.

Of course, teachers must help students learn to interact fruitfully. To this end, teachers can model clear descriptions and supportive questioning or helping techniques. In a classroom situation, some students may solve problems at the board while others solve them at their seats. Students can make drawings or use notations to indicate how they thought about or solved a problem. Selected students can then describe their solution methods, and peers can ask questions to clarify and to give listeners a role. Sometimes, pairs of students may explain their solutions, with the less-advanced partner explaining first and the other partner then expanding and clarifying. Students usually attend better if only two or three of their fellow students explain their solution method for a given problem. More students can solve at the board, but the teacher can select the methods or the students for the class to hear at that time. It is useful to vary the verbal level of such explainers. Doing so assists all students in becoming better explainers by hearing and helping classmates expand upon a range of explanations. The goal in all of this discussion is to advance everyone's thinking and monitoring of their own understanding and that of other students rather than to conduct simple turn taking, though of course over time, all students can have opportunities to explain.

Seeking and Giving Help

Students must have enough confidence not only to engage with problems and try to solve them, but also to seek help when they are stuck. The dialogue that occurs in pair or class situations can help generate self-regulating speech that a student can produce while problem solving. Such helping can also increase the metacognitive awareness of the helper as he or she takes into consideration the thinking of the student being helped.

The Framework of *How People Learn*: Seeking a Balanced Classroom Environment

The framework of *How People Learn* suggests that classroom environments should at the same time be learner-centered, knowledge-centered, assessment-centered, and community-centered (see Chapter 1). These features map easily to the preceding discussion of the three principles, as well as to the chapters that follow. The instruction described is learner-centered in that it draws out and builds on student thinking. It is also knowledge-centered in that it focuses simultaneously on the conceptual understanding and the procedural knowledge of a topic, which students must master to be proficient, and the learning paths that can lead from existing to more advanced understanding. It is assessment-centered in that there are frequent opportunities for students to reveal their thinking on a topic so the teacher can shape instruction in response to their learning, and students can be made aware of their own progress. And it is community-centered in that the norms of the classroom community value student ideas, encourage productive interchange, and promote collaborative thinking.

Effective teaching and learning depend, however, on balance among these features of the classroom environment. There must be continual connections between the learner-centered focus on student knowledge and the more formal knowledge networks that are the goals of teaching in a domain. Traditional teaching has tended to emphasize the knowledge networks and pay insufficient attention to conceptual supports and the need to build on learner knowledge. Many students learn rote knowledge that cannot be used adequately in solving problems. On the other hand, an overemphasis on learner-centered teaching results in insufficient attention to connections with valued knowledge networks, the crucially important guiding roles of teachers and of learning accessible student methods, and the need to consolidate knowledge. Four such excesses are briefly discussed here.

First, some suggest that students must invent all their mathematical ideas and that we should wait until they do so rather than teach ideas. This view, of course, ignores the fact that all inventions are made within a supportive culture and that providing appropriate supports can speed such inventions. Too much focus on student-invented methods per se can hold students back; those who use time-consuming methods that are not easily generalized need to be helped to move on to more rapid and generalizable "good-enough" methods. A focus on sense making and understanding of the methods that are used is the balanced focus, rather than an emphasis on whether the method was invented by the student using it.

Second, classroom discussions may not be sufficiently guided by the teacher through the learning path. Students may talk on and on, meandering without much focus. Descriptions of student thinking may have a turn-taking, "every method is equally wonderful" flavor so that other students do not listen carefully or ask questions, but passively await their turn to talk. Different student methods may be described, but their advantages and disadvantages, or at least their similar and different features, are not discussed. There may be no building toward student-to-student talk, but everything said may be directed toward the teacher.

Third, the use of real-world situations and conceptual supports may consist more of a series of activities in which the mathematical ideas are not sufficiently salient and not connected enough to the standard math notations and vocabulary. The result may be a scattershot approach involving many different activities rather than careful choices of core representations or bridging contexts that might guide students through a coherent learning path.

Fourth, learning may not be consolidated enough because of an excessive focus on the initial learning activities. Time for consolidation of learning, with feedback loops should errors arise, is vital for mathematical fluency.

The recent Third International Mathematics and Science Study showed that teaching in the United States is still overwhelmingly traditional. However, the above caveats need to be kept in mind as teachers move forward in implementing the principles of *How People Learn*.

NEXT STEPS

There are some curricula that implement, at least partially, the principles of *How People Learn*. Even without extensive curricular support, however, teachers can substantially improve their practice by understanding and using these principles. This is particularly true if they can examine their own teaching practices, supported by a teaching–learning community of like-minded colleagues. Such a community can help teachers create learning paths for themselves that can move them from their present teaching practices to practices that conform more fully to the principles of *How People Learn* and thereby create more effective classrooms. Two such teacher communities, involving video clubs and lesson study, respectively, are summarized in Boxes 5-7 and 5-8. A third approach to a teacher learning community is to organize teacher discussions around issues that arise from teaching a curriculum that supports conceptual approaches. Box 5-9 describes research summarizing one productive focus for such discussions—the use of openings in the curriculum where teachers can focus on student questions or misunderstandings.

BOX 5-7 Learning to Use Student Thinking in Teacher Video Clubs

Research indicates that teachers can develop their ability to attend to and interpret student thinking not only in the midst of class discussions, but also outside of class as they reflect on students' ideas. One model for doing so is the use of video clubs in which teachers meet together to watch and discuss video excerpts from their classrooms.[20] By providing teachers opportunities to examine student thinking without the pressure of having to respond immediately, video clubs can help prompt the development of new techniques for analyzing student thinking among teachers—techniques that teachers can then bring back to their classrooms.

BOX 5-8 Lesson Study: Learning Together How to Build on Student Knowledge

Lesson study is "a cycle in which teachers work together to consider their long-term goals for students, bring those goals to life in actual 'research lessons,' and collaboratively observe, discuss, and refine the lessons."[21] Lesson study has been a major form of teacher professional development in Japan for many decades, and in recent years has attracted the attention of U.S. teachers, school administrators, and educational researchers.[22] It is a simple idea. Teachers collaboratively plan a lesson that is taught by one group member while others observe and carefully collect data on student learning and behavior. The student data are then used to reflect on the lesson and revise it as needed. Lesson study is a teacher-led process in which teachers collaboratively identify a concept that is persistently difficult for students, study the best available curriculum materials in order to rethink their teaching of this topic, and plan and teach one or more "research lessons" that enable them to see student reactions to their redesigned unit. Ideally, a lesson study group allows teachers to share their expertise and knowledge, as well as questions related to both teaching and subject matter. Lesson study groups may also draw on knowledgeable outsiders as resources for content knowledge, group facilitation, and so on.

NOTE: Resources, including a handbook, videotapes, listserve, and protocols for teachers who wish to engage in lesson study, can be found at the websites of the Lesson Study Research Group at Teachers College, Columbia University: (http://www.tc.columbia.edu/lessonstudy/) and the Mills College Lesson Study Group (www.lessonresearch.net). See also Lewis (2002).

BOX 5-9 **Teachers as Curriculum Designers: Using Openings in the Curriculum to Determine Learning Paths**

Even when using a prepared curriculum, teachers have an important role as curriculum designers. In a study of two elementary teachers using a new textbook, Remillard[23] found that teachers made regular decisions about what parts of the teacher's guide to read, which suggestions to follow and to what ends, how to structure students' mathematical activities, and how to respond to students' questions and ideas. The decisions teachers made had a substantial impact on the curriculum experienced by students. In other words, written curriculum alone does not determine students' experiences in the classroom; this is the role of the teacher.

Remillard and Geist[24] use the term "openings in the curriculum" to denote those instances during instruction in which things do not go as described in the preset curriculum. These openings are often prompted by students' questions or teachers' observations about student understanding or misunderstanding. The authors argue that teachers must navigate these openings by (1) carefully analyzing student work and thinking, (2) weighing possible options for proceeding against one's goals for student learning, and (3) taking responsive action that is open to ongoing examination and adjustment. They suggest that teaching with curriculum guides can be improved as teachers recognize and embrace their role while navigating openings in the curriculum to determine learning paths for students.

Similarly, Remillard[25] found that teachers came to reflect on their beliefs and understandings related to their teaching and its content while involved in the very work of deciding what to do next by interpreting students' understanding with respect to their goals for the students and particular instructional tasks. Thus, some of the most fruitful opportunities for teacher learning when using a new curriculum occurred when teachers were engaged in the work of navigating openings in the curriculum.

It will take work by teachers, administrators, researchers, parents, and politicians to bring these new principles and goals to life in classrooms and to create the circumstances in which this can happen. Nonetheless, there are enough examples of the principles in action to offer a vision of the new kinds of learning that can be accessible to all students and to all teachers. Some materials to support teachers in these efforts do exist, and more are being developed. Helpful examples of the three principles in action are given in the chapters that follow. It is important to note, once again, that other projects have generated examples that implement the principles of *How People Learn*. Some of these examples can be found in the authors' references to that research and in the suggested teacher reading list. All of this work indicates that we have begun the crucial journey into mathematical proficiency for all and that the principles of *How People Learn* can guide us on this journey.

NOTES

1. Holt, 1964, pp. 143-144.
2. National Research Council, 2001.
3. See Fuson, 1986a, 1986b, 1990; Fuson and Briars, 1990; Fuson and Burghardt, 1993, 1997; Fuson et al., 1994, 2000; Fuson and Smith, 1997; Fuson, Smith, and Lott, 1977; Fuson, Wearne et al., 1997; Fuson, Lo Cicero et al., 1997; Lo Cicero et al., 1999; Fuson et al., 2000; Ron, 1998.
4. Carey, 2001; Gelman, 1990; Starkey et al., 1990; Wynn, 1996; Canfield and Smith, 1996.
5. Case et al., 1999; Ginsburg, 1984; Saxe, 1982.
6. Carraher, 1986; Carraher et al., 1985.
7. Lave, 1988; Sternberg, 1999.
8. De la Rocha, 1986.
9. Ceci and Liker, 1986; Ceci, 1996.
10. National Council of Teachers of Mathematics, 2000.
11. National Research Council, 2001.
12. See, e.g., Hatano and Inagaki, 1996; Resnick, 1987; Stigler and Heibert, 1997.
13. Stigler and Heibert, 1999.
14. National Research Council, 2004.
15. See, e.g., Tobias, 1978.
16. Hufferd-Ackles et al., 2004.
17. Sherin, 2000a, 2002.
18. See, e.g., Bransford et al., 1989.
19. See, e.g., Schwartz and Moore, 1998.
20. Sherin, 2000b, 2001.
21. Lewis, 2002, p. 1.
22. Fernandez, 2002; Lewis, 2002; Stigler and Heibert, 1999.
23. Remillard, 1999, 2000.
24. Remillard and Geist, 2002.
25. Remillard, 2000.

REFERENCES

Anghileri, J. (1989). An investigation of young children's understanding of multiplication. *Educational Studies in Mathematics, 20,* 367-385.
Ashlock, R.B. (1998). *Error patterns in computation.* Upper Saddle River, NJ: Prentice-Hall.
Baek, J.-M. (1998). Children's invented algorithms for multidigit multiplication problems. In L.J. Morrow and M.J. Kenney (Eds.), *The teaching and learning of algorithms in school mathematics.* Reston, VA: National Council of Teachers of Mathematics.

Baroody, A.J., and Coslick, R.T. (1998). *Fostering children's mathematical power: An investigative approach to k-8 mathematics instruction.* Mahwah, NJ: Lawrence Erlbaum Associates.

Baroody, A.J., and Ginsburg, H.P. (1986). The relationship between initial meaningful and mechanical knowledge of arithmetic. In J. Hiebert (Ed.), *Conceptual and procedural knowledge: The case of mathematics* (pp. 75-112). Mahwah, NJ: Lawrence Erlbaum Associates.

Beishuizen, M. (1993). Mental strategies and materials or models for addition and subtraction up to 100 in Dutch second grades. *Journal for Research in Mathematics Education, 24,* 294-323.

Beishuizen, M., Gravemeijer, K.P.E., and van Lieshout, E.C.D.M. (Eds.). (1997). *The role of contexts and models in the development of mathematical strategies and procedures.* Utretch, The Netherlands: CD-B Press/The Freudenthal Institute.

Bergeron, J.C., and Herscovics, N. (1990). Psychological aspects of learning early arithmetic. In P. Nesher and J. Kilpatrick (Eds.), *Mathematics and cognition: A research synthesis by the International Group for the Psychology of Mathematics Education.* Cambridge, England: Cambridge University Press.

Bransford, J.D., Franks, J.J., Vye, N.J., and Sherwood, R.D. (1989). New approaches to instruction: Because wisdom can't be told. In S. Vasniadou and A. Ortony (Eds.), *Similarity and analogical reasoning* (pp. 470-497). New York: Cambridge University Press.

Brophy, J. (1997). Effective instruction. In H.J. Walberg and G.D. Haertel (Eds.), *Psychology and educational practice* (pp. 212-232). Berkeley, CA: McCutchan.

Brownell, W.A. (1987). AT Classic: Meaning and skill—maintaining the balance. *Arithmetic Teacher, 34*(8), 18-25.

Canfield, R.L., and Smith, E.G. (1996). Number-based expectations and sequential enumeration by 5-month-old infants. *Developmental Psychology, 32,* 269-279.

Carey, S. (2001). Evolutionary and ontogenetic foundations of arithmetic. *Mind and Language, 16*(1), 37-55.

Carpenter, T.P., and Moser, J.M. (1984). The acquisition of addition and subtraction concepts in grades one through three. *Journal for Research in Mathematics Education, 15*(3), 179-202.

Carpenter, T.P., Fennema, E., Peterson, P.L., Chiang, C.P., and Loef, M. (1989). Using knowledge of children's mathematics thinking in classroom teaching: An experimental study. *American Educational Research Journal, 26*(4), 499-531.

Carpenter, T.P., Franke, M.L., Jacobs, V., and Fennema, E. (1998). A longitudinal study of invention and understanding in children's multidigit addition and subtraction. *Journal for Research in Mathematics Education, 29,* 3-20.

Carraher, T.N. (1986). From drawings to buildings: Mathematical scales at work. *International Journal of Behavioural Development, 9,* 527-544.

Carraher, T.N., Carraher, D.W., and Schliemann, A.D. (1985). Mathematics in the streets and in schools. *British Journal of Developmental Psychology, 3,* 21-29.

Carroll, W.M. (2001). *A longitudinal study of children using the reform curriculum everyday mathematics.* Available: http://everydaymath.uchicago.edu/educators/references.shtml [accessed September 2004].

Carroll, W.M., and Fuson, K.C. (1999). *Achievement results for fourth graders using the standards-based curriculum everyday mathematics*. Unpublished document, University of Chicago, Illinois.

Carroll, W.M., and Porter, D. (1998). Alternative algorithms for whole-number operations. In L.J. Morrow and M.J. Kenney (Eds.), *The teaching and learning of algorithms in school mathematics* (pp. 106-114). Reston, VA: National Council of Teachers of Mathematics.

Case, R. (1985). *Intellectual development: Birth to adulthood*. New York: Academic Press.

Case, R. (1992). *The mind's staircase: Exploring the conceptual underpinnings of children's thought and knowledge*. Mahwah, NJ: Lawrence Erlbaum Associates.

Case, R. (1998). *A psychological model of number sense and its development*. Paper presented at the annual meeting of the American Educational Research Association, April, San Diego, CA.

Case, R., and Sandieson, R. (1988). A developmental approach to the identification and teaching of central conceptual structures in mathematics and science in the middle grades. In M. Behr and J. Hiebert (Eds.), *Research agenda in mathematics education: Number concepts and in the middle grades* (pp. 136-270). Mahwah, NJ: Lawrence Erlbaum Associates.

Case, R., Griffin, S., and Kelly, W.M. (1999). Socioeconomic gradients in mathematical ability and their responsiveness to intervention during early childhood. In D.P. Keating and C. Hertzman (Eds.), *Developmental health and the wealth of nations: Social, biological, and educational dynamics* (pp. 125-149). New York: Guilford Press.

Ceci, S.J. (1996). *On intelligence: A bioecological treatise on intellectual development*. Cambridge, MA: Harvard University Press.

Ceci, S.J., and Liker, J.K. (1986). A day at the races: A study of IQ, expertise, and cognitive complexity. *Journal of Experimental Psychology, 115*(3), 255-266.

Cotton, K. (1995). *Effective schooling practices: A research synthesis*. Portland, OR: Northwest Regional Lab.

Davis, R.B. (1984). *Learning mathematics: The cognitive science approach to mathematics education*. Norwood, NJ: Ablex.

De la Rocha, O.L. (1986). The reorganization of arithmetic practice in the kitchen. *Anthropology and Education Quarterly, 16*(3), 193-198.

Dixon, R.C., Carnine, S.W., Kameenui, E.J., Simmons, D.C., Lee, D.S., Wallin, J., and Chard, D. (1998). *Executive summary. Report to the California State Board of Education, review of high-quality experimental research*. Eugene, OR: National Center to Improve the Tools of Educators.

Dossey, J.A., Swafford, J.O., Parmantie, M., and Dossey, A.E. (Eds.). (2003). Multidigit addition and subtraction methods invented in small groups and teacher support of problem solving and reflection. In A. Baroody and A. Dowker (Eds.), *The development of arithmetic concepts and skills: Constructing adaptive expertise*. Mahwah, NJ: Lawrence Erlbaum Associates.

Fernandez, C. (2002). Learning from Japanese approaches to professional development. The case of lesson study. *Journal of Teacher Education, 53*(5), 393-405.

Fraivillig, J.L., Murphy, L.A., and Fuson, K.C. (1999). Advancing children's mathematical thinking in everyday mathematics reform classrooms. *Journal for Research in Mathematics Education, 30*, 148-170.

Fuson, K.C. (1986a). Roles of representation and verbalization in the teaching of multidigit addition and subtraction. *European Journal of Psychology of Education, 1*, 35-56.

Fuson, K.C. (1986b). Teaching children to subtract by counting up. *Journal for Research in Mathematics Education, 17*, 172-189.

Fuson, K.C. (1990). Conceptual structures for multiunit numbers: Implications for learning and teaching multidigit addition, subtraction, and place value. *Cognition and Instruction, 7*, 343-403.

Fuson, K.C. (1992a). Research on learning and teaching addition and subtraction of whole numbers. In G. Leinhardt, R.T. Putnam, and R.A. Hattrup (Eds.), *The analysis of arithmetic for mathematics teaching* (pp. 53-187). Mahwah, NJ: Lawrence Erlbaum Associates.

Fuson, K.C. (1992b). Research on whole number addition and subtraction. In D. Grouws (Ed.), *Handbook of research on mathematics teaching and learning* (pp. 243-275). New York: Macmillan.

Fuson, K.C. (2003). Developing mathematical power in whole number operations. In J. Kilpatrick, W.G. Martin, and D. Schifter (Eds.), *A research companion to principles and standards for school mathematics* (pp. 68-94). Reston, VA: National Council of Teachers of Mathematics.

Fuson, K.C., and Briars, D.J. (1990). Base-ten blocks as a first- and second-grade learning/teaching approach for multidigit addition and subtraction and place-value concepts. *Journal for Research in Mathematics Education, 21*, 180-206.

Fuson, K.C., and Burghardt, B.H. (1993). Group case studies of second graders inventing multidigit addition procedures for base-ten blocks and written marks. In J.R. Becker and B.J. Pence (Eds.), *Proceedings of the fifteenth annual meeting of the North American chapter of the international group for the psychology of mathematics education* (pp. 240-246). San Jose, CA: The Center for Mathematics and Computer Science Education, San Jose State University.

Fuson, K.C., and Burghardt, B.H. (1997). Group case studies of second graders inventing multidigit subtraction methods. In *Proceedings of the 19th annual meeting of the North American chapter of the international group for the psychology of mathematics education* (pp. 291-298). San Jose, CA: The Center for Mathematics and Computer Science Education, San Jose State University.

Fuson, K.C., and Fuson, A.M. (1992). Instruction to support children's counting on for addition and counting up for subtraction. *Journal for Research in Mathematics Education, 23*, 72-78.

Fuson, K.C., and Kwon, Y. (1992). Korean children's understanding of multidigit addition and subtraction. *Child Development, 63*(2), 491-506.

Fuson, K.C., and Secada, W.G. (1986). Teaching children to add by counting with finger patterns. *Cognition and Instruction, 3*, 229-260.

Fuson, K.C., and Smith, T. (1997). Supporting multiple 2-digit conceptual structures and calculation methods in the classroom: Issues of conceptual supports, instructional design, and language. In M. Beishuizen, K.P.E. Gravemeijer, and E.C.D.M. van Lieshout (Eds.), *The role of contexts and models in the development of mathematical strategies and procedures* (pp. 163-198). Utrecht, The Netherlands: CD-B Press/The Freudenthal Institute.

Fuson, K.C., Stigler, J., and Bartsch, K. (1988). Grade placement of addition and subtraction topics in Japan, mainland China, the Soviet Union, Taiwan, and the United States. *Journal for Research in Mathematics Education, 19*(5), 449-456.

Fuson, K.C., Perry, T., and Kwon, Y. (1994). Latino, Anglo, and Korean children's finger addition methods. In J.E.H. van Luit (Ed.), *Research on learning and instruction of mathematics in kindergarten and primary school,* (pp. 220-228). Doetinchem/Rapallo, The Netherlands: Graviant.

Fuson, K.C., Perry, T., and Ron, P. (1996). Developmental levels in culturally different finger methods: Anglo and Latino children's finger methods of addition. In E. Jakubowski, D. Watkins, and H. Biske (Eds.), *Proceedings of the 18th annual meeting of the North American chapter for the psychology of mathematics education* (2nd edition, pp. 347-352). Columbus, OH: ERIC Clearinghouse for Science, Mathematics, and Environmental Education.

Fuson, K.C., Lo Cicero, A., Hudson, K., and Smith, S.T. (1997). Snapshots across two years in the life of an urban Latino classroom. In J. Hiebert, T. Carpenter, E. Fennema, K.C. Fuson, D. Wearne, H. Murray, A. Olivier, and P. Human (Eds.), *Making sense: Teaching and learning mathematics with understanding* (pp. 129-159). Portsmouth, NH: Heinemann.

Fuson, K.C., Smith, T., and Lo Cicero, A. (1997). Supporting Latino first graders' ten-structured thinking in urban classrooms. *Journal for Research in Mathematics Education, 28*, 738-760.

Fuson, K.C., Wearne, D., Hiebert, J., Murray, H., Human, P., Olivier, A., Carpenter, T., and Fennema, E. (1997). Children's conceptual structures for multidigit numbers and methods of multidigit addition and subtraction. *Journal for Research in Mathematics Education, 28*, 130-162.

Fuson, K.C., De La Cruz, Y., Smith, S., Lo Cicero, A., Hudson, K., Ron, P., and Steeby, R. (2000). Blending the best of the 20th century to achieve a mathematics equity pedagogy in the 21st century. In M.J. Burke and F.R. Curcio (Eds.), *Learning mathematics for a new century* (pp. 197-212). Reston, VA: National Council of Teachers of Mathematics.

Geary, D.C. (1994). *Children's mathematical development: Research and practical applications.* Washington, DC: American Psychological Association.

Gelman, R. (1990). First principles organize attention to and learning about relevant data: Number and the animate-inanimate distinction as examples. *Cognitive Science, 14*, 79-106.

Ginsburg, H.P. (1984). *Children's arithmetic: The learning process.* New York: Van Nostrand.

Ginsburg, H.P., and Allardice, B.S. (1984). Children's difficulties with school mathematics. In B. Rogoff and J. Lave (Eds.), *Everyday cognition: Its development in social contexts* (pp. 194-219). Cambridge, MA: Harvard University Press.

Ginsburg, H.P., and Russell, R.L. (1981). Social class and racial influences on early mathematical thinking. *Monographs of the Society for Research in Child Development* 44(6, serial #193). Malden, MA: Blackwell.

Goldman, S.R., Pellegrino, J.W., and Mertz, D.L. (1988). Extended practice of basic addition facts: Strategy changes in learning-disabled students. *Cognition and Instruction, 5*(3), 223-265.

Goldman, S.R., Hasselbring, T.S., and the Cognition and Technology Group at Vanderbilt (1997). Achieving meaningful mathematics literacy for students with learning disabilities. *Journal of Learning Disabilities, March 1*(2), 198-208.

Greer, B. (1992). Multiplication and division as models of situation. In D. Grouws (Ed.), *Handbook of research on mathematics teaching and learning* (pp. 276-295). New York: Macmillan.

Griffin, S., and Case, R. (1997). Re-thinking the primary school math curriculum: An approach based on cognitive science. *Issues in Education, 3*(1), 1-49.

Griffin, S., Case, R., and Siegler, R.S. (1994). Rightstart: Providing the central conceptual structures for children at risk of school failure. In K. McGilly (Ed.), *Classroom lessons: Integrating cognitive theory and classroom practice* (pp. 13-48). Mahwah, NJ: Lawrence Erlbaum Associates.

Grouws, D. (1992). *Handbook of research on mathematics teaching and learning.* New York: Teachers College Press.

Hamann, M.S., and Ashcraft, M.H. (1986). Textbook presentations of the basic addition facts. *Cognition and Instruction, 3*, 173-192.

Hart, K.M. (1987). Practical work and formalisation, too great a gap. In J.C. Bergeron, N. Hersovics, and C. Kieren (Eds.), *Proceedings from the eleventh international conference for the psychology of mathematics education* (vol. 2, pp. 408-415). Montreal, Canada: University of Montreal.

Hatano, G., and Inagaki, K. (1996). *Cultural contexts of schooling revisited. A review of the learning gap from a cultural psychology perspective.* Paper presented at the Conference on Global Prospects for Education: Development, Culture, and Schooling, University of Michigan.

Hiebert, J. (1986). *Conceptual and procedural knowledge: The case of mathematics.* Mahwah, NJ: Lawrence Erlbaum Associates.

Hiebert, J. (1992). Mathematical, cognitive, and instructional analyses of decimal fractions. In G. Leinhardt, R. Putnam, and R.A. Hattrup (Eds.), *The analysis of arithmetic for mathematics teaching* (pp. 283-322). Mahwah, NJ: Lawrence Erlbaum Associates.

Hiebert, J., and Carpenter, T.P. (1992). Learning and teaching with understanding. In D. Grouws (Ed.), *Handbook of research on mathematics teaching and learning* (pp. 65-97). New York: Macmillan.

Hiebert, J., and Wearne, D. (1986). Procedures over concepts: The acquisition of decimal number knowledge. In J. Hiebert (Ed.), *Conceptual and procedural knowledge: The case of mathematics* (pp. 199-223). Mahwah, NJ: Lawrence Erlbaum Associates.

Hiebert, J., Carpenter, T., Fennema, E., Fuson, K.C., Murray, H., Olivier, A., Human, P., and Wearne, D. (1996). Problem solving as a basis for reform in curriculum and instruction: The case of mathematics. *Educational Researcher, 25*(4), 12-21.

Hiebert, J., Carpenter, T., Fennema, E., Fuson, K.C., Wearne, D., Murray, H., Olivier, A., and Human, P. (1997). *Making sense: Teaching and learning mathematics with understanding.* Portsmouth, NH: Heinemann.

Holt, J. (1964). *How children fail.* New York: Dell.

Hufferd-Ackles, K., Fuson, K., and Sherin, M.G. (2004). Describing levels and components of a math-talk community. *Journal for Research in Mathematics Education, 35*(2), 81-116.

Isaacs, A.C., and Carroll, W.M. (1999). Strategies for basic-facts instruction. *Teaching Children Mathematics, 5*(9), 508-515.

Kalchman, M., and Case, R. (1999). Diversifying the curriculum in a mathematics classroom streamed for high-ability learners: A necessity unassumed. *School Science and Mathematics, 99*(6), 320-329.

Kameenui, E.J., and Carnine, D.W. (Eds.). (1998). *Effective teaching strategies that accommodate diverse learners.* Upper Saddle River, NJ: Prentice-Hall.

Kerkman, D.D., and Siegler, R.S. (1993). Individual differences and adaptive flexibility in lower-income children's strategy choices. *Learning and Individual Differences, 5*(2), 113-136.

Kilpatrick, J., Martin, W.G., and Schifter, D. (Eds.). (2003). *A research companion to principles and standards for school mathematics.* Reston, VA: National Council of Teachers of Mathematics.

Knapp, M.S. (1995). *Teaching for meaning in high-poverty classrooms.* New York: Teachers College Press.

Lampert, M. (1986). Knowing, doing, and teaching multiplication. *Cognition and Instruction, 3*, 305-342.

Lampert, M. (1992). Teaching and learning long division for understanding in school. In G. Leinhardt, R.T. Putnam, and R.A. Hattrup (Eds.), *The analysis of arithmetic for mathematics teaching* (pp. 221-282). Mahwah, NJ: Lawrence Erlbaum Associates.

Lave, J. (1988). *Cognition in practice: Mind, mathematics and culture in everyday life.* London, England: Cambridge University Press.

LeFevre, J., and Liu, J. (1997). The role of experience in numerical skill: Multiplication performance in adults from Canada and China. *Mathematical Cognition, 3*(1), 31-62.

LeFevre, J., Kulak, A.G., and Bisantz, J. (1991). Individual differences and developmental change in the associative relations among numbers. *Journal of Experimental Child Psychology, 52*, 256-274.

Leinhardt, G., Putnam, R.T., and Hattrup, R.A. (Eds.). (1992). The *analysis of arithmetic for mathematics teaching.* Mahwah, NJ: Lawrence Erlbaum Associates.

Lemaire, P., and Siegler, R.S. (1995). Four aspects of strategic change: Contributions to children's learning of multiplication. *Journal of Experimental Psychology: General, 124*(1), 83-97.

Lemaire, P., Barrett, S.E., Fayol, M., and Abdi, H. (1994). Automatic activation of addition and multiplication facts in elementary school children. *Journal of Experimental Child Psychology, 57*, 224-258.

Lewis, C. (2002). *Lesson study: A handbook of teacher-led instructional change.* Philadelphia, PA: Research for Better Schools.

Lo Cicero, A., Fuson, K.C., and Allexaht-Snider, M. (1999). Making a difference in Latino children's math learning: Listening to children, mathematizing their stories, and supporting parents to help children. In L. Ortiz-Franco, N.G. Hernendez, and Y. De La Cruz (Eds.), *Changing the faces of mathematics: Perspectives on Latinos* (pp. 59-70). Reston, VA: National Council of Teachers of Mathematics.

McClain, K., Cobb, P., and Bowers, J. (1998). A contextual investigation of three-digit addition and subtraction. In L. Morrow (Ed.), *Teaching and learning of algorithms in school mathematics* (pp. 141-150). Reston, VA: National Council of Teachers of Mathematics.

McKnight, C.C., and Schmidt, W.H. (1998). Facing facts in U.S. science and mathematics education: Where we stand, where we want to go. *Journal of Science Education and Technology, 7*(1), 57-76.

McKnight, C.C., Crosswhite, F.J., Dossey, J.A., Kifer, E., Swafford, J.O., Travers, K.T., and Cooney, T.J. (1989). *The underachieving curriculum: Assessing U.S. school mathematics from an international perspective.* Champaign, IL: Stipes.

Miller, K.F., and Paredes, D.R. (1990). Starting to add worse: Effects of learning to multiply on children's addition. *Cognition, 37,* 213-242.

Moss, J., and Case, R. (1999). Developing children's understanding of rational numbers: A new model and experimental curriculum. *Journal for Research in Mathematics Education, 30*(2), 122-147.

Mulligan, J., and Mitchelmore, M. (1997). Young children's intuitive models of multiplication and division. *Journal for Research in Mathematics Education, 28*(3), 309-330.

National Council of Teachers of Mathematics. (1989). *Curriculum and evaluation standards for school mathematics.* Reston, VA: National Council of Teachers of Mathematics.

National Council of Teachers of Mathematics. (1991). *Professional standards for teaching mathematics.* Reston, VA: National Council of Teachers of Mathematics.

National Council of Teachers of Mathematics. (2000). *Principles and standards for school mathematics.* Reston, VA: National Council of Teachers of Mathematics.

National Research Council. (2001). *Adding it up: Helping children learn mathematics.* Mathematics Learning Study Committee, J. Kilpatrick, J. Swafford, and B. Findell (Eds.). Center for Education, Division of Behavioral and Social Sciences and Education. Washington, DC: National Academy Press.

National Research Council. (2002). *Helping children learn mathematics.* Mathematics Learning Study Committee, J. Kilpatrick, J. Swafford, and B. Findell (Eds.). Center for Education, Division of Behavioral and Social Sciences and Education. Washington, DC: The National Academies Press.

National Research Council. (2004). *Learning and instruction: A SERP research agenda.* Panel on Learning and Instruction. M.S. Donovan and J.W. Pellegrino (Eds.). Division of Behavioral and Social Sciences and Education. Washington, DC: The National Academies Press.

Nesh, P., and Kilpatrick, J. (Eds.). (1990). Mathematics *and cognition: A research synthesis by the International Group for the Psychology of Mathematics Education.* Cambridge, MA: Cambridge University Press.

Nesher, P. (1992). Solving multiplication word problems. In G. Leinhardt, R.T. Putnam, and R.A. Hattrup (Eds.), *The analysis of arithmetic for mathematics teaching* (pp. 189-220). Mahwah, NJ: Lawrence Erlbaum Associates.

Peak, L. (1996). *Pursuing excellence: A study of the U.S. eighth-grade mathematics and science teaching, learning, curriculum, and achievement in an international context*. Washington, DC: National Center for Education Statistics.

Remillard, J.T. (1999). Curriculum materials in mathematics education reform: A framework for examining teachers' curriculum development. *Curriculum Inquiry, 29*(3), 315-342.

Remillard, J.T. (2000). Can curriculum materials support teachers' learning? *Elementary School Journal, 100*(4), 331-350.

Remillard, J.T., and Geist, P. (2002). Supporting teachers' professional learning though navigating openings in the curriculum. *Journal of Mathematics Teacher Education, 5*(1), 7-34.

Resnick, L.B. (1987). *Education and learning to think.* Committee on Mathematics, Science, and Technology Education, Commission on Behavioral and Social Sciences and Education. Washington, DC: National Academy Press.

Resnick, L.B. (1992). From protoquantities to operators: Building mathematical competence on a foundation of everyday knowledge. In G. Leinhardt, R.T. Putnam, and R.A. Hattrup (Eds.), *The analysis of arithmetic for mathematics teaching* (pp. 373-429). Mahwah, NJ: Lawrence Erlbaum Associates.

Resnick, L.B., and Omanson, S.F. (1987). Learning to understand arithmetic. In R. Glaser (Ed.), *Advances in instructional psychology* (vol. 3, pp. 41-95). Mahwah, NJ: Lawrence Erlbaum Associates.

Resnick, L.B., Nesher, P., Leonard, F., Magone, M., Omanson, S., and Peled, I. (1989). Conceptual bases of arithmetic errors: The case of decimal fractions. *Journal for Research in Mathematics Education, 20*(1), 8-27.

Ron, P. (1998). My family taught me this way. In L.J. Morrow and M.J. Kenney (Eds.), *The teaching and learning of algorithms in school mathematics* (pp. 115-119). Reston, VA: National Council of Teachers of Mathematics.

Saxe, G.B. (1982). Culture and the development of numerical cognition: Studies among the Oksapmin of Papua New Guinea. In C.J. Brainerd (Ed.), *Progress in cognitive development research: Children's logical and mathematical cognition* (vol. 1, pp. 157- 176). New York: Springer-Verlag.

Schmidt, W., McKnight, C.C., and Raizen, S.A. (1997). *A splintered vision: An investigation of U.S. science and mathematics education.* Dordrecht, The Netherlands: Kluwer.

Schwartz, D.L., and Moore, J.L. (1998). The role of mathematics in explaining the material world: Mental models for proportional reasoning. *Cognitive Science, 22*, 471-516.

Secada, W.G. (1992). Race, ethnicity, social class, language, and achievement in mathematics. In D. Grouws (Ed.), *Handbook of research on mathematics teaching and learning* (pp. 623-660). New York: Macmillan.

Sherin, M.G. (2000a). Facilitating meaningful discussions about mathematics. *Mathematics Teaching in the Middle School, 6*(2), 186-190.

Sherin, M.G. (2000b). Taking a fresh look at teaching through video clubs. *Educational Leadership, 57*(8), 36-38.

Sherin, M.G. (2001). Developing a professional vision of classroom events. In T. Wood, B.S. Nelson, and J. Warfield (Eds.), *Beyond classical pedagogy: Teaching elementary school mathematics* (pp. 75-93). Mahwah, NJ: Lawrence Erlbaum Associates.

Sherin, M.G. (2002). A balancing act: Developing a discourse community in a mathematics classroom. *Journal of Mathematics Teacher Education, 5*, 205-233.

Shuell, T.J. (2001). Teaching and learning in a classroom context. In N.J. Smelser and P.B. Baltes (Eds.), *International encyclopedia of the social and behavioral sciences* (pp. 15468-15472). Amsterdam: Elsevier.

Siegler, R.S. (1988). Individual differences in strategy choices: Good students, not-so-good students, and perfectionists. *Child Development, 59*(4), 833-851.

Siegler, R.S. (2003). Implications of cognitive science research for mathematics education. In J. Kilpatrick, W.G. Martin, and D.E. Schifter (Eds.), *A research companion to principles and standards for school mathematics* (pp. 1289-1303). Reston, VA: National Council of Teachers of Mathematics.

Simon, M.A. (1995). Reconstructing mathematics pedagogy from a constructivist perspective. *Journal for Research in Mathematics Education, 26*, 114-145.

Starkey, P., Spelke, E.S., and Gelman, R. (1990). Numerical abstraction by human infants. *Cognition, 36*, 97-127.

Steffe, L.P. (1994). Children's multiplying schemes. In G. Harel and J. Confrey (Eds.), *The development of multiplicative reasoning in the learning of mathematics* (pp. 3-39). New York: State University of New York Press.

Steffe, L.P., Cobb, P., and Von Glasersfeld, E. (1988). *Construction of arithmetical meanings and strategies.* New York: Springer-Verlag.

Sternberg, R.J. (1999). The theory of successful intelligence. *Review of General Psychology, 3*(4), 292-316.

Stigler, J.W., and Hiebert, J. (1999). *Teaching gap.* New York: Free Press.

Stigler, J.W., Fuson, K.C., Ham, M., and Kim, M.S. (1986). An analysis of addition and subtraction word problems in American and Soviet elementary mathematics textbooks. *Cognition and Instruction, 3*(3), 153-171.

Stipek, D., Salmon, J.M., Givvin, K.B., Kazemi, E., Saxe, G., and MacGyvers, V.L. (1998). The value (and convergence) of practices suggested by motivation research and promoted by mathematics education reformers. *Journal for Research in Mathematics Education, 29*, 465-488.

Thornton, C.A. (1978). Emphasizing thinking in basic fact instruction. *Journal for Research in Mathematics Education, 9*, 214-227.

Thornton, C.A., Jones, G.A., and Toohey, M.A. (1983). A multisensory approach to thinking strategies for remedial instruction in basic addition facts. *Journal for Research in Mathematics Education, 14*(3), 198-203.

Tobias, S. (1978). *Overcoming math anxiety.* New York: W.W. Norton.

Van de Walle, J.A. (1998). *Elementary and middle school mathematics: Teaching developmentally, third edition.* New York: Longman.

Van de Walle, J.A. (2000). *Elementary school mathematics: Teaching developmentally, fourth edition.* New York: Longman.

Wynn, K. (1996). Infants' individuation and enumeration of actions. *Psychological Science, 7*, 164-169.

Zucker, A.A. (1995). Emphasizing conceptual understanding and breadth of study in mathematics instruction. In M.S. Knapp (Ed.), *Teaching for meaning in high-poverty classrooms*. New York: Teachers College Press.

SUGGESTED READING LIST FOR TEACHERS

Carpenter, T.P. Fennema, E., Franke, M.L., Empson, S.B., and Levi, L.W. (1999). *Children's mathematics: Cognitively guided instruction*. Portsmouth, NH: Heinemann.

Fuson, K.C. (1988). Subtracting by counting up with finger patterns. (Invited paper for the Research into Practice Series.) *Arithmetic Teacher*, 35(5), 29-31.

Hiebert, J., Carpenter, T., Fennema, E., Fuson, K.C., Wearne, D., Murray, H., Olivier, A., and Human, P. (1997). *Making sense: Teaching and learning mathematics with understanding*. Portsmouth, NH: Heinemann.

Jensen, R.J. (Ed.). (1993). *Research ideas for the classroom: Early childhood mathematics*. New York: Macmillan.

Knapp, M.S. (1995). *Teaching for meaning in high-poverty classrooms*. New York: Teachers College Press.

Leinhardt, G., Putnam, R.T., and Hattrup, R.A. (Eds.). (1992). *The analysis of arithmetic for mathematics teaching*. Mahwah, NJ: Lawrence Erlbaum Associates.

Lo Cicero, A., De La Cruz, Y., and Fuson, K.C. (1999). Teaching and learning creatively with the Children's Math Worlds Curriculum: Using children's narratives and explanations to co-create understandings. *Teaching Children Mathematics*, 5(9), 544-547.

Owens, D.T. (Ed.). (1993). *Research ideas for the classroom: Middle grades mathematics*. New York: Macmillan.

Schifter, D. (Ed.). (1996). *What's happening in math class? Envisioning new practices through teacher narratives*. New York: Teachers College Press.

Wagner, S. (Ed.). (1993). *Research ideas for the classroom: High school mathematics*. New York: Macmillan.

6

Fostering the Development of Whole-Number Sense: Teaching Mathematics in the Primary Grades

Sharon Griffin

After 15 years of inquiry into children's understanding and learning of whole numbers, I can sum up what I have learned very simply. To teach math, you need to know three things. You need to know where you are now (in terms of the knowledge children in your classroom have available to build upon). You need to know where you want to go (in terms of the knowledge you want all children in your classroom to acquire during the school year). Finally, you need to know what is the best way to get there (in terms of the learning opportunities you will provide to enable all children in your class to achieve your stated objectives). Although this sounds simple, each of these points is just the tip of a large iceberg. Each raises a question (e.g., Where are we now?) that I have come to believe is crucial for the design of effective mathematics instruction. Each also points to a body of knowledge (the iceberg) to which teachers must have access in order to answer that question. In this chapter, I explore each of these icebergs in turn in the context of helping children in the primary grades learn more about whole numbers.

Readers will recognize that the three things I believe teachers need to know to teach mathematics effectively are similar in many respects to the knowledge teachers need to implement the three *How People Learn* principles (see Chapter 1) in their classrooms. This overlap should not be surprising. Because teaching and learning are two sides of the same coin and because effective teaching is defined primarily in terms of the learning it supports, we cannot talk about one without talking about the other. Thus when I address each of the three questions raised above, I will at the same time offer preschool and elementary mathematics teachers a set of resources they can use to implement the three principles of *How People Learn* in their classrooms and, in so doing, create classrooms that are student-centered, knowledge-centered, community-centered, and assessment-centered.

Addressing the three principles of *How People Learn* while exploring each question occurs quite naturally because the bodies of knowledge that underlie effective mathematics teaching provide a rich set of resources that teachers can use to implement these principles in their classrooms. Thus, when I explore question 1 (Where are we now?) and describe the number knowledge children typically have available to build upon at several specific age levels, I provide a tool (the Number Knowledge test) and a set of examples of age-level thinking that teachers can use to enact Principle 1—*eliciting, building upon, and connecting student knowledge*—in their classrooms. When I explore question 2 (Where do I want to go?) and describe the knowledge networks that appear to be central to children's mathematics learning and achievement and the ways these networks are built in the normal course of development, I provide a framework that teachers can use to enact Principle 2—*building learning paths and networks of knowledge*—in their classrooms. Finally, when I explore question 3 (What is the best way to get there?) and describe elements of a mathematics program that has been effective in helping children acquire whole-number sense, I provide a set of learning tools, design principles, and examples of classroom practice that teachers can use to enact Principle 3—*building resourceful, self-regulating mathematical thinkers and problem solvers*—in their classrooms. Because the questions I have raised are interrelated, as are the principles themselves, teaching practices that may be effective in answering each question and in promoting each principle are not limited to specific sections of this chapter, but are noted throughout.

I have chosen to highlight the questions themselves in my introduction to this chapter because it was this set of questions that motivated my inquiry into children's knowledge and learning in the first place. By asking this set of questions every time I sat down to design a math lesson for young children, I was able to push my thinking further and, over time, construct better answers and better lessons. If each math teacher asks this set of questions on a regular basis, each will be able to construct his or her own set of answers for the questions, enrich our knowledge base, and improve mathematics teaching and learning for at least one group of children. By doing so, each teacher will also embody the essence of what it means to be a resourceful, self-regulating mathematics teacher. The questions themselves are thus more important than the answers. But the reverse is also true:

although good questions can generate good answers, rich answers can also generate new and better questions.

I now turn to the answers I have found useful in my own work with young children. By addressing question 2 (Where do I want to go?) first, I hope to give readers a sense of the general direction in which we are heading before I turn to question 1 (Where are we now?) and provide a detailed description of the knowledge children generally have available to build upon at each age level between 4 and 8. While individual children differ a great deal in the rate at which they acquire number knowledge, teachers are charged with teaching a class of students grouped by age. It is therefore helpful in planning instruction to focus on the knowledge typical among children of a particular age, with the understanding that there will be considerable variation. In a subsequent section, I use what we have learned about children's typical age-level understandings to return to the issue of the knowledge to be taught and to provide a more specific answer for question 2.

DECIDING WHAT KNOWLEDGE TO TEACH

All teachers are faced with a dizzying array of mathematics concepts and skills they are expected to teach to groups of students who come to their classrooms with differing levels of preparedness for learning. This is true even at the preschool level. For each grade level, the knowledge to be taught is prescribed in several documents—the national standards of the National Council of Teachers of Mathematics (NCTM), state and district frameworks, curriculum guides—that are not always or even often consistent. Deciding what knowledge to teach to a class as a whole or to any individual child in the class is no easy matter.

Many primary school teachers resolve this dilemma by selecting number sense as the one set of understandings they want all students in their classrooms to acquire. This makes sense in many respects. In the NCTM standards, number sense is the major learning objective in the standard (numbers and operations) to which primary school teachers are expected to devote the greatest amount of attention. Teachers also recognize that children's ability to handle problems in other areas (e.g., algebra, geometry, measurement, and statistics) and to master the objectives listed for these standards is highly dependent on number sense. Moreover, number sense is given a privileged position on the report cards used in many schools, and teachers are regularly required to evaluate the extent to which their students "demonstrate number sense." In one major respect, however, the choice of number sense as an instructional objective is problematic. Although most teachers and lay people alike can easily recognize number sense when they see it, defining what it is and how it can be taught is much more difficult.

Consider the responses two kindergarten children provide when asked the following question from the Number Knowledge test (described in full later in this chapter): "If you had four chocolates and someone gave you three more, how many would you have altogether?"

Alex responds by scrunching up his brow momentarily and saying, "seven." When asked how he figured it out, he says, "Well, 'four' and 'four' is 'eight' [displaying four fingers on one hand and four on the other hand to demonstrate]. But we only need three more [taking away one finger from one hand to demonstrate]. So I went—'seven,' 'eight.' Seven is one less than eight. So the answer is seven."

Sean responds by putting up four fingers on one hand and saying (under his breath), "Four. Then three more—'five, six, seven.'" In a normal tone of voice, Sean says "seven." When asked how he figured it out, Sean is able to articulate his strategy, saying, "I started at four and counted—'five, six, seven'" (tapping the table three times as he counts up, to indicate the quantity added to the initial set).

It will be obvious to all kindergarten teachers that the responses of both children provide evidence of good number sense. The knowledge that lies behind that sense may be much less apparent, however. What knowledge do these children have that enables them to come up with the answer in the first place and to demonstrate number sense in the process? Scholars have studied children's mathematical thinking and problem solving, tracing the typical progression of understanding or developmental pathway for acquiring number knowledge.[1] This research suggests that the following understandings lie at the heart of the number sense that 5-year-olds such as Alex and Sean are able to demonstrate on this problem: (1) they know the counting sequence from "one" to "ten" and the position of each number word in the sequence (e.g., that "five" comes after "four" and "seven" comes before "eight"); (2) they know that "four" refers to a set of a particular size (e.g., it has one fewer than a set of five and one more than a set of 3), and thus there is no need to count up from "one" to get a sense of the size of this set; (3) they know that the word "more" in the problem means that the set of four chocolates will be increased by the precise amount (three chocolates) given in the problem; (4) they know that each counting number up in the counting sequence corresponds precisely to an increase of one unit in the size of a set; and (5) it therefore makes sense to count on from "four" and to say the next three numbers up in the sequence to figure out the answer (or, in Alex's case, to retrieve the sum of four plus four from memory, arrive at "eight," and move one number back in the sequence). This complex knowledge network—called a *central conceptual structure for whole number*—is described in greater detail in a subsequent section.

The knowledge that Alex and Sean demonstrate is not limited to the understandings enumerated above. It includes computational fluency (e.g., ease and proficiency in counting) and awareness of the language of quantity (e.g., that "altogether" indicates the joining of two sets), which were acquired earlier and provided a base on which the children's current knowledge was constructed. Sean and Alex also demonstrate impressive metacognitive skills (e.g., an ability to reflect on their own reasoning and to communicate it clearly in words) that not only provide evidence of number sense, but also contributed to its development.

Finally, children who demonstrate this set of competencies also show an ability to answer questions about the joining of two sets when the contexts vary considerably, as in the following problems: "If you take four steps and then you take three more, how far have you gone?" and "If you wait four hours and then you wait three more, how long have you waited?" In both of these problems, the quantities are represented in very different ways (as steps along a path, as positions on a dial), and the language used to describe the sum ("How far?" "How long?") differs from that used to describe the sum of two groups of objects ("How many?"). The ability to apply number knowledge in a flexible fashion is another hallmark of number sense.

Each of the components of number sense mentioned thus far is described in greater detail in a subsequent section of this chapter. For now it is sufficient to point out that the network of knowledge the components represent—the central conceptual structure for whole number—has been found to be central to children's mathematics learning and achievement in at least two ways. First, as mentioned above, it enables children to make sense of a broad range of quantitative problems in a variety of contexts (see Box 6-1 for a discussion of research that supports this claim). Second, it provides the base—the building block—on which children's learning of more complex number concepts, such as those involving double-digit numbers, is built (see Box 6-2 for research support for this claim). Consequently, this network of knowledge is an important set of understandings that should be taught. In choosing number sense as a major learning goal, teachers demonstrate an intuitive understanding of the essential role of this knowledge network and the importance of teaching a core set of ideas that lie at the heart of learning and competency in the discipline (learning principle 2). Having a more explicit understanding of the factual, procedural, and conceptual understandings that are implicated and intertwined in this network will help teachers realize this goal for more children in their classrooms.

Once children have consolidated the set of understandings just described for the oral counting sequence from "one" to "ten," they are ready to make sense of written numbers (i.e., numerals). Now, when they are exposed to

BOX 6-1 The Central Conceptual Structure Hypothesis: Support for the First Claim

A central conceptual structure is a powerful organizing knowledge network that is extremely broad in its range of application and that plays a central role in enabling individuals to master the problems that the domain presents. The word "central" implies (1) that the structure is vital to successful performance on a range of tasks, ones that often transcend individual disciplinary boundaries; and (2) that future learning in these tasks is dependent on the structure, which often forms the initial core around which all subsequent learning is organized.

To test the first of these claims, Griffin and Case selected two groups of kindergarten children who were at an age when children typically have acquired the central conceptual structure for whole number, but had not yet done so.[2] All the children were attending schools in low-income, inner-city communities. In the first part of the kindergarten year, all the children were given a battery of developmental tests to assess their central conceptual understanding of whole number (Number Knowledge test) and their ability to solve problems in a range of other areas that incorporate number knowledge, including scientific reasoning (Balance Beam test), social reasoning (Birthday Party task), moral reasoning (Distributive Justice task), time telling (Time test), and money knowledge (Money test). On this test administration, no child in either group passed the Number Knowledge test, and fewer than 20 percent of the children passed any of the remaining tests.

One group of children (the treatment group) was exposed to a mathematics program called Number Worlds that had been specifically designed to teach the central conceptual structure for whole number. The second group of children (a matched control group) received a variety of other forms of mathematics instruction for the same time period (about 10 weeks). The performance of these two groups on the second administra-

the symbols that correspond to each number name and given opportunities to connect name to symbol, they will bring all the knowledge of what that name means with them, and it will accrue to the symbol. They will thus be able to read and write number symbols with meaning. To build a learning path that matches children's observed progression of understanding, this would be a reasonable next step for teachers to take. Finally, with experience in using this knowledge network, children eventually become capable

tion of the same tests at the end of the kindergarten year is presented in the following table. The treatment group—those exposed to the Number Worlds curriculum—improved substantially in all test areas, far surpassing the performance of the control group. Because no child in the treatment group had received any training in any of the areas tested in this battery besides number knowledge, the strong post-training performance of the treatment group on these tasks can be attributed to the construction of the central conceptual structure for whole number, as demonstrated in the children's (post-training) performance on the Number Knowledge test. Other factors that might have accounted for these findings, such as more individual attention and/or instructional time given to the treatment group, were carefully controlled in this study.

Percentages of Children Passing the Second Administration of the Number Knowledge Test and Five Numerical Transfer Tests

Test[a]	Control Group (N = 24)	Treatment Group (N = 23)
Number Knowledge (5/6)	25	87
Balance Beam (2/2)	42	96
Birthday Party (2/2)	42	96
Distributive Justice (2/2)	37	87
Time Telling (4/5)	21	83
Money Knowledge (4/6)	17	43

[a]Number of items out of total used as the criterion for passing the test are given in parentheses.

of applying their central conceptual understandings to two distinct quantitative variables (e.g., tens and ones, hours and minutes, dollars and cents) and of handling two quantitative variables in a coordinated fashion. This ability permits them to solve problems involving double-digit numbers and place value, for example, and introducing these concepts at this point in time (sometime around grade 2) would be a reasonable next step for teachers to

BOX 6-2 The Central Conceptual Structure Hypothesis: Support for the Second Claim

To test the second centrality claim—that future learning is dependent on the acquisition of the central conceptual structure for whole number—Griffin and Case conducted a follow-up study using the same sample of children as that in Box 6-1.[3] Children in both the treatment and control groups had graduated to a variety of first-grade classrooms in a number of different schools. Those who had remained in the general geographic area were located 1 year later and given a range of assessments to obtain measures of their mathematics learning and achievement in grade 1. Their teachers, who were blind to the children's status in the study, were also asked to rate each child in their classroom on a number of variables.

The results, displayed in the following table, present an interesting portrait of the importance of the central conceptual structure (assessed by performance at the 6-year-old level of the Number Knowledge test) for children's learning and achievement in grade 1. Recall that 87 percent of the treatment group had passed this level of the number knowledge test at the end of kindergarten compared with 25 percent of the control group. As the table indicates, most of the children in the control group (83 percent) had acquired this knowledge by the end of grade 1, but it appears to have been too late to enable many of them to master the grade 1 arithmetic tasks that require conceptual understanding (e.g., the Oral Arithmetic test; the Word Problems; test and teacher ratings of number sense, number meanings, and number use). On all of these measures, children who had acquired the central conceptual structure before the start of the school year did significantly better.

On the more traditional measures of mathematics achievement (e.g., the Written Arithmetic test and teacher ratings of addition and subtraction) that rely more on procedural knowledge than conceptual understanding, the performance of children in the control group was stronger. It was still inferior, however, in absolute terms to the performance of children in the treatment group.

Possibly the most interesting finding of all is the difference between the two groups on tests that tap knowledge not typically taught until grade 2 (e.g., the 8-year-old level of the Number Knowledge test and the 8-year-old level of the Word Problems test). On both of these tests, a number of children in the treatment group demonstrated that they had built upon their central conceptual structure for whole number during their first-grade experience and were beginning to construct the more elaborate understandings required to mentally solve double-digit arithmetic problems. Few children in the control group demonstrated this level of learning.

**Percentages of Children Passing the Number Knowledge
Test and Measures of Arithmetic Learning and
Achievement at the End of Grade 1**

Test	Control Group (N = 12)	Treatment Group (N= 11)	Significance of difference[a]
Number Knowledge Test			
6-year-old level	83	100	ns
8-year-old level	0	18	[a]
Oral Arithmetic Test	33	82	[a]
Written Arithmetic Test	75	91	ns
Word Problems Test			
6-year-old level	54	96	[a]
8-year-old level	13	46	[a]
Teacher Rating			
Number sense	24	100	[a]
Number meaning	42	88	[a]
Number use	42	88	[a]
Addition	66	100	ns
Subtraction	66	100	ns

ns= not significant; [a] = significant at the .01 level or better.

take in building learning paths that are finely attuned to children's observed development of number knowledge.

In this brief example, several developmental principles that should be considered in building learning paths and networks of knowledge (learning principle 2) for the domain of whole numbers have come to light. They can be summarized as follows:

- Build upon children's current knowledge. This developmental principle is so important that it was selected as the basis for one of the three primary learning principles (principle 1) of *How People Learn*.
- Follow the natural developmental progression when selecting new knowledge to be taught. By selecting learning objectives that are a natural next step for children (as documented in cognitive developmental research and described in subsequent sections of this chapter), the teacher will be creating a learning path that is developmentally appropriate for children, one that fits the progression of understanding as identified by researchers. This in turn will make it easier for children to construct the knowledge network that is expected for their age level and, subsequently, to construct the higher-level knowledge networks that are typically built upon this base.
- Make sure children consolidate one level of understanding before moving on to the next. For example, give them many opportunities to solve oral problems with real quantities before expecting them to use formal symbols.
- Give children many opportunities to use number concepts in a broad range of contexts and to learn the language that is used in these contexts to describe quantity.

I turn now to question 1 and, in describing the knowledge children typically have available at several successive age levels, paint a portrait of the knowledge construction process uncovered by research—the step-by-step manner in which children construct knowledge of whole numbers between the ages of 4 and 8 and the ways individual children navigate this process as a result of their individual talent and experience. Although this is the subject matter of cognitive developmental psychology, it is highly relevant to teachers of young children who want to implement the developmental principles just described in their classrooms. Because young children do not reflect on their own thinking very often or very readily and because they are not skilled in explaining their reasoning, it is difficult for a teacher of young children to obtain a picture of the knowledge and thought processes each child has available to build upon. The results of cognitive developmental research and the tools that researchers use to elicit children's understandings can thus supplement teachers' own knowledge and expertise in important ways, and help teachers create *learner-centered classrooms* that build effectively on students' current knowledge. Likewise, having a rich picture of the step-by step manner in which children typically construct knowledge of whole numbers can help teachers create *knowledge-centered classrooms* and learning pathways that fit children's spontaneous development.

BUILDING ON CHILDREN'S CURRENT UNDERSTANDINGS

What number knowledge do children have when they start preschool around the age of 4? As every preschool teacher knows, the answer varies widely from one child to the next. Although this variation does not disappear as children progress through the primary grades, teachers are still responsible for teaching a whole classroom of children, as well as every child within it, and for setting learning objectives for their grade level. It can be a great help to teachers, therefore, to have some idea of the range of understandings they can expect for children at their grade level and, equally important, to be aware of the mistakes, misunderstandings, and partial understandings that are also typical for children at this age level.

To obtain a portrait of these age-level understandings, we can consider the knowledge children typically demonstrate at each age level between ages 4 and 8 when asked the series of oral questions provided on the Number Knowledge test (see Box 6-3). The test is included here for discussion purposes, but teachers who wish to use it to determine their student's current level of understanding can do so.

Before we start, a few features of the Number Knowledge test deserve mention. First, because this instrument has been called a test in the developmental research literature, the name has been preserved in this chapter. However, this instrument differs from school tests in many ways. It is administered individually, and the questions are presented orally. Although right and wrong answers are noted, children's reasoning is equally important, and prompts to elicit this reasoning (e.g., How do you know? How did you figure that out?) are always provided on a subset of items on the test, especially when children's thinking and/or strategy use is not obvious when they are solving the problems posed. For these reasons, the "test" is better thought of as a tool or as a set of questions teachers can use to elicit children's conceptions about number and quantity and to gain a better understanding of the strategies children have available to solve number problems. When used at the beginning (and end) of the school year, it provides a good picture of children's entering (and exit) knowledge. It also provides a model for the ongoing, formative assessments that are conducted throughout the school year in *assessment-centered classrooms*.

Second, as shown in Box 6-3, the test is divided into three levels, with a preliminary (warm-up) question. The numbers associated with each level

BOX 6-3 **Number Knowledge Test**

Preliminary

Let's see if you can count from 1 to 10. Go ahead.

Level 0 (4-year-old level): Go to Level 1 if 3 or more correct.

1. Can you count these chips and tell me how many there are? (Place 3 counting chips in front of child in a row.)

2a. (Show stacks of chips, 5 vs. 2, same color.) Which pile has more?
2b. (Show stacks of chips, 3 vs. 7, same color.) Which pile has more?

3a. This time I'm going to ask you which pile has less.
(Show stacks of chips, 2 vs. 6, same color.) Which pile has less?
3b. (Show stacks of chips, 8 vs. 3, same color.) Which pile has less?

4. I'm going to show you some counting chips (Show a line of 3 red and 4 yellow chips in a row, as follows: R Y R Y R Y Y). Count just the yellow chips and tell me how many there are.

5. (Pick up all chips from the previous question.) Here are some more counting chips (show mixed array [not in a row] of 7 yellow and 8 red chips.) Count just the red chips and tell me how many there are.

Level 1 (6-year-old level): Go to Level 2 if 5 or more correct.

1. If you had 4 chocolates and someone gave you 3 more, how many chocolates would you have altogether?

2. What number comes right after 7?

3. What number comes two numbers after 7?

4a. Which is bigger: 5 or 4?
4b. Which is bigger: 7 or 9?

5a. This time, I'm going to ask you about smaller numbers.
Which is smaller: 8 or 6?
5b. Which is smaller: 5 or 7?

6a. Which number is closer to 5: 6 or 2? (Show visual array after asking the question.)

6b. Which number is closer to 7: 4 or 9? (Show visual array after asking the question.)

7. How much is 2 + 4? (OK to use fingers for counting.)

8. How much is 8 take away 6? (OK to use fingers for counting.)

9a. (Show visual array 8 5 2 6. Ask child to point to and name each numeral.) When you are counting, which of these numbers do you say first?

9b. When you are counting, which of these numbers do you say last?

Level 2 (8-year-old level): Go to Level 3 if 5 or more correct.

1. What number comes 5 numbers after 49?

2. What number comes 4 numbers before 60?

3a. Which is bigger: 69 or 71?
3b. Which is bigger: 32 or 28?

4a. This time I'm going to ask you about smaller numbers. Which is smaller: 27 or 32?
4b. Which is smaller: 51 or 39?

5a. Which number is closer to 21: 25 or 18? (Show visual array after asking the question.)
5b. Which number is closer to 28: 31 or 24? (Show visual array after asking the question.)

6. How many numbers are there in between 2 and 6? (Accept either 3 or 4.)

7. How many numbers are there in between 7 and 9? (Accept either 1 or 2.)

8. (Show visual array 12 54.) How much is 12 + 54?

9. (Show visual array 47 21.) How much is 47 take away 21?

(0, 1, 2) are drawn from the cognitive developmental tradition and are meant to suggest that the knowledge demonstrated at Level 0 is foundational for the knowledge demonstrated at Level 1, which represents a new, higher-order knowledge structure and a major reorganization of children's thought. The knowledge demonstrated at Level 2 represents an even more sophisticated version of this knowledge structure. The ages associated with each level of the test represent the midpoint in the 2-year age period during which this knowledge is typically constructed and demonstrated. Thus, the 4-year-old level captures children's thinking between the ages of 3 and 5 years, and the 6-year-old level captures children's thinking between the ages of 5 and 7 years. Finally, the age norms given in the test are the age ranges within which children in developed societies (drawn primarily from middle-income homes) typically pass that level of the test. But even when the norm is accurate for a group of children, it is important to remember that the knowledge possessed by individual children can differ by as much as 2 years (e.g., from knowledge typical of a 3- and a 5-year-old among the group at age 4). The test thus provides a set of broad developmental milestones for the majority of U.S. children, although the extent to which these levels hold true for children from vastly different sociocultural groups remains to be determined. (Directions for administering and scoring the test are provided in Box 6-4.)

Understandings of 4-Year-Olds

By the age of 4 to 5, most children can accurately count a set of three chips that are placed in front of them (Level 0, #1) and tell how many there are. They typically do so by touching the chips in a systematic fashion, usually proceeding from left to right; by saying "one," "two," "three" as they do so; and by giving the last number said, "three," as the answer. Fewer children (but still the majority) can also solve the more challenging counting problems at this level. They can count a set of four yellow chips that are intermixed with three red chips in a row (Level 0, #4) by counting just the yellow chips in the row or by physically moving the yellow chips into a separate space to make counting easier, and tell you how many there are. They can also count a set of eight red chips that are intermixed with seven white chips in a randomly distributed array (Level 0, #5), using one of the strategies just mentioned. Children who are successful with these items have learned to isolate the partial set to be counted, either mentally or physically, and to count items in this set in a systematic fashion, making sure that they know which chip they counted first and that they touch each chip only once when counting.

Children who are unsuccessful often fail to count systematically. They say the counting words and touch the chips, but these strategies are not

BOX 6-4 Directions for Administering and Scoring the Number Knowledge Test

Administration: The Number Knowledge test is an oral test. It is administered individually, and it requires an oral response. Paper and pencil are not permitted. Use of a follow-up question — "How did you figure that out?"— for Questions 1, 3, and 7 at Level 1 and Questions 1, 2, and 8 at Level 2 provides additional insight into children's reasoning and strategy use.

Scoring: One point is assigned for each item passed at Levels 0, 1, and 2. For all two-part items, both (a) and (b) must be passed to earn a point.

Props Needed: For Level 0: 12 red and 8 yellow counting chips, at least 1/8" thick (other contrasting colors can be substituted). For Levels 1 and 2: visual displays (see samples below). Each image should be at least twice the size of the samples shown here.

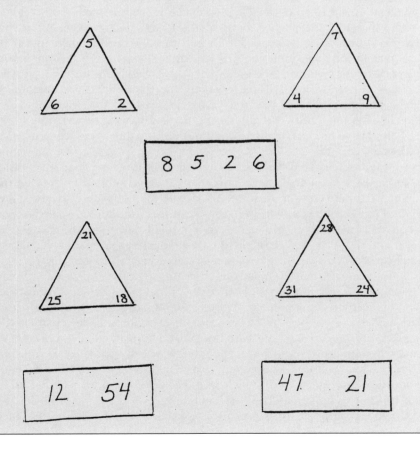

aligned, so they say more words than chips touched or skip some chips while counting, or (particularly on item #5) forget which chip they started with and count one or more chips twice. Children who make these errors are demonstrating some knowledge of counting. They are typically able to say the string of counting words in the correct sequence, and they know what must be done to figure out the answer to the question (e.g., touch the objects present while saying the words). What they do not yet understand is that the chips must be touched in a certain order and manner to coincide precisely with their recitation of the counting words. An even less sophisticated response is given by children who have not yet learned to say the counting words in the correct sequence and who may count the four red chips in item #4 by saying, "one," "two," "five," seven."

By the age of 4, most children can also compare two stacks of chips that differ in height in obvious, perceptually salient ways (Level 0, #2 and #3) and tell which pile has more or less. Children who can do this can solve the same problem when the question is phrased "Which pile is bigger (or smaller)?" and can solve similar problems involving comparisons of length (when the chips are aligned along a table) and of weight (when the chips are placed on a balance scale), provided the differences between the sets are visually obvious. Children who fail these items often look genuinely puzzled by the question, and either sit quietly waiting for further instruction or start to play with the chips by taking the stacks apart and moving the chips about. It appears that the words "more–less" (or "bigger–smaller," "longer–shorter," "heavier–lighter") and the comparison process that underlies them have no meaning for these children, and they are uncertain how to respond.

Although most children of this age can handle these quantity comparisons easily, they fail to achieve more than a chance rate of success when the differences between the sets are not visually obvious, and counting is required to determine which set has more or less. Although 4-year-olds have acquired some fairly sophisticated counting skills (as suggested above), they tend not to use counting to make quantity judgments, instead relying almost exclusively on visual cues in answering this sort of question.

If 4-year-olds can do these things, what might that suggest about what they know? Using this test and other performance assessments, researchers have constructed hypotheses about children's knowledge, which can be summarized as follows. By the age of 4, most children have constructed an initial *counting schema* (i.e., a well-organized knowledge network) that enables them to count verbally from one to five, use the one-to-one correspondence rule, and use the cardinality rule.[4] By the same age, most have also constructed an initial *quantity schema* that gives them an intuitive understanding of relative amount (they can compare two groups of objects that differ in size and tell which has a lot or a little) and of the transformations that change this amount (they know that one group will get bigger or smaller if objects are added to it or taken away). Most preschoolers can also use words to talk about these quantity relations and transformations.[5] As suggested earlier, however, most preschoolers do not use these schemas in a coordinated or integrated fashion.[6] It is as if they were stored in separate files in children's minds.

Understandings of 5-Year-Olds

A major change takes place for children when they can begin to solve problems involving small (single-digit) numbers and quantities without having real objects available to count. For the typical child this happens some time during the kindergarten year, between ages 5 and 6. With this change, children behave as if they are using a "mental counting line" inside their heads and/or their fingers to keep track of how many items they have counted. When asked how many chocolates they would have if they had four and someone gave them three more (Level 1, #1), the majority of children aged 5 to 6 can figure out the answer. The most advanced children will say that they just knew the answer was seven because four and three makes seven. More typically, children in this age range will use their fingers and one of three counting strategies to solve the problem. They may use the count-on strategy (the most sophisticated counting strategy) by starting their count at "four," often holding up four fingers to represent the first set, and then counting on "five," "six," "seven," often putting up three additional fingers to represent the second set. Alternatively, they may use the less sophisticated count-up-from-one strategy by starting their count at "one," putting up four fingers in sequence as they count up to four (to mark off the first set), and then continuing to count up to seven as they raise three additional fingers (to mark off the second set). Children who are unsure of this strategy will use it to put up seven fingers, counting as they do so, and will then use their noses or nods of their heads to count the fingers they have raised and thus determine that the answer to the question is seven.

Although it may take children 1 or 2 years to move from the least to the most sophisticated of these strategies, children using these approaches are in all cases demonstrating their awareness that the counting numbers refer to real-world quantities and can be used, in the absence of countable objects, to solve simple addition problems involving the joining of two sets. Children who respond to the same question by saying "I don't know" or by taking a wild guess and saying "one hundred" appear to lack this awareness. In between these two extremes are children who make a common error and say the answer is "five," thus demonstrating *some* understanding of addition (i.e., that the answer must be larger than four) but an incomplete understanding of how to use counting numbers to find the answer.

Kindergarten children use the same range of strategies to figure out what number comes two numbers after seven (Level 1, #3). Some use the count-on strategy to solve this problem and say, "seven [pause], eight, nine. The answer is nine." Others count up from one to get the same answer. Two common errors that children make on this problem shed light on what successful children appear to know about the number sequence. The first error involves starting at seven, saying two counting words—"seven, eight"—and explaining that eight is the answer. The second error is to say that the answer is "eight and nine" and to repeat this answer when prompted with the question, "Well, which is it—eight or nine?" Both of these answers show an understanding of the *order* of counting words but a weak (or incomplete) understanding of the position of each word in the number sequence and what position entails in terms of quantity. Finally, children who say "I don't know" to this question appear to lack either sufficient knowledge of the counting sequence or sufficient understanding of the term "after" to even attempt the problem.

At this age level, children are also able to tell which of two single-digit *numbers* is bigger or smaller (Level 1, #4 and #5). This is a large leap from the previous (4-year-old) level, at which children could compare quantities that were physically present as long as the differences between them were visible to the naked eye. This new competence implies the presence of a sophisticated set of understandings. Children who are successful with these items appear to know (1) that numbers indicate quantity and therefore (2) that numbers themselves have magnitude, (3) that the word "bigger" or "more" is sensible in this context, (4) that the numbers seven and nine occupy fixed positions in the counting sequence, (5) that seven comes before nine when one is counting up, (6) that numbers that come later in the sequence—are higher up—indicate larger quantities, and (7) that nine is therefore bigger (or more) than seven. Children who lack these understandings typically guess hesitantly. (Note that because children can get the right answer to these questions 50 percent of the time by guessing, they must pass both parts of each question to receive credit for these items on the test.)

Understandings of 6-Year-Olds

The last three items on Level 1 of the test are typically not passed until children are 6 years old, in first grade, and have had the benefit of some formal schooling. The addition problem "How much is two plus four?" and the subtraction problem "How much is eight take away six?" are particularly challenging because they are stated formally, in a decontextualized fashion, and because the quantity to be added or subtracted is larger than three, making it difficult for children to easily count up or back a few numbers to figure out the answer. The most sophisticated response children provide to the addition question is to count on from the largest addend (intuitively using the commutative principle) and to say "four [pause], five, six." Although many children use this strategy, many others start with the first addend in the stated problem (two); they then have the cumbersome job of counting on four more, making sure they count correctly at the same time they are keeping track of how many they have counted. It is not surprising that this strategy results in more errors in counting than does the first strategy.

Although some children make wild guesses in response to these questions, two other examples of a partial understanding are provided more frequently when children say, after pausing to think, that the answer is "five." Although five appears to be a favorite number for many children, regardless of the context, it is also a reasonable answer for both of these questions. If it reflects an awareness that the answer to the addition problem must be bigger than four (the largest addend), and the answer to the subtraction problem must be smaller than eight (the first subtrahend), it suggests a partial understanding of addition and subtraction.

The final item at Level 1 (#9) presents children with a conflicting cue (i.e., four numerals presented in a random order—8, 5, 6, 2) and gives them a chance to show just how solid their understanding of the counting sequence is: "When you're counting, which of these numbers do you say first (and last)?" Children can easily solve this problem if their experience with counting is extensive and their knowledge solid. If this is not the case, they are easily confused and give the first (or last) numeral listed in the display as their answer. As with all other items at this level of the test, the majority (about 60 percent) of children in developed societies acquire the knowledge needed for success sometime between the ages of 5 and 7.

Again we can ask what knowledge undergirds these performances. Scholars hypothesize that, around the age of 5 to 6, as children's knowledge of counting and quantity becomes more elaborate and differentiated it also gradually becomes more integrated, eventually merging in a single knowledge network termed here as a *central conceptual structure for whole number,* or a *mental counting line structure.*[7] This structure is illustrated in Figure 6-1. The figure can be thought of as a blueprint showing the important pieces of knowledge children have acquired (depicted by words or pictures in the figure) and the ways these pieces of knowledge are interrelated (depicted by arrows in the figure).

The top row of the figure illustrates children's knowledge of the counting words and suggests that they can not only say those words in sequence, but also understand the position of each word in the sequence and tell what number comes next, after, or before any number from one to ten. The second row shows that children know they touch each object once and only once when counting. The third row shows that children know the precise

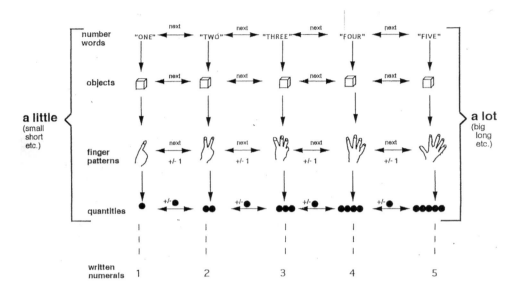

FIGURE 6-1 Mental counting line structure—a blueprint showing the important pieces of knowledge children have acquired (words or pictures) and the ways these pieces are interrelated (arrows).

finger patterns associated with each counting word; as indicated by the horizontal and vertical arrows that connect finger displays to each other and to the counting words, they also know that the finger display contains one more finger each time they count up by one and contains one less finger each time they count down by one. The fourth row suggests that children have acquired similar understandings with respect to objects (and other real-world quantities). The fifth row is connected to all the others with dotted lines to show that children acquire knowledge of the numerals that are associated with each counting word somewhat later, and this knowledge is not a vital component of the central conceptual structure. What is vital, however, are the brackets that contain the first four rows and connect the knowledge indicated within them (i.e., knowledge of counting) to several words used to make quantity judgments. These connectors show that children at this age can use their knowledge of counting to make precise judgments about relative amount.

With this higher-order knowledge structure, children come to realize that a question about addition or subtraction can be answered, in the absence of any concrete set of objects, simply by counting forward or backward along the counting string. They also come to realize that a simple verbal statement about a transformation, such as "I have four things, and then I get three more," has an automatic entailment with regard to quantity. One does not even need to see the objects involved or know anything else about them. These simple understandings actually mark a major revolution in children's understanding, which changes the world of formal mathematics from something that can occur only "out there" to something that can occur inside their own heads and under their own control. As this change takes place, children begin to use their counting skills in a wide range of other contexts. In effect, children realize that counting is something one can do to determine the relative value of two objects on a wide variety of dimensions (e.g., width, height, weight, musical tonality).[8]

Around age 6 to 7, supported by their entry into formal schooling, children typically learn the written numerals (though this is taught to some children earlier). When this new understanding is linked to their central conceptual understanding of number, children understand that the numerals are symbols for number words, both as ordered "counting tags" and as indicators of set size (i.e., numerical cardinality).

Understandings of 7-Year-Olds

Around the age of 7 to 8, in grade 2, children are able to solve the same sorts of problems they could solve previously for single-digit numbers, but for double-digits numbers. When asked what number comes five numbers after forty-nine (Level 2, #1) or four numbers before sixty (Level 2, #2), the majority of second graders can figure out the answer. They do so by counting up from forty-nine (or down from sixty), often subvocally and, less frequently than at the previous stage, using their fingers to keep track of how many they have counted up (or down). When children make errors on these problems, they demonstrate the same sorts of partial understandings that were described earlier. That is, they may show a strong partial understanding of double-digit numbers by making a counting error (e.g., counting the number from which they start as the first number added or subtracted), or a weak understanding by saying, "I don't know. That's a big number. I haven't learned them yet." Between these two extremes are children who know intuitively that the answer to each problem must be in the fifties but are unsure how to count up or down.

At this age level, children can also tell which of two double-digit numbers is bigger or smaller (Level 2, #3 and #4). To do so, they must recognize that numbers in the tens place of each problem (e.g., sixty-nine versus seventy-one) have a much greater value than numbers in the ones place, and thus outweigh the value of even big numbers such as nine that occur in the units position. In short, children who succeed on these items recognize that any number in the seventies is automatically bigger than any number in the sixties "because you have to go through all the numbers in the sixties before you even hit seventy." A common error children make—which reveals an absence of this awareness—is to choose consistently on the basis of the value of the unit digits and to say, for example, that sixty-nine is bigger than seventy-one because nine is larger than one.

Finally, typically toward the end of this age period, children are able to figure out how many whole numbers are in between two and six (Level 2, #7) and in between seven and nine (Level 2, #8). These are complex single-digit problems that require the use of two mental counting lines, one with the numbers involved in the problem and one with the numbers involved in the solution. Children who are successful with the first item often start the solution process by looking fixedly ahead and saying "two" [pause] "six," as if they were looking at an imaginary counting line and marking the numbers two and six on this line. They then proceed to count the numbers in between by nodding their heads; saying "three," "four," "five" (sometimes using their fingers to keep track of the second number line, in which "three" is one, "four" is two, and "five" is three); and providing "three" as the answer. This behavior suggests they are using one mental counting line as an operator to count the numbers on a second mental number line that shows the beginning and end points of the count. By contrast, children who are unsuccessful with this item often give "five" as the answer and explain this answer by saying that five is in between two and six. Although this answer demonstrates an understanding of the order of numbers in the counting sequence, it completely ignores the part of the question that asks, "How many numbers are there in between?" Other children look stunned when this question is posed, as if it is not a meaningful thing to ask, and respond "I don't know," suggesting that they have not yet come to understand that numbers have a fixed position in the counting sequence and can themselves be counted.

Understandings of 8-Year-Olds

The last two items at Level 2 are more complex than the previous items, and they are frequently not solved until children are 8 years old. Children succeed on the problem "How much is 12 plus 54?" most easily by reducing one of these numbers to a benchmark value, carrying the amount that was taken away in their heads, adding the new values, and then adding on the amount that was carried (e.g., "ten and fifty-four is sixty-four; add two; the answer is sixty-six"). Use of this strategy implies a good understanding of the additive composition of double-digit numbers and of the value of using benchmark numbers to make addition and subtraction easier.

Other children solve these problems more laboriously, with less sophisticated strategies. Some count on from fifty-four by ones until they have marked twelve fingers, essentially ignoring the base-ten value of these numbers and treating them as units. Others try to line the numbers up in their heads into the typical vertical format used on worksheets in the classroom. They then add the numbers in the ones column—"two and four is six"—and the numbers in the tens column—"five and one is six"—and, with much mental effort, say that the answer is sixty-six. Children using this solution strategy are essentially performing two single-digit addition operations in succession and are not demonstrating a good understanding of the base-ten features of double-digit numbers. As with all the other test problems, there are always some children who take a wild guess and produce an answer that is not even in the ballpark or who look puzzled and say, more or less forlornly, "I don't know. I haven't learned that yet."

Again we can ask what knowledge underlies these performances. Researchers have suggested that, around the age of 7 to 8 years, children's central conceptual understandings become more elaborate and more differentiated, permitting them to represent two distinct quantitative dimensions, such as tens and ones, in a coordinated fashion. With this new structure, called a *bidimensional central conceptual structure for number,* children are able to understand place value (e.g., represent the tens dimension and the ones dimension in the base-ten number system and work with these dimensions in a coordinated fashion). They are also able to solve problems involving two quantitative dimensions across multiple contexts, including time (hours and minutes), money (dollars and cents), and math class (tens and ones).[9]

ACKNOWLEDGING TEACHERS' CONCEPTIONS AND PARTIAL UNDERSTANDINGS

As illustrated in the foregoing discussion, the questions included on the Number Knowledge test can provide a rich picture of the number understandings, partial understandings, and problem-solving strategies that children in several age groups bring to instruction.

The test can serve another function as well, however, which is worth discussing in the present context: it can provide an opportunity for teachers to examine their own mathematical knowledge and to consider whether any of the partial understandings children demonstrate are ones they share as well. My own understanding of number has grown considerably over the past several years as a result of using this test with hundreds of children, listening to what they say, and examining how their explanations and understandings change as they grow older. Three insights in particular have influenced my teaching.

Insight #1: Math Is Not About Numbers, but About Quantity

It is easy to endorse the myth that math is about numbers because numbers, after all, are everywhere in math. What my work with children has taught me is that math is about quantity, and numbers express those quantities. As the age-level descriptions of children's understandings suggest, numbers acquire meaning for children when they recognize that each number refers to a particular quantity (which may be represented in a variety of different ways) and when they realize that numbers provide a means of describing quantity and quantity transformations more precisely than is possible using everyday language such as "lots," "little," or "more." This realization—that numbers are tools that can be used to describe, predict, and explain real-world quantities and quantity transactions—gives children a tremendous boost in mastering and using the number system. To help children construct this understanding, therefore, it is crucial to introduce numbers to children in the context of the quantities (e.g., objects, pictures of objects) and quantity representations (e.g., dot set patterns, number lines, thermometers, bar graphs, dials) that will give these numbers meaning as quantities.

Insight #2: Counting Words Is the Crucial Link Between the World of Quantity and the World of Formal Symbols

Numbers are expressed in our culture in two quite different ways: orally, as a set of counting words, and graphically, as a set of formal symbols. Because children start using the counting words so early—learning to say "one–two–three" almost as soon as they learn to talk—it may be tempting to think that they should abandon this early form of expression when they start their formal schooling and learn to use the graphic symbol system instead. But children have spent most of their preschool years using the counting words in the context of their real-world exploration and ever so slowly building up a network of meaning for each word. Why should they be deprived of this rich conceptual network when they start their school-based math instruction and be required, instead, to deal with a set of symbols that have no inherent meaning? Mathematics instruction that takes advantage of this prior knowledge and experience—rather than denying it or presenting math as distinct from these everyday experiences—is bound to be more accessible to children.

In my own work, I have found that the key to helping children acquire meanings for symbols is providing opportunities for them to connect the symbol system to the (more familiar) counting words. This is best accomplished when children have previously acquired a solid set of connections between the counting words themselves and the quantities to which they refer. Many third graders are still constructing this latter understanding (e.g., acquiring an awareness of the links between double-digit counting numbers and the quantities to which they refer). Thus, to enable children to use their current understandings to build new ones, it is crucial that they have ample opportunities to use the oral language system to make sense of quantitative problems and that they be introduced to the graphic equivalents of that system in this familiar context.

Insight #3: Acquiring an Understanding of Number Is a Lengthy, Step-by-Step Process

I used to think (or at least I liked to believe) that if I designed an especially elegant lesson that made the concept I was attempting to teach transparent for children, I could produce an "aha" experience and enable the children to grasp a connection that was previously unavailable to them. I now realize that this goal (or wish) is not only unrealistic, but also unobtainable if the concept to be learned is not within reach of the child's current level of understanding. As the earlier age-level descriptions of children's understanding suggest, the acquisition of number knowledge is, by its very nature, a step-by-step process, with each new understanding building systematically and incrementally on previous understandings. Although I still believe in the value of carefully designed, elegant lessons, my goals, while still ambitious, are more limited. Now, I hope that a lesson or series of lessons will enable a child to move up one level at a time in his or her understanding, to deepen and consolidate each new understanding before moving on to the next, and to gradually construct a set of understandings that are more sophisticated and "higher-level" than the ones available at the start. I now recognize that such a process takes time and that each child may move through the process at his or her own pace.

REVISITING QUESTION 2: DEFINING THE KNOWLEDGE THAT SHOULD BE TAUGHT

Now that we have a better idea of the knowledge children have available to work with at several age levels and the manner in which this knowledge is constructed, it is possible to paint a more specific portrait of the knowledge that should be taught in school, at each grade level from preschool through second grade, to ensure that each child acquires a well-developed whole-number sense. As suggested previously, the knowledge taught to each child should be based, at least in part, on his or her existing understandings (Principle 1). However, because teachers are required to teach whole classrooms of children (as well as individuals), they need a set of general learning objectives for each grade level that will be appropriate for the range of children involved. Two sets of objectives are paramount for this purpose. The first is to ensure that all children in the class attain the developmental milestones—the central conceptual structures for whole number—described earlier; the second is to ensure that all children become familiar with the major ways in which number and quantity are represented and talked about so they can recognize and make sense of number problems they encounter across contexts.

The framework presented in the previous section leads to a clear set of learning goals for each grade level from prekindergarten through grade 2 that are within reach of the majority of children at that level and that teachers can use to "teach" the developmental milestones (i.e., to ensure that children who have not yet acquired these central conceptual understandings have an opportunity to do so). Using this framework, it can be suggested that a major goal for the preschool year is to ensure that children acquire a well-developed counting schema and a well-developed quantity schema. A major goal for the kindergarten year is to ensure that children acquire a well-consolidated central conceptual structure for single-digit numbers. A major goal for first grade is to help children link this structure to the formal symbol system and to construct the more elaborated knowledge network this entails. Finally, a major goal for second grade is to help children acquire the bidimensional central conceptual structure for double-digit numbers that underlies a solid understanding of the base-ten system.

These grade-level goals (see Box 6-5) not only specify knowledge networks to be taught at specific grade levels to foster the development of whole-number sense, but also form a "number sense" learning pathway—a sequence of learning objectives teachers can use to individualize instruction for children who are progressing at a rate that is faster or slower than that of the rest of the class. The second body of knowledge to be taught—knowledge of the major ways number and quantity are represented and talked about—can be defined most clearly in the context of the tools developed to teach it, as discussed in the following section.

HOW CAN THIS KNOWLEDGE BE TAUGHT?: THE CASE OF NUMBER WORLDS

During the past two decades, several innovative programs and approaches to mathematics teaching have been developed to teach whole-number concepts and to put the principles of *How People Learn* into curricular action.[10] The program described here—Number Worlds—was designed specifically to teach the knowledge described above. It is also the one with which I am most familiar. As codeveloper of this program, I was involved in its inception in 1988 under the name Rightstart. In the ensuing years, I have continued to participate in the program's development, revising it annually to achieve a better fit with teachers' needs and learning goals, conducting program evaluations to assess its effects on children's learning and achievement, and ultimately producing the expanded set of prekindergarten–grade 2 programs now called Number Worlds.[11] Like the other programs and approaches referred to above, Number Worlds was designed specifically to (1) build on children's existing understandings (learning principle 1), (2) help children construct new knowledge, both factual and conceptual, that is organized so as to facilitate retrieval and application (learning principle 2), and (3) require and teach metacognitive strategies (learning principle 3). Like each of the other programs and approaches referred to above, Number Worlds provides a distinctive way of thinking about mathematics and mathematics teaching.

To maximize opportunities for all children to achieve the knowledge objectives of the Number Worlds program, a set of design principles drawn from the *How People Learn* research base was adopted and used to create each of the more than 200 activities included in the program. The principles that are most relevant to the present discussion are listed below. In the ensuing discussion, each design principle is described more fully and illustrated with one or more activities from the Number Worlds program:

1. Activities should expose children to the major ways number is represented and talked about in developed societies.

2. Activities should provide opportunities to link the "world of quantity" with the "world of counting numbers" and the "world of formal symbols."

3. Activities should provide visual and spatial analogs of number representations that children can actively explore in a hands-on fashion.

4. Activities should be affectively engaging and capture children's imagination so knowledge constructed is embedded not only in their minds, but also in their hopes, fears, and passions.

5. Activities should provide opportunities for children to acquire computational fluency as well as conceptual understanding.

6. Activities should encourage or require the use of metacognitive processes (e.g., problem solving, communication, reasoning) that will facilitate knowledge construction.

Design Principle 1: Exposing Children to Major Forms of Number Representation

Number is represented in our culture in five major ways: through objects, dot set patterns, segments on a line, segments on a scale (or bar graph),

BOX 6-5 Learning Goals for Prekindergarten Through Grade 2

Grade Level	Knowledge Networks That All Children Should Acquire	Examples of Specific Competencies within Each Network[a]
Prekindergarten	Initial counting schema	Can count verbally from one to five (or ten). Can use the one-to one correspondence rule. Knows the cardinal value of each number.
	Initial quantity schema	Understands relative amount (a lot–a little). Knows that an amount gets bigger if objects added and smaller if objects taken away.
Kindergarten	Central conceptual structure for single-digit numbers	Knows the relative value of numbers. Knows that set size increases by one with each counting number up in the sequence.

and segments or points on a dial. Children who are familiar with these forms of representation and the language used to talk about number in these contexts have a much easier time making sense of the number problems they encounter inside and outside of school. The Number Worlds program provides one example of how these forms of representation can be taught. In so doing, it illustrates what a *knowledge-centered classroom* might look like in the area of elementary mathematics.

At each grade level in this program, children explore five different lands. Learning activities developed for each land share a particular form of number representation while simultaneously addressing specific knowledge goals (i.e., the developmental milestones) for each grade level. The five forms of representation and the lands in which they appear are illustrated in Figure 6-2. As the figure suggests, the first land to which children are exposed is Object Land, where numbers are represented by the bundling of several

		Can use the counting numbers alone to solve addition and subtraction problems.
Grade 1	Central conceptual structure linked to formal symbol system	Knows the symbols associated with each number word and the names and symbols for addition, subtraction, and equality.
Grade 2	Central conceptual structure for double-digit numbers	Understands place value (e.g., a two in the ones place means two and a two in the tens place means 20); can solve double-digit addition and subtraction problems mentally.

<hr>

[a] Additional, more concrete, examples of the sorts of problems children can solve when they have acquired each knowledge network can be found in the Number Knowledge Test (Box 6-1). See the 4-year-old level items for the prekindergarten network; the 6-year-old level items (1 through 6) for the kindergarten network; the remaining 6-year-old level items for the grade 1 network; and the 8-year-old level items for the grade 2 network.

objects, such as pennies or fingers, into groups. This is the first way in which numbers were represented historically and the first that children learn naturally.[12] In Object Land, children first work with real objects (e.g., "How many crackers will you have left after you eat one? After you eat one more?") and then move on to working with pictures of objects (e.g., "Are there enough hats so that each clown will have one? How many more do you need? How do you know?").

The second land to which children are introduced is Picture Land, where numbers are represented as stylized, semiabstract dot set patterns that are equivalent to mathematical sets. These patterns provide a link between the world of movable objects and the world of abstract symbols. Unlike the real objects they represent, dot set pictures cannot be placed physically in one-to-one correspondence for easier comparison. Instead, a child must make a mental correspondence between two sets, for example by noticing that the

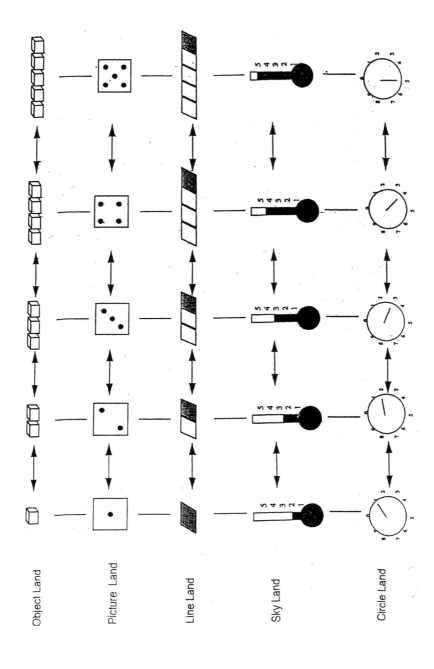

FIGURE 6-2 The five forms of representation and the lands in which they appear.

pattern for five is the same as that for four, except that the five pattern has one extra dot in the center. As children engage in Picture Land activities (e.g., by playing an assortment of card and dice games similar in format to War, Fish, and Concentration), they gradually come to think of these patterns as forming the same sort of ordered series as do the number words themselves. Numerals, another way of representing numbers, are also part of Picture Land, and are used extensively in the activity props that are provided at all grade levels and, by the children themselves, in the upper levels of the program. Tally marks are used as well in this land to record and compare quantities.

A third way to represent numbers is as segments along a line—for example, the lines that are found on board games such as Chutes and Ladders. The language that is used for numbers in this context is the language of distance. In Line Land, children come to understand (by playing games on a Human Game Mat and on an assortment of smaller number line game boards) that a number such as "four" can refer not only to a particular place on a line, but also to a number of moves *along* the line. One can talk about going four numbers forward from the number four on one's fourth turn. Perhaps the most important transition that children must make as they move from the world of small countable objects to that of abstract numbers and numerical operations is to treat the physical addition or subtraction of objects as equivalent to movement forward or backward along a line. All children eventually make this correspondence; until they do, however, they are unable to move from physical to mental operations with any insight.

Yet another way to represent numbers is with bar graphs and scales, such as thermometers. In Sky Land (a name chosen as a child-friendly substitute for the word "scale," as in "reach for the sky"), this sort of representation is always used in a vertical direction, such that bigger numbers are higher up. These forms of representation make a convenient context for introducing children to the use of numbers as a measure, as a way to keep track of continuous quantity in standard units. Systems for measuring continuous quantity have the same long history as do systems for enumerating discrete objects, and it is important to develop children's intuitions for the properties of the former systems from the outset.[13]

Dials are the final representation of number included in Number Worlds. Sundials and clocks are more sophisticated ways of representing numbers since they incorporate the cyclic quality—a path that repeats itself—possessed by certain real-world dimensions, such as time and the natural rhythm of the seasons. In Circle Land, children develop spatial intuitions (e.g., by playing games on a skating rink configuration that requires them to chart progress within and across revolutions to determine a winner) that become the foundation for understanding many concepts in mathematics dealing with circular motion (e.g., pie charts, time, and number bases).

Although the five forms of number representation have been introduced in a fixed order here, from easiest to most difficult, an important goal of the Number Worlds program is to help children appreciate the equivalence of these forms of representation and of the language used to talk about number in these contexts. To this end, children are encouraged to explore all lands and all number representations early in the school year by beginning with activities in each land that target lower-level knowledge objectives (labeled Level 1 activities) and by proceeding throughout the year to activities in each land that target higher-level knowledge objectives (labeled Level 3 activities). By moving back and forth across lands throughout the year, children gradually come to appreciate, for example, that "nine" is bigger than "seven" by a precise amount and that this difference holds whether these numbers are represented as groups of objects, as positions along a path, or as points on a scale. They also come to appreciate that this difference is the same whether it is talked about as "more" in one context, as "farther along" in another, or as "higher up" in a third. For adults, these various manifestations of the whole-number counting system are easily seen to be equivalent. To very young children, they are quite different, so different that they might appear to be from different "worlds." Helping children construct an organized knowledge network in which these ideas are interconnected (learning principle 2) is thus a major goal of Number Worlds.

Design Principle 2: Providing Opportunities to Link the "World of Quantity" with the "World of Counting Numbers" and the "World of Formal Symbols"

Although every activity created for the Number Worlds program provides opportunities to link the "world of quantity" with the "world of counting numbers" and the "world of formal symbols"—or to link two of these worlds—the three activities described in this section illustrate this principle nicely, at the simplest level. Readers should note that the remaining design principles are also illustrated in these examples, but to preserve the focus are not highlighted in this section.

Plus Pup

Plus Pup is an Object Land activity that is used in both the preschool and kindergarten programs to provide opportunities for children to (1) count a set of objects and identify how many there are, and (2) recognize that when one object is added, the size of the set is increased by one (see Figure 6-3). To play this game, the teacher and children put a certain number of cookies into a lunch bag to bring to school, carefully counting the cookies as they do so, and being sure they remember how many cookies they placed

FIGURE 6-3 Plus Pup—an Object Land activity used to provide opportunities for children to understand addition problems.

inside the bag. Next, the teacher (or a child volunteer) takes a little walk (as if going to school) and encounters Plus Pup along the way (by picking up the Plus Pup card). As the icon on the card suggests, Plus Pup gives the cookie carrier one more cookie. The bag is opened up slightly to receive a real cookie and is then promptly closed. The challenge children confront is this: How many cookies are in the bag now? How can we figure this out?

If the teacher is patient and allows children to explore these questions as genuine problems, a range of solution strategies are often provided as children play and replay the game with different quantities of cookies. The first and most obvious solution children suggest (and implement) is to open the bag, take the cookies out, and count them. This provides opportunities for the teacher to draw children's attention to the quantity transaction that has occurred to produce this amount. For example, the teacher may say, "We have five cookies now. How do we know how many Plus Pup gave us? How can we figure this out?" If no answers are forthcoming, the teacher can prompt the children by asking, "Does anyone remember how many cookies we had at the start?"—thus leading them to make sense of the quantity transaction that has occurred (i.e., the initial amount, the amount added, the end total) by describing the entire process in their own words.

As children replay this game, they gradually come to realize that they can use the counting numbers themselves, with or without their fingers, to solve this sort of problem, and that dumping the cookies out of the bag to count them is unnecessary. When children begin to offer this solution strategy, the teacher can shift the focus of her questions to ask, "Who can predict how many cookies are in the bag now? How do you know?" After predictions and explanations (or proofs) have been offered, the children can be allowed to examine the contents of the bag "to confirm or verify their predictions." Although preschoolers are often unfamiliar with these scientific terms when first introduced, it is not long before they understand the meaning of the terms in this context and use these words themselves, feeling very pleased with the air of sophistication this language bestows on their own mathematical activity. By encouraging problem solving and communication, this activity, like all activities in the program, makes children's thinking visible, and in so doing provides the basis for ongoing assessment that is the hallmark of *assessment-centered classrooms.*

The rationale that was created for this activity is as follows: "In this activity, a giving pup icon is used to give children a meaningful mental image of the addition operation. This image will serve as a conceptual bridge and help children build strong connections between an increase in quantity in the real world and the +1 symbol that describes this increase in the world of formal mathematics" (Object Land: Lesson #7). Although children are not expected to make explicit use of the +1 symbol in either the preschool or kindergarten program, it is available for those who are ready to take advantage of it. To our delight, children who have been exposed to this activity in their preschool or kindergarten year spontaneously remember Plus Pup when they encounter more complex addition problems later on, providing evidence they have indeed internalized the set of connections (among name, icon, and formal symbol) to which they were exposed earlier and are able to use this knowledge network to help them make sense of novel addition problems.

Minus Mouse

Once children have become familiar with Plus Pup and what Plus Pup does, they are introduced to Minus Mouse (see Figure 6-4). The format of

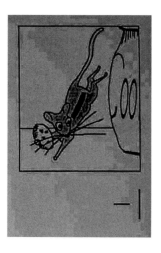

FIGURE 6-4 Minus Mouse—an Object Land activity used to provide opportunities for children to understand subtraction problems.

this activity is identical to that of the former except, of course, that whereas Plus Pup will add one cookie to the bag, Minus Mouse will take one away. The challenge children are asked to deal with in this activity is this: "How many cookies will we have left?" How can we figure this out? The similarly in format between these two activities and the repetition that results proves not to be the deterrent to children that adults might expect. Most young children prefer the comfort of the familiar to the excitement of the novel. Indeed, they appear to thrive on the opportunities this similarity provides for them to anticipate what might happen and, with confidence, make predictions about those outcomes.

Plus Pup Meets Minus Mouse

Once children have become familiar with Minus Mouse and reasonably adept at solving the problems this activity presents for a range of single-digit quantities, the teacher makes the problem more complex by including both Plus Pup and Minus Mouse in the same activity. This time, when the cookie carrier walks to school, he or she draws a card from a face-down pack and either Plus Pup or Minus Mouse will surface. The challenge this time is to interpret the icon with its associated symbol, to determine the action that should be performed (adding one more cookie to the bag or taking one away), and to figure out how to solve the problem of how many cookies are in the bag now and how we can figure this out. Children who have become reasonably competent at counting on (from the initial amount) to solve Plus Pup problems and counting back (from the initial amount) to solve Minus Mouse problems will now have to employ these strategies in a much more flexible fashion. They will also have to pay much closer attention to the meaning of the icon and its associated symbol and what this entails in terms of the quantity transaction to be performed. Both of these challenges pose bigger problems for children than adults might expect; thus, by providing opportunities for children to confront and resolve these challenges, this activity scaffolds the development of whole-number sense.

All three of the above activities can provide multiple opportunities for teachers to assess each child's current level of understanding as reflected in the solutions constructed (or not constructed) for each of the problems posed, the explanations provided, and the strategies employed (e.g., emptying the cookies out of the bag to determine how many or using the counting numbers instead, with or without fingers, to solve the problem). These informal assessments, in turn, can help teachers determine the quantity of cookies that would provide an appropriate starting place for the next round of each activity and the sorts of questions that should be posed to individual children to help them advance their knowledge. By using assessment in this formative fashion—to create learning opportunities that are finely attuned to children's current understandings and that help them construct new knowledge at the next level up—teachers are creating classrooms that are, at one and the same time, *learner-centered, knowledge-centered,* and *assessment-centered.*

Design Principle 3: Providing Visual and Spatial Analogs of Number Representations That Children Can Actively Explore in a Hands-On Fashion

Because the central conceptual understandings that the program was designed to teach involve the coordination of spatial and numeric concepts, it was deemed important to provide several opportunities for children to explore the number system in a variety of spatial contexts, to scaffold this coordination. The spatial contexts that were created for the Number Worlds program often take the form of game boards on which number is depicted as a position on a line, scale, or dial and on which quantity is depicted as segments on these line, scale, and dial representations. By using a pawn to represent "self" as player and by moving through these contexts to solve problems posed by the game, children gain a vivid sense of the relationship between movement along a line, scale, or dial and increases and decreases in quantity. This experience is illustrated in the following activities.

The Skating Party Game

This game is played in Circle Land at the kindergarten level. It was designed to help children realize that a dial (or a circular path) is another device for representing quantity, and that the same relationships that apply between numbers and movement on a number line apply also to numbers and movement in this context (see Figure 6-5). In this game, a dial is represented as a circular path. By including 10 segments on this path, numbered 0 to 9, this prop provides opportunities for children to acquire an intuitive understanding of the cyclical nature of the base-ten number system. This understanding is explicitly fostered and built upon in activities children encounter later on, at higher levels of the program. The explicit learning objectives that were developed for the Skating Party game are as follows: (1) identify or compute set size, and associate set size with a position on a dial (i.e., a circular path); (2) associate increasing a quantity with moving around a dial; and (3) compare positions on a dial to identify which have more, less, or the same amount, and use this knowledge to solve a problem.

These objectives are achieved as children engage in game play and respond to questions that are posed by the teacher (or by a child serving as group leader). With four children sharing one game board, children start

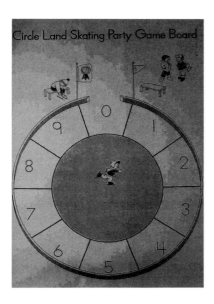

FIGURE 6-5   Skating Party game board—a Circle Land activity used to provide a hands-on representation for children to explore the relationship between movement and increases and decreases in quantity.

game play by placing their pawns at the starting gate. They then take turns rolling a die, counting the dots, and moving their pawns that many spaces around the dial. Each time they complete a revolution around the dial, they collect an Award card. At the end of the game, children count and compare their Award cards, and the child with the most cards is the first winner, followed by the child with the second most, who is the second winner, and so on. In one variation of this game, the Award cards collected by each group of four children are computed and compared, and a group winner is declared.

Questions are posed at several points in game play, and the sorts of questions that are put to individual children are most productive if they are finely tuned to each child's current level of understanding (learning principle 1). For example, when all children have their pawns on the board, they can be asked, "Who is farther around? Who has gone the least distance? How much farther do you need to go to win an Award card?" These questions are always followed by "How do you know?" or "How did you figure that out?" Plenty of time needs to be allowed for children to come up with answers that make sense to them and for them to share their answers with each other. When children are counting their Award cards, they can be asked, "How many times did you go around the rink? Who has the most Award cards? How come that child went around the rink more times than this child if everyone had the same number of turns?" The last question is the most challenging of this set, and beginning players often attribute going around the rink more times to skating faster (rather than to rolling a lot of high numbers).

Eventually children will make this connection, and they can be encouraged to do so by being asked to pay close attention to movement around the rink the next time they play. For example, the teacher might say, "Did that child really skate faster? Let's watch next time we play and see." In encouraging children to construct their own answers to the question by reflecting on their own activity, teachers are encouraging the use of metacognitive processes and allowing children to take charge of their own learning (learning principle 3).

In a follow-up activity, the teacher adds another level of complexity to this game by providing an illustrated set of skating cards that show either "+1, You skate well"; "–1, You stumbled"; or "0," blank symbol and image (see Figures 6-6a and 6-6b). In this version of the game, children play as before, but in addition, they draw a skating card from the face-down deck after every turn and follow the instructions on the card to move one space forward or backward around the rink, or to stay where they are. This version of the game provides opportunities for children to meet an additional learning objective—identifying how many there will be if a set is increased or decreased by one (or by two in a challenge activity). This objective, in turn, is met most easily if the teacher scaffolds children's learning by providing opportunities for them to talk about the quantity transactions they are performing. For example, when a child draws a card, the teacher can ask, "Where are you now? What does that card tell you to do? How far around the rink will you be after you do that? Is that closer to the finish line

FIGURE 6-6 An illustrated set of skating cards used in the Circle Land Skating Party game.

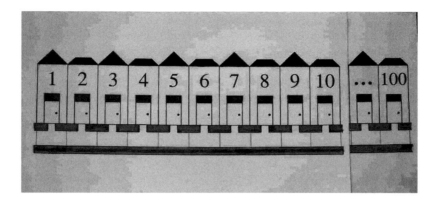

FIGURE 6-7 Neighborhood Number Line game board—used to help children understand the base-ten number system.

or farther away from it? How do you know?" By answering and discussing these questions and by confirming or disconfirming their thoughts and predictions with real actions, children gradually build up a solid intuitive understanding of the links among the world of quantity (in spatial contexts), the world of counting numbers, and the world of formal symbols.

Rosemary's Magic Shoes

This game provides an illustration of a spatial context developed for Line Land in the second-grade program to help children build an understanding of the base-ten number system. The prop itself—the Neighborhood Number Line—comprises 10 blocks of houses, each containing 10 houses that attach with Velcro to create a linear neighborhood of 100 houses that is 15 feet long when fully assembled (see Figure 6-7). This prop is used extensively in the first-grade program as well, to teach several concepts implicit in the 1–100 number sequence. The character created for this game, a professional monster-tracker called Rosemary, has a pair of magic shoes that allows her to leap over 10 houses in a single bound. For Rosemary's shoes to work, however, she first must tell them how many times to jump 10 houses and how many times to walk past 1 house.

To play this game, children take turns picking a number tile that indicates a house where the presence of a monster has been suspected. Using Rosemary's magic shoes, they then move to the house as quickly and efficiently as possible; check for monsters (by drawing a card from a face-down deck that indicates the monsters' presence or absence); and, if indicated, place a sticker on the house to show that it is a "monster-free zone." In later versions of this game, children are required to keep a written record of Rosemary's movements, using the formal symbol system to do so. In all versions of this game, they are required to watch each player carefully to see if the oral directions given (e.g., "Magic shoes, jump over 5 blocks and walk to the eighth house") were followed precisely, to consider whether other ways of getting to the same house (#58) might have been more efficient, and to share their thinking with the class.

With exposure to this game, children gradually come to realize that they can leap over 10 houses (i.e., count up or down by tens) from any number in the sequence, not just from the decade markers (e.g., 10, 20, 30). They also come to realize that they need not always move in a forward direction (e.g., count up) to reach a particular number, that it might be more efficient to move to the closest tens marker and go back a few steps (e.g., jump over 6 blocks and walk back two steps to get to house #58). With these realizations and opportunities to put them into practice, children gain fluency in computing the distance between any two numbers in the 1-100 sequence and in moving fluently from one location (or number) to the next, using benchmark values to do so. They also gain an appreciation of the relative value of numbers in this sequence (e.g., that 92 is a long way away from 9) and can recognize immediately that the sum of 9 + 2 could not possibly be 92, an error that is not uncommon for this age group. The knowledge gains that have just been described—the acquisition of procedural fluency, factual knowledge, and conceptual understanding—appear to be greatly facilitated by the provision of spatial analogs of the number system that children can actively explore in a hands-on fashion (design principle 3 as set forth in this chapter), coupled with opportunities to explain their thinking, to communicate with their peers, and to reflect on their own activity (learning principle 3).

Design Principle 4: Engaging Children's Emotions and Capturing Their Imagination So Knowledge Constructed Is Embedded Not Only in Their Minds, but Also in Their Hopes, Fears, and Passions

Each of the activities described thus far has been engaging for children and has captured their imagination. The one described in this section possibly achieves this purpose to a greater extent than most others. It also provides an example of how the Number Worlds program addresses a major learning goal for first grade: helping children link their central conceptual structure for whole number to the formal symbol system.

FIGURE 6-8 Dragon Quest game board—a Picture Land activity that uses numerals and operation signs to achieve the game's goals.

Dragon Quest

Dragon Quest was developed for Picture Land in the first-grade program (see Figure 6-8). Although the game is played on a line and children can use objects to solve the problems posed by the game, the major representation of number that children must work with in this game to achieve the game's goals are numerals and operation signs. For this reason, this game is classified as a Picture Land activity. Children are introduced to Phase 1 of this activity by being told a story about a fire-breathing dragon that has been terrorizing the village where the children live. The children playing the game are heroes who have been chosen to seek out the dragon and put out his fire. To extinguish this dragon's fire (as opposed to that of other, more powerful dragons they will encounter in later phases), a hero will need at least 10 pails of water. If a hero enters the dragon's area with less than 10 pails of water, he or she will become the dragon's prisoner and can be rescued only by one of the other players.

To play the game, children take turns rolling a die and moving their playing piece along the colored game board. If they land on a well pile (indicated by a star), they can pick a card from the face-down deck of cards that illustrate, with images and symbols (e.g., + 4), a certain number of pails of water. Children are encouraged to add up their pails of water as they receive them and are allowed to use a variety of strategies to do so, ranging from mental math (which is encouraged) to the use of tokens to keep track of the quantity accumulated. The first child to reach the dragon's lair with at least 10 pails of water can put out the dragon's fire and free any teammates who have become prisoners.

Needless to say, this game is successful in capturing children's imagination and inducing them to engage in the increasing series of challenges posed by later versions. As they do so, most children acquire increasingly sophisticated number competencies. For example, they become capable of performing a series of successive addition and subtraction operations in their heads when spill cards (e.g., – 4) are added to the set of cards in the well pile. When they encounter more-powerful dragons whose fire can be extinguished only with 20 buckets of water, they become capable of performing these operations with larger sets of numbers and with higher numbers. When they are required to submit formal proof to the mayor of the village that they have amassed sufficient pails of water to put out the dragon's fire before they are allowed to do so, they become capable of writing a series of formal expressions to record the number of pails received and spilled over the course of the game. In such contexts, children have ample opportunity to use the formal symbol system in increasingly efficient ways to make sense of quantitative problems they encounter in the course of their own activity.

Design Principle 5: Providing Opportunities for Children to Acquire Computational Fluency As Well As Conceptual Understanding

Although opportunities to acquire computational fluency as well as conceptual understanding are built into every Number Worlds activity, computational fluency is given special attention in the activities developed for the Warm-Up period of each lesson. In the prekindergarten and kindergarten programs, these activities typically take the form of count-up and count-down games that are played in each land, with a prop appropriate for that land. This makes it possible for children to acquire fluency in counting and, at the same time, to acquire a conceptual understanding of the changes in quantity that are associated with each successive number up (or down) in the counting sequence. This is illustrated in an activity, developed for Sky Land, that is always introduced after children have become reasonably fluent in the count-up activity that uses the same prop.

Sky Land Blastoff

In this activity, children view a large, specially designed thermometer with a moveable red ribbon that is set to 5 (or 10, 15, or 20, depending on children's competence) (see Figure 6-9). Children pretend to be on a rocket ship and count down while the teacher (or a child volunteer) moves the red ribbon on the thermometer to correspond with each number counted. When the counting reaches "1," all the children jump up and call "Blastoff!" The sequence of counting is repeated if a counting mistake is made or if anyone jumps up too soon or too late. The rationale that motivated this activity is as follows: "Seeing the level of red liquid in a thermometer drop while counting down will give children a good foundation for subtraction by allowing

FIGURE 6-9 A specially designed thermometer for the Sky Land Blastoff activity—to provide an understanding of the changes in quantity associated with each successive number (up) or down in the counting sequence.

them to see that a quantity decreases in scale height with each successive number down in the sequence. This will also lay a foundation for measurement" (Sky Land: Activity #2).

This activity is repeated frequently over the course of the school year, with the starting point being adjusted over time to accommodate children's growing ability. Children benefit immensely from opportunities to perform (or lead) the count-down themselves and/or to move the thermometer ribbon while another child (or the rest of the class) does the counting. When children become reasonably fluent in basic counting and in serial counting (i.e., children take turns saying the next number down), the teacher adds a level of complexity by asking them to predict where the ribbon will be if it is on 12, for example, and they count down (or up) two numbers, or if it is on 12 and the temperature drops (or rises) by 2 degrees. Another form of complexity is added over the course of the school year when children are asked to demonstrate another way (e.g., finger displays, position on a human game mat) to represent the quantity depicted on the thermometer and the way this quantity changes as they count down. By systematically increasing the complexity of these activities, teachers expose children to a learning path that is finely attuned to their growing understanding (learning principle 1) and that allows them to gradually construct an important network of conceptual and procedural knowledge (learning principle 2).

In the programs for first and second grade, higher-level computation skills (e.g., fluent use of strategies and procedures to solve mental arithmetic problems) are fostered in the Warm-Up activities. In Guess My Number, for example, the teacher or a child picks a number card and, keeping it hidden, generates two clues that the rest of the class can use to guess the number (e.g., it is bigger than 25 and smaller than 29). Guessers are allowed to ask one question, if needed, to refine their prediction (e.g., "Is it an odd number?" "Is it closer to 25 or to 29?").

Generating good clues is, of course, more difficult than solving the problem because doing so requires a refined sense of the neighborhood of numbers surrounding the target number, as well as their relationship to this number. In spite of the challenges involved, children derive sufficient enjoyment from this activity to persevere through the early stages and to acquire a more refined number sense, as well as greater computational fluency, in the process. In one lovely example, a first-grade student provided the following clues for the number he had drawn: "It is bigger than 8 and it is 1 more than 90 smaller than 100." The children in the class were stymied by these clues until the teacher unwittingly exclaimed, "Oh, I see, you're using the neighborhood number line," at which point all children followed suit, counted down 9 blocks of houses, and arrived at a correct prediction, "9."

Design Principle 6: Encouraging the Use of Metacognitive Processes (e.g., Problem Solving, Communication, Reasoning) That Will Facilitate Knowledge Construction

In addition to opportunities for problem solving, communication, and reasoning that are built into the activities themselves (as illustrated in the examples provided in this chapter), three additional supports for these processes are included in the Number Worlds program. The first is a set of question cards developed for specific stages of each small-group game. The questions (e.g., "How many buckets of water do you have now?") were designed to draw children's attention to the quantity displays they create during game play (e.g., buckets of water collected and spilled) and the changes in quantity they enact (e.g., collecting four more buckets), and to prompt them to think about these quantities and describe them, performing any computations necessary to answer the question. Follow-up questions that are also included (e.g., "How did you figure that out?") prompt children to reflect on their own reasoning and to put it into words, using the language of mathematics to do so. Although the question cards are typically used by the teacher (or a teacher's aide) at first, children can gradually take over this function and, in the process, take greater control over their own learning (learning principle 3). This transition is facilitated by giving one child in the group the official role of Question Poser each time the game is played. By giving children important roles in the learning process (e.g., Question-Poser, Facilitator, Discussion Leader, Reporter) and by allowing them to be teachers as well as learners, teachers can create the sort of *community-centered classroom* that is described in Chapters 1 and 5.

The second support is a set of dialogue prompts included in the teacher's guide, which provides a more general set of questions (e.g., "Who has gone the farthest? How do you know?") than those provided with the game. Although both sets of questions are highly useful in prompting children to use metacognitive processes to make mathematical sense of their own activity, they provide no guidance on how a teacher should respond to the answers children provide. Scaffolding good math talk is still a significant challenge for most primary and elementary teachers. Having a better understanding of the sorts of answers children give at different age levels, as well as increased opportunities to listen to children explain their thinking, can be helpful in building the expertise and experience needed for the exceedingly difficult task of constructing follow-up questions for children's answers that will push their mathematical thinking to higher levels.

The third support for metacognitive processes that is built into the Number Worlds program is a Wrap-Up period that is provided at the end of each lesson. In Wrap-Up, the child who has been assigned the role of Reporter for the small-group problem-solving portion of the lesson (e.g., game play) describes the mathematical activity his or her group did that day and what they learned. The Reporter then takes questions from the rest of the class, and any member of the Reporter's team can assist in providing answers. It is during this portion of the lesson that the most significant learning occurs because children have an opportunity to reflect on aspects of the number system they may have noticed during game play, explain these concepts to their peers, and acquire a more explicit understanding of the concepts in the process. Over time, Wrap-Up comes to occupy as much time in the math lesson as all the preceding activities (i.e., the Warm-Up activities and small-group problem-solving activities) put together.

With practice in using this format, teachers become increasingly skilled at asking good questions to get the conversation going and, immediately thereafter, at taking a back seat in the discussion so that children have ample opportunity to provide the richest answers they are capable of generating at that point in time. (Some wonderful examples of skilled teachers asking good questions in elementary mathematics classrooms are available in the video and CD-ROM products of the Institute for Learning [www.institutefor learning.org].) This takes patience, a willingness to turn control of the discussion over to the children, and faith that they have something important to say. Even at the kindergarten level, children appear to be better equipped to rise to this challenge than many teachers, who, having been taught that they should assume the leadership role in the class, often feel that they should dominate the discussion. Teachers who can rise to this challenge have found that their faith is amply rewarded by the sophistication of the explanations children provide, even at the kindergarten level; by the opportunities this occasion provides for assessing children's growth and current understandings; and by the learning and achievement gains children demonstrate on standard measures.

WHAT SORTS OF LEARNING DOES THIS APPROACH MAKE POSSIBLE?

The Number Worlds program was developed to address three major learning goals: to enable children to acquire (1) conceptual knowledge of number as well as procedural knowledge (e.g., computational fluency); (2) number sense (e.g., an ability to use benchmark values, an ability to solve problems in a range of contexts); and (3) an interest in and positive attitude toward mathematics. Program evaluation for the most part has focused on assessing the extent to which children who have been exposed to the program have been able to demonstrate gains on any of these fronts. The results of several evaluation studies are summarized below.

The Number Worlds program has now been tried in several different communities in Canada and in the United States. For research purposes, the groups of students followed have always been drawn from schools serving low-income, predominantly inner-city communities. This decision was based on the assumption that if the program works for children known to be at risk for school failure, there is a good chance that it will work as well, or even better, for those from more affluent communities. Several different forms of evaluation have been conducted.

In the first form of evaluation, children who had participated in the kindergarten level of the program (formerly called Rightstart) were compared with matched controls who had taken part in a math readiness program of a different sort. On tests of mathematical knowledge, on a set of more general developmental measures, and on a set of experimental measures of learning potential, children who had participated in the Number Worlds program consistently outperformed those in the control groups (see Box 6-1 for findings from one of these studies).[14] In a second type of evaluation, children who had taken part in the kindergarten level of the program (and who had graduated into a variety of more traditional first-grade classrooms) were followed up 1 year later and evaluated on an assortment of mathematical and scientific tests, using a double-blind procedure. Once again, those who had participated in the Number Worlds program in kindergarten were found to be superior on virtually all measures, including teacher evaluations of "general number sense" (see Box 6-2).[15]

The expansion of the Number Worlds program to include curricula for first and second grades permitted a third form of evaluation—a longitudinal study in which children were tracked over a 3-year period. At the beginning of the study and the end of each year, children who had participated in the Number Worlds program were compared with two other groups: (1) a second low-socioeconomic-status group that had originally been tested as having superior achievement in mathematics, and (2) a mixed-socioeconomic-status (largely middle-class) group that had also demonstrated a higher level of performance at the outset and attended an acclaimed magnet school with a special mathematics coordinator and an enriched mathematics program. These three groups are represented in the figure of Box 6-6, and the differences between the magnet school students and the students in the low-socioeconomic-status groups can be seen in the different start positions of the lines on the graph. Over the course of this study, which extended from the beginning of kindergarten to the end of second grade, children who had taken part in the Number Worlds program caught up with, and gradually outstripped, the magnet school group on the major measure used throughout this study—the Number Knowledge test (see Box 6-6). On this measure, as well as on a variety of other mathematics tests (e.g., measures of number sense), the Number Worlds group outperformed the second low-socioeconomic-status group from the end of kindergarten onward. On tests of procedural knowledge administered at the end of first grade, they also compared very favorably with groups from China and Japan that were tested on the same measures.[16]

These findings provide clear evidence that a program based on the principles of *How People Learn* (i.e., the Number Worlds program) works for the population of children most in need of effective school-based instruction—those living in poverty. In a variety of studies, the program enabled children from diverse cultural backgrounds to start their formal learning of arithmetic on an equal footing with their more-advantaged peers. It also enabled them to keep pace with their more-advantaged peers (and even outperform them on some measures) as they progressed through the first few years of formal schooling and to acquire the higher-level mathematics concepts that are central for continued progress in this area. In addition to the mathematics learning and achievement demonstrated in these studies, two other findings are worthy of note: both teachers and children who have used the Number Worlds program consistently report a positive attitude toward the teaching and learning of math. For teachers, this often represents a dramatic change in attitude. Math is now seen as fun, as well as useful, and both teachers and children are eager to do more of it.

BOX 6-6 Comparing Number Worlds and Control Group Outcomes

As the figure below shows, the magnet school group began kindergarten with substantially higher scores on the Number Knowledge test than those of children in the Number Worlds and control groups. The gap indicated a developmental lag that exceeded one year, and for many children in the Number Worlds group was closer to 2 years. By the end of the kindergarten year, however, the Number Worlds children had narrowed this gap to a small fraction of its initial size. By the end of the second grade, the Number Worlds children actually outperformed the magnet school group. In contrast, the initial gap between the control group and the magnet school group did not narrow over time. The control group children did make steady progress over the 3 years; however, they were never able to catch up.

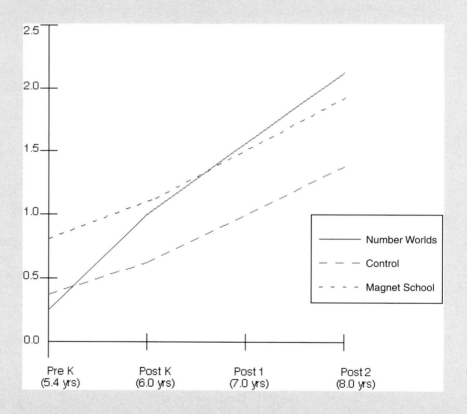

Mean developmental level scores on Number Knowledge test at four time periods.

SUMMARY AND CONCLUSION

It was suggested at the beginning of this chapter that the teaching of whole-number concepts could be improved if each math teacher asked three questions on a regular basis: (1) Where am I now? (in terms of the knowledge children in their classrooms have available to build upon); (2) Where do I want to go? (in terms of the knowledge they want all children in their classrooms to acquire during the school year); and (3) What is the best way to get there? (in terms of the learning opportunities they will provide to enable all children in their class to reach the chosen objectives). The challenges these questions pose for primary and elementary teachers who have not been exposed in their professional training to the knowledge base needed to construct good answers were also acknowledged. Exposing teachers to this knowledge base is a major goal of the present volume. In this chapter, I have attempted to show how the three learning principles that lie at the heart of this knowledge base—and that are closely linked to the three questions posed above—can be used to improve the teaching and learning of whole numbers.

To illustrate learning Principle 1 (eliciting and building upon student knowledge), I have drawn from the cognitive developmental literature and described the number knowledge children typically demonstrate at each age level between ages 4 and 8 when asked a series of questions on an assessment tool—the Number Knowledge Test—that was created to elicit this knowledge. To address learning Principle 2 (building learning paths and networks of knowledge), I have again used the cognitive developmental literature to identify knowledge networks that lie at the heart of number sense (and that should be taught) and to suggest learning paths that are consistent with the goals for mathematics education provided in the NCTM standards.[17] To illustrate learning Principle 3 (building resourceful, self-regulating mathematics thinkers and problem solvers), I have drawn from a mathematics program called Number Worlds that was specifically developed to teach the knowledge networks identified for Principle 2 and that relied heavily on the findings of *How People Learn* to achieve this goal. Other programs that have also been developed to teach number sense and to put the principles of *How People Learn* into action have been noted in this chapter, and teachers are encouraged to explore these resources to obtain a richer picture of how Principle 3 can be realized in mathematics classrooms.

In closing, I would like to acknowledge that it is not an easy task to develop a practice that embodies the three learning principles outlined herein. Doing so requires continuous effort over a long period of time, and even when this task has been accomplished, teaching in the manner described in this chapter is hard work. Teachers can take comfort in the fact the these efforts will pay off in terms of children's mathematics learning and achievement; in the positive attitude toward mathematics that students will acquire and carry with them throughout their lives; and in the sense of accomplishment a teacher can derive from the fruits of these efforts. The well-deserved professional pride that this can engender, as well as the accomplishments of children themselves, will provide ample rewards for these efforts.

ACKNOWLEDGMENTS

The development of the Number Worlds program and the research that is described in this chapter were made possible by the generous support of the James S. McDonnell Foundation. The author gratefully acknowledges this support, as well as the contributions of all the teachers and children who have used the program in various stages of development, and who have helped shape its final form.

NOTES

1. Referenced in Griffin and Case, 1997.
2. Griffin and Case, 1996a.
3. Ibid.
4. Gelman, 1978.
5. Starkey, 1992.
6. Siegler and Robinson, 1982.
7. Case and Griffin, 1990; Griffin et al., 1994.
8. Griffin et al., 1995.
9. Griffin et al., 1992.
10. Ball, 1993; Carpenter and Fennema, 1992; Cobb et al., 1988; Fuson, 1997; Hiebert, 1997; Lampert, 1986; Schifter and Fosnot, 1993.
11. Griffin and Case, 1996b; Griffin, 1997, 1998, 2000.
12. Schmandt-Basserat, 1978.
13. Damerow et al., 1995.
14. Griffin et al., 1994, 1995.
15. Also see Griffin et al., 1994; Griffin and Case, 1996a.
16. Griffin and Case, 1997.
17. National Council of Teachers of Mathematics, 2000.

REFERENCES

Ball, D.L. (1993). With an eye on the mathematical horizon: Dilemmas of teaching elementary school mathematics. *Elementary School Journal, 93*(4), 373-397.

Carpenter, T., and Fennema, E. (1992). Cognitively guided instruction: Building on the knowledge of students and teachers. *International Journal of Research in Education, 17*(5), 457-470.

Case, R., and Griffin, S. (1990). Child cognitive development: The role of central conceptual structures in the development of scientific and social thought. In E.A. Hauert (Ed.), *Developmental psychology: Cognitive, perceptuo-motor, and neurological perspectives* (pp. 193-230). North-Holland, The Netherlands: Elsevier.

Cobb, P., Yackel, E., and Wood, T. (1988). A constructivist approach to second grade mathematics. In E. von Glasserfeld (Ed.), *Constructivism in mathematics education*. Dordecht, The Netherlands: D. Reidel.

Dehaene, S., and Cohen, L. (1995). Towards an anatomical and functional model of number processing. *Mathematical Cognition, 1*, 83-120.

Damerow, P., Englund, R.K., and Nissen, H.J. (1995). The first representations of number and the development of the number concept. In R. Damerow (Ed.), *Abstraction and representation: Essays on the cultural evolution of thinking* (pp. 275-297). Book Series: Boston studies in the philosophy of science, vol. 175. Dordrecht, The Netherlands: Kluwer Academic.

Fuson, K. (1997). Snapshots across two years in the life of an urban Latino classroom. In J. Hiebert (Ed.), *Making sense: Teaching and learning mathematics with understanding*. Portsmouth, NH: Heinemann.

Gelman, R. (1978). Children's counting: What does and does not develop. In R.S. Siegler (Ed.), *Children's thinking: What develops* (pp. 213-242). Mahwah, NJ: Lawrence Erlbaum Associates.

Griffin, S. (1997). *Number worlds: Grade one level*. Durham, NH: Number Worlds Alliance.

Griffin, S. (1998). *Number worlds: Grade two level*. Durham, NH: Number Worlds Alliance.

Griffin, S. (2000). *Number worlds: Preschool level*. Durham, NH: Number Worlds Alliance.

Griffin, S. (in press). Evaluation of a program to teach number sense to children at risk for school failure. *Journal for Research in Mathematics Education*.

Griffin, S., and Case, R. (1996a). Evaluating the breadth and depth of training effects when central conceptual structures are taught. *Society for Research in Child Development Monographs, 59*, 90-113.

Griffin, S., and Case, R. (1996b). *Number worlds: Kindergarten level*. Durham, NH: Number Worlds Alliance.

Griffin, S., and Case, R. (1997). Re-thinking the primary school math curriculum: An approach based on cognitive science. *Issues in Education, 3*(1), 1-49.

Griffin, S., Case, R., and Sandieson, R. (1992). Synchrony and asynchrony in the acquisition of children's everyday mathematical knowledge. In R. Case (Ed.), *The mind's staircase: Exploring the conceptual underpinnings of children's thought and knowledge* (pp. 75-97). Mahwah, NJ: Lawrence Erlbaum Associates.

Griffin, S., Case, R., and Siegler, R. (1994). Rightstart: Providing the central conceptual prerequisites for first formal learning of arithmetic to students at-risk for school failure. In K. McGilly (Ed.), *Classroom lessons: Integrating cognitive theory and classroom practice* (pp. 24-49). Cambridge, MA: Bradford Books MIT Press.

Griffin, S., Case, R., and Capodilupo, A. (1995). Teaching for understanding: The importance of central conceptual structures in the elementary mathematics curriculum. In A. McKeough, I. Lupert, and A. Marini (Eds.), *Teaching for transfer: Fostering generalization in learning* (pp. 121-151). Mahwah, NJ: Lawrence Erlbaum Associates.

Hiebert, J, (1997). *Making sense: Teaching and learning mathematics with understanding.* Portsmouth, NH: Heinemann.

Lampert, M. (1986). Knowing, doing, and teaching multiplication. *Cognition and Instruction 3*(4), 305-342.

National Council of Teachers of Mathematics. (2000). *Principles and standards for school mathematics.* Reston, VA: National Council of Teachers of Mathematics.

Schifter, D., and Fosnot, C. (1993). *Reconstructing mathematics education.* New York: Teachers College Press.

Schmandt-Basserat, D. (1978). The earliest precursor of writing. *Scientific American, 238*(June), 40-49.

Siegler, R.S., and Robinson, M. (1982). The development of numerical understanding. In H.W. Reese and R. Kail (Eds.), *Advances in child development and behavior.* New York: Academic Press.

Starkey, P. (1992). The early development of numerical reasoning. *Cognition and Instruction, 43,* 93-126.

7

Pipes, Tubes, and Beakers: New Approaches to Teaching the Rational-Number System

Joan Moss

© 1977 United Features Syndicate, Inc.

PEANUTS reprinted by permission of United Feature Syndicate, Inc.

Poor Sally. Her anger and frustration with fractions are palpable. And they no doubt reflect the feelings and experiences of many students. As mathematics education researchers and teachers can attest, students are often vocal in their expression of dislike of fractions and other representations of rational numbers (percents and decimals). In fact, the rational-number system poses problems not only for youngsters, but for many adults as well.[1] In a recent study, masters students enrolled in an elementary teacher-training program were interviewed to determine their knowledge and understanding of basic rational-number concepts. While some students were confident and produced correct answers and explanations, the majority had difficulty with the topic. On attempting to perform an operation involving fractions, one student, whose sentiments were echoed by many, remarked, "Oh fractions! I know there are lots of rules but I can't remember any of them and I never understood them to start with."[2]

We know from extensive research that many people—adults, students, even teachers—find the rational-number system to be very difficult.[3] Introduced in early elementary school, this number system requires that students reformulate their concept of number in a major way. They must go beyond whole-number ideas, in which a number expresses a fixed quantity, to understand numbers that are expressed in relationship to other numbers. These new proportional relationships are grounded in multiplicative reasoning that is quite different from the additive reasoning that characterizes whole numbers (see Box 7-1).[4] While some students make the transition smoothly, the majority, like Sally, become frustrated and disenchanted with mathematics.[5] Why is this transition so problematic?

A cursory look at some typical student misunderstandings illuminates the kinds of problems students have with rational numbers. The culprit appears to be the continued use of whole-number reasoning in situations where it does not apply. When asked which number is larger, 0.059 or 0.2, a majority of middle school students assert that 0.059 is bigger, arguing that the number 59 is bigger than the number 2.[6] Similarly, faulty whole-number reasoning causes students to maintain, for example, that the fraction 1/8 is larger than 1/6 because, as they say, "8 is a bigger number than 6."[7] Not surprisingly, students struggle with calculations as well. When asked to find the sum of 1/2 and 1/3, the majority of fourth and sixth graders give the answer 2/5. Even after a number of years working with fractions, some eighth graders make the same error, illustrating that they still mistakenly count the numerator and denominator as separate numbers to find a sum.[8] Clearly whole-number reasoning is very resilient.

Decimal operations are also challenging.[9] In a recent survey, researchers found that 68 percent of sixth graders and 51 percent of fifth and seventh graders asserted that the answer to the addition problem 4 + .3 was .7.[10] This example also illustrates that students often treat decimal numbers as whole numbers and, as in this case, do not recognize that the sum they propose as a solution to the problem is smaller than one of the addends.

The introduction of rational numbers constitutes a major stumbling block in children's mathematical development.[11] It marks the time when many students face the new and disheartening realization that they no longer understand what is going on in their mathematics classes.[12] This failure is a cause for concern. Rational-number concepts underpin many topics in advanced mathematics and carry significant academic consequences.[13] Students cannot succeed in algebra if they do not understand rational numbers. But rational numbers also pervade our daily lives.[14] We need to be able to understand them to follow recipes, calculate discounts and miles per gallon, exchange money, assess the most economical size of products, read maps, interpret scale drawings, prepare budgets, invest our savings, read financial statements, and examine campaign promises. Thus we need to be able to

BOX 7-1 **Additive and Multiplicative Reasoning**

Lamon,[15] whose work on proportional reasoning and rational number has made a great contribution to our understanding of students' learning, elucidates the distinction between relative and absolute reasoning. She asks the learner to consider the growth of two fictitious snakes: String Bean, who is 4 feet long when the story begins, and Slim, who is 5 feet long. She tells us that after 5 years, both snakes have grown. String Bean has grown from 4 to 7 feet, and Slim has grown from 5 to 8 feet (see the figure below). She asks us to compare the growth of these two snakes and to answer the question, "Who grew more?"

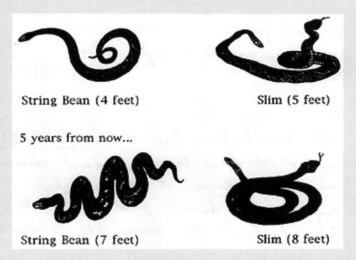

Lamon suggests that there are two answers. First, if we consider absolute growth, both snakes grew 3 feet, so both grew the same amount. The second answer deals with relative growth; from this perspective, String Bean grew the most because he grew 3/4 of his length, while Slim grew only 3/5 of his length. If we compare the two fractions, 3/4 is greater than 3/5, and so we conclude that String Bean has grown proportionally more than Slim.

Lamon asks us to note that while the first answer, about the *absolute* difference, involves addition, the second answer, about the *relative* difference, is solved through multiplication. In this way she shows that absolute thinking is *additive*, while relative thinking is *multiplicative*.

understand rational numbers not only for academic success, but also in our lives as family members, workers, and citizens.

Do the principles of learning highlighted in this book help illuminate the widespread problems observed as students grapple with rational number? Can they point to more effective approaches to teaching rational number? We believe the answer to both these questions is "yes." In the first section below we consider each of the three principles of *How Students Learn*, beginning with principle 2—the organization of a knowledge network that emphasizes core concepts, procedural knowledge, and their connections. We then turn to principle 1—engaging student preconceptions and building on existing understandings. Finally we consider metacognitive instruction as emphasized in principle 3.

The second section focuses on instruction in rational number. It begins with a description of frequently used instructional approaches and the ways in which they diverge from the above three principles. We then describe an experimental approach to teaching rational number that has proven to be successful in helping students in fourth, fifth, and sixth grades understand the interconnections of the number system and become adept at moving among and operating with the various representations of rational number. Through a description of lessons in which the students engaged and protocols taken from the research classrooms, we set out the salient features of the instructional approach that played a role in shaping a learning-centered classroom environment. We illustrate how in this environment, a focus on the interconnections among decimals, fractions, and percents fosters students' ability to make informed decisions on how to operate effectively with rational numbers. We also provide emerging evidence of the effectiveness of the instructional approach. The intent is not to promote our particular curriculum, but rather to illustrate the ways in which it incorporates the principles of *How People Learn*, and the observed changes in student understanding and competence with rational numbers that result.

RATIONAL-NUMBER LEARNING AND THE PRINCIPLES OF *HOW PEOPLE LEARN*

The Knowledge Network: New Concepts of Numbers and New Applications (Principle 2)

What are the core ideas that define the domain of rational numbers? What are the new understandings that students will have to construct? How does a beginning student come to understand rational numbers?

Let us look through the eyes of a young student who is just beginning to learn about rational number. Until this point, all of her formal instruction in arithmetic has centered on learning the whole-number system. If her learning has gone well, she can solve arithmetic problems competently and easily makes connections between the mathematics she is learning and experiences of her daily life. But in this next phase of her learning, the introduction of rational number, there will be many new and intertwined concepts, new facts, new symbols that she will have to learn and understand—a new knowledge network, if you will. Because much of this new learning is based on multiplicative instead of whole-number relations, acquiring an understanding of this new knowledge network may be challenging, despite her success thus far in mathematics. As with whole-number arithmetic, this domain connects to everyday life. But unlike whole numbers, in which the operations for the most part appear straightforward, the operations involved in the learning of rational numbers may appear to be less intuitive, at odds with earlier understandings (e.g., that multiplication always makes things bigger), and hence more difficult to learn.

New Symbols, New Meanings, New Representations

One of the first challenges facing our young student is that a particular rational number can take many forms. Until now her experience with symbols and their referents has been much simpler. A number—for example, four—is represented exclusively by one numeral, 4. Now the student will need to learn that a rational number can be expressed in different ways—as a decimal, fraction, and percent. To further complicate matters, she will have to learn that a rational-number quantity can be represented by an infinite number of equivalent common and decimal fractions. Thus a rational number such as one-fourth can be written as 1/4, 2/8, 3/12, 4/16, 0.25, 0.250, and so on.

Not only does the learning of rational number entail the mastery of these forms and of the new symbol systems that are implied, but the learner is also required to move among these various forms flexibly and efficiently.[16] Unfortunately, this flow between representations does not come easily.[17] In fact, even mature students are often challenged when they try to understand the relations among the representations.[18] To illustrate how difficult translating between fractions and decimals can be, I offer two examples taken from our research.

In a recent series of studies, we interviewed fourth, sixth, and eighth graders on a number of items that probed for rational-number understanding. One of the questions we asked was how the students would express the quantity 1/8 as a decimal. This question proved to be very challenging for many, and although the students' ability increased with age and experience, more than half of the sixth and eighth graders we surveyed asserted that as a decimal, 1/8 would be 0.8 (rather than the correct answer, 0.125).

In the next example, an excerpt taken from an interview conducted as part of a pretest, Wyatt, a traditionally trained fifth-grade student, discussed ordering a series of rational numbers presented to him in mixed representations.

Interviewer	Here are 3 numbers: 2/3, 0.5, and 3/4. Could you please put these numbers in order from smallest to largest?
Wyatt	Well, to start with, I think that the decimal 0.5 is bigger than the fractions because it's a decimal, so it's just bigger, because fractions are really small things.

The response that 1/8 would equal 0.8 should be familiar to many who have taught decimals and fractions. As research points out, students have a difficult time understanding the quantities involved in rational number and thus do not appear to realize the unreasonableness of their assertion.[19] As for Wyatt's assertion in the excerpt above that decimals and fractions cannot be compared, this answer is representative of the reasoning of the majority of the students in this class before instruction. Moreover, it reflects more general research findings.[20] Since most traditional instruction in rational number presents decimals, fractions, and percents separately and often as distinct topics, it is not surprising that students find this task confusing. Indeed, the notion that a single quantity can have many representations is a major departure from students' previous experience with whole numbers; it is a difficult set of understandings for them to acquire and problem-laden for many.[21]

But this is not the only divergence from the familiar one-to-one correspondence of symbol to referent that our new learner will encounter. Another new and difficult idea that challenges the relatively simple referent-to-symbol relation is that in the domain of rational number, a single rational number can have several conceptually distinct meanings, referred to as "subconstructs." Now our young student may well become completely confused.

The Subconstructs or the Many Personalities of Rational Number

What is meant by conceptually distinct meanings? As an illustration, consider the simple fraction 3/4. One meaning of this fraction is as a *part–whole* relation in which 3/4 describes 3 of 4 equal-size shares. A second interpretation of the fraction 3/4 is one that is referred to as the *quotient* interpretation. Here the fraction implies division, as in 4 children sharing 3 pies. As a ratio, 3/4 might mean there are, for example, 3 red cars for every 4 green cars (this is not to be confused with the part–whole interpretation that 3/7 of the cars are red). Rational numbers can also indicate a *measure.* Here rational number is a fixed quantity, most frequently accompanied by a number line, that identifies a situation in which the fraction 1/4 is used repeatedly to determine a distance (e.g., 3/4 of an inch = 1/4, 1/4, 1/4). Finally, there is the interpretation of rational number as a *multiplicative operator,* behaving as an operation that reduces or enlarges the size of another quantity (e.g., the page has been reduced to 3/4 its original size).

The necessity of coordinating these different interpretations requires a deep understanding of the concepts and interrelationships among them. On the one hand, a student must think of rational numbers as a division of two whole numbers (quotient interpretation); on the other, she must also come to know these two numbers as an entity, a single quantity (measure), often to be used in another operation. These different interpretations, generally referred to as the "subconstructs" of rational number, have been analyzed extensively[22] and are a very important part of the knowledge network that the learner will construct for rational number.

Reconceptualizing the Unit and Operations

While acquiring a knowledge network for rational-number understanding means that new forms of representation must be learned (e.g., decimals, fractions) and different interpretations coordinated, the learner will encounter many other new ideas—ideas that also depart from whole numbers. She will have to come to understand that rational numbers are "dense"—meaning that between any two rationals we can find an infinity of other numbers. In the whole-number domain, number is discrete rather than continuous, and the main operation is counting. This is a very big change indeed.[23]

Another difficult new set of understandings concerns the fundamental change that students will encounter in the nature of the unit. In whole numbers, the unit is always explicit (6 refers to 6 units). In rational numbers, on the other hand, the unit is often implied. But it is the unstated unit that gives meaning to the represented quantities, operations, and the solutions. Consider the student trying to interpret what is meant by the task of multiplying, for example, 1/2 times 1/8. If the student recognizes that the "1/8" in the problem refers to 1/8 of one whole, she may reason correctly that half of the quantity 1/8 is 1/16. However since the 1 is not stated but implied, our young student may err and, thinking the unit is 8, consider the answer to be 1/4 (since 4 is one-half of 8)—a response given by 75 percent of traditionally instructed fourth and sixth graders students in our research projects.

New Conceptualizations: Understanding Numbers As Multiplicative Relations

Clearly the transition to learning rational numbers is challenging. Fundamentally, students must construct new meanings for numbers and operations. Development of the network of understandings for rational numbers requires a core conceptual shift: numbers must be understood in multiplicative relationship.

As a final illustration, I offer one more example of this basic shift. Again, consider the quantity 3/4 from our new learner's perspective. All of our student's prior learning will lead her to conclude that the 3 and 4 in 3/4 are two separate numbers that define separate quantities. Her knowledge of whole numbers will provide an additive understanding. Thus she will know that 3 and 4 are contiguous on the number line and have a difference of 1. But to interpret 3/4 as a rational number instead of considering these two numbers to be independent, as many students mistakenly continue to do,[24] our student must come to understand this fraction as a new kind of quantity that is defined multiplicatively by the relative amount conveyed by the symbols. Suddenly numbers are no longer simple. When placed in the context of a fraction, 3 and 4 become a quantity between 0 and 1. Obvious to adults, this numerical metamorphosis can be confusing to children.

How can children learn to make the transition to the complex world of rational numbers in which the numbers 3 and 4 exist in a relationship and are less than 1? Clearly, instruction will need to support a major conceptual change. Looking at students' prior conceptions and relevant understandings can provide footholds to support that conceptual change.[25]

Students' Errors and Misconceptions Based on Previous Learning (Principle 1)

As the above examples suggest, students come to the classroom with conceptions of numbers grounded in their whole-number learning that lead them astray in the world of rational numbers. If instruction is to change those conceptions, it is important to understand thoroughly how students reason as they puzzle through rational-number problems. Below I present verbatim interviews that are representative of faulty understandings held by many students.

In the following excerpt, we return to our fifth grader, Wyatt. His task was to order a series of rational numbers in mixed representations. Recall his earlier comments that these representations could not be compared. Now as the interview continues, he is trying to compare the fractions 2/3 and 3/4. The interview proceeds:

Interviewer	What about 2/3 and 3/4? Which of those is bigger?
Wyatt	Well, I guess that they are both the same size because they both have one piece missing.
Interviewer	I am not sure I understand what you mean when you say that there is one piece missing.
Wyatt	I'll show you. [Wyatt draws two uneven circles, roughly partitions the first in four parts, and then proceeds to shade three parts. Next he divides the second circle into three parts and shades two of them (see Figure 7-1). O.K., here is 3/4 and 2/3. You see they both have one part missing. [He points to the unshaded sections in both circular regions.] You see one part is left out, so they are both the same.

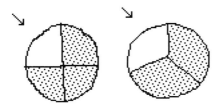

FIGURE 7-1

Wyatt's response is typical in asserting that 2/3 and 3/4 must be the same size. Clearly he has not grasped the multiplicative relations involved in rational numbers, but makes his comparisons based on operations from his whole-number knowledge. When he asserts that 2/3 and 3/4 are the same size because there is "one piece missing," Wyatt is considering the difference of 1 in additive terms rather than considering the multiplicative relations that underlie these numbers.

Additive reasoning is also at the basis of students' incorrect answers on many other kinds of rational-number tasks. Mark, a sixth grader, is working on a scaling problem in which he is attempting to figure out how the length and width of an enlarged rectangle are related to the measurements of a smaller, original rectangle. His challenge is to come up with a proportional relation and, in effect, solve a "missing-term problem" with the following relations: 8 is to 6 as 12 is to what number?

Interviewer	I have two pictures of rectangles here (see Figure 7-2). They are exactly the same shape, but one of them is bigger than the other. I

made this second one bigger by taking a picture of the first one and then enlarging it just a bit. As you can see, the length of the first rectangle is 8 cm and the width is 6 cm. Unfortunately, we know only the length of the second one. That is 12 cm. Can you please tell me what you think the width is?

Mark   Well, if the first one (rectangle) is 8 cm and 6 cm, then the next one is 12 cm and 10 cm. Because in the 8 and 6 one (rectangle) you subtract 2 from the 8 (to get the difference of the width and the length). So in the bigger rectangle you have to subtract 2 from the 12. So that's 10. So the width of the big rectangle is 10.

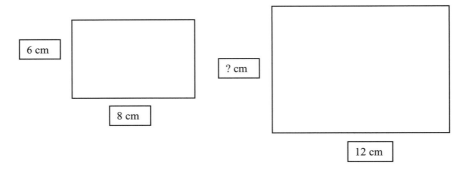

FIGURE 7-2

Mark's error in choosing 10 instead of the correct answer of 9 is certainly representative of students in his age group—in fact, many adults use the same kind of faulty reasoning.[26] Mark clearly attempts to assess the relations, but he uses an additive strategy to come up with a difference of 2. To answer this problem correctly, Mark must consider the multiplicative relations involved (the rectangle was enlarged so that the proportional relationship between the dimensions remains constant)—a challenge that eludes many.

It is this multiplicative perspective that is difficult for students to adopt in working with rational numbers. The misconception that Mark, the sixth grader, displays in asserting that the height of the newly sized rectangle is 10 cm instead of the correct answer of 9 cm shows this failure clearly. Wyatt certainly was not able to look at the relative amount in trying to distinguish between the quantities 2/3 and 3/4. Rather, he reasoned in absolute terms about the circles, that ". . . both have one piece missing."

Metacognition and Rational Number (Principle 3)

A metacognitive approach to instruction helps students monitor their understanding and take control of their own learning.[27] The complexity of rational number—the different meanings and representations, the challenges of comparing quantities across the very different representations, the unstated unit—all mean that students must be actively engaged in sense making to solve problems competently.[28] We know, however, that most middle school children do not create appropriate meanings for fractions, decimals, and percents; rather, they rely on memorized rules for symbol manipulation.

The student errors cited at the beginning of this chapter indicate not only the students' lack of understanding of rational number, but also their failure to monitor their operations and judge the reasonableness of their responses.[29] If classroom teaching does not support students in developing metacognitive skills—for example, by encouraging them to explain their reasoning to their classmates and to compare interpretations, strategies, and solutions—the consequences can be serious. Student can stop expecting math to make sense. Indeed for many students, rational number marks the point at which they draw this conclusion.

INSTRUCTION IN RATIONAL NUMBER

Why does instruction so often fail to change students' whole-number conceptions? Analyses of commonly used textbooks suggest that the principles of *How People Learn* are routinely violated. First, it has been noted that—in contrast to units on whole-number learning—topics in rational number are typically covered quickly and superficially. Yet the major conceptual shift required will take time for students to master thoroughly. Within the allotted time, too little is devoted to teaching the conceptual meaning of rational number, while procedures for manipulating rational numbers receive greater emphasis.[30] While procedural competence is certainly important, it must be anchored by conceptual understanding. For a great many students, it is not.

Other aspects of the knowledge network are shortchanged as well, including the presentation and teaching of the notation system for decimals, fractions, and percents. Textbooks typically treat the notation system as something that is obvious and transparent and can simply be given by definition at a lesson's outset. Further, operations tend to be taught in isolation and divorced from meaning. Virtually no time is spent in relating the various representations—decimals, fractions, percents—to each other.[31]

While these are all significant problems and oversights, however, there are more basic problems with traditional instruction. The central problem with most textbook instruction, many researchers agree,[32] is the failure of textbooks to provide a grounding for the major conceptual shift to multiplicative reasoning that is essential to mastering rational number. To support this claim, let us look at how rational number is typically introduced in traditional practice.

Pie Charts and a Part–Whole Interpretation of Rational Numbers

Most of us learned fractions with the model of a pie chart, and for many people, fractions remain inextricably linked to a picture of a partly shaded shape. Instruction traditionally begins with the presentation of pictures of circles (pies) and rectangles (cakes) that are partitioned and partially shaded. First, students are asked to count the number of parts in the whole shape and then the number of parts shaded. They then use these counts as the basis for naming and symbolically representing fractions. They learn that the top number, the numerator, always indicates how many pieces are shaded and that the bottom number, the denominator, always tells how many pieces there are in all. Next, using these same sorts of pictures (see Figure 7-3), instruction continues with simple addition and subtraction operations: "Two shaded 1/4 pieces (the bottom half of the circle) + 1 shaded 1/4 piece (the top left piece of the circle) = 3 shaded 1/4 pieces or 3/4."

From a psychological perspective, this introduction is sound because it is based on students' present knowledge and aligned with their experiences both in and out of school. We know that students' formal mathematics programs have been based on counting, and that from everyday experience, students know about cutting equal pieces of pies and cakes. Thus, the act of assessing partitioned regions is well within their experience.

From a mathematical point of view, the rationale for this introduction is

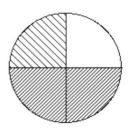

FIGURE 7-3

2⁄4 + 1⁄4 = 3⁄4

also clear. Mathematically, this approach promotes an understanding of one particular aspect of rational number—the way rational numbers indicate parts of a whole. This part–whole subconstruct is one of the basic interpretations of rational numbers.

However, this introduction is grounded in *additive* thinking. It reinforces the very concept that students must change to master rational number. Children tend to treat the individual parts that result from a partition as discrete objects. The four pieces into which a pie is cut are just four pieces. Although the representation does have the potential to bring out the multiplicative relations inherent in the numbers—considering the shaded parts in relation to the whole—this is not what students naturally extract from the situations presented given their strong preconceptions regarding additive relationships.[33]

Recall that Wyatt, the fifth grader, asserted that 2/3 and 3/4 were the "same sized" number, supporting his erroneous claim with reference to pie charts. He explained that the picture showed they were both missing one piece. His lack of focus on the different relations that are implied in these two fractions is evident from his interpretation.

Alternative Instructional Approaches: Ratio and Sharing

For some time now, researchers have wondered whether alternative instructional approaches can help students overcome this misunderstanding. As Kieren[34] points out, ". . . rather than relying on children's well developed additive instincts we must find the intuitions and schemes that go beyond those that support counting. Whole number understandings are carefully built over a number of years; now we must consider how rational number understanding develops and is fostered."

But what would such instruction look like? Over the last several years, a number of innovative approaches have been developed that highlight the multiplicative relations involved, a few of which are highlighted here. Kieren[35] has developed a program for teaching fractions that is based on the multiplicative operations of splitting. As part of his approach he used paper folding rather than pie charts as its primary problem situation. In this approach, both the operator and measure subconstructs are highlighted. Confrey's[36] 3-year developmental curriculum uses a number of contexts for ratio, including cooking, shadows, gears, and ramps.[37] Streefland's[38] approach to teaching fractions is also driven by an emphasis on ratio. His basic image is of equal shares and quotients. In his procedure for teaching fractions, children are presented with realistic situations in which they are asked to share a quantity of something, such as chocolate bars or pancakes (e.g., five children sharing two bars). To represent these situations, children use a notation system that they devise themselves, which emphasizes proportional rather than additive relations. Mack's[39] approach is to engage the students in part–whole activities as a starting point, and to ground these concepts in realistic situations in which students are pressed to consider the multiplicative relations. Finally, Lamon[40] has devised programs that address each of the subconstructs separately. All of these programs and others developed by the Rational Number Project have demonstrated a significant impact on the participating students.

Below I present a different approach to teaching rational number that I developed with my colleague Robbie Case. Our approach, shown through controlled experimental trials to be effective in helping students in the fourth, fifth, and sixth grades[41] gain a strong initial grounding in the number system, also highlights multiplicative understanding, with an additional focus on the interrelations among fractions, decimals, and percents.[42] While there is no one best method or best set of learning activities for rational number,[43] our approach provides an opportunity to describe how instruction in rational number can be built around the principles of *How People Learn* that are the theme of this volume.

First, as will be elaborated, our curriculum is based on our analyses of students' prior understandings (Principle 1). Our instructional strategy is to help students to further develop these informal understandings and then integrate them into a developmentally sequenced set of activities designed to help them develop a network of concepts and relations for rational numbers (Principle 2). Finally, as will be illustrated throughout our accounts of the lessons, a central feature of this program is the fostering of a metacognitive approach to rational number (Principle 3). By providing students with an understanding of the interconnections among decimals, fractions, and percents, our curriculum helps them develop the ability to make informed decisions on how best to operate with rational numbers.

Pipes, Tubes, and Beakers: A New Approach to Rational-Number Learning

Percents as a Starting Point

In our curriculum, rather than teaching fractions and decimals first, we introduce percents—which we believe to be a "privileged" proportion in that it only involves fractions of the base 100.[44] We do this through students' everyday understandings. We situate the initial learning of percent in linear measurement contexts, in which students are challenged to consider the relative lengths of different quantities. As will be shown below, our initial activities direct students' attention to ideas of relative amount and proportion from the very beginning of their learning of rational number. For example, we use beakers of water: "If I fill this beaker 50 percent full, approximately where will the line be? Now fill this bigger beaker 50 percent full. Do you notice that although they are both 50 percent full, there is more water in this bigger one?" These ideas of percents and proportion serve as an anchoring concept for the subsequent learning of decimals and fractions, and then for an overall understanding of the number system as a whole.

Starting Point: Visual Proportional Estimation and Halving and Doubling

Our starting point in developing our curriculum was to consider students' informal knowledge and the intuitions they have developed that could serve as a foundation. (As has been shown many times in this chapter, students have previous understandings and knowledge of mathematics that are not productive for rational-number understanding.) To this end, we highlighted two kinds of understandings that students have generally developed by this age. One is an ability to estimate proportions visually such as halves;[45] the other is an ability to work with successive halving[46] (see Box 7-2).

BOX 7-2 **Students' Informal Knowledge**

Proportional Understandings

While we know that formal proportional reasoning is slow to develop[47] it has nonetheless been shown that children from a very early age have a strong propensity for making proportional evaluations that are nonnumerical and based on perceptual cues. For example, young children have little difficulty perceiving narrow, upright containers in proportional terms. Although they can see which of two such containers has more liquid in it in absolute terms, they can also see which has more in proportional terms. That is to say, they can see which one is fuller.[48]

Halving and Doubling

The ability to do repeated halving is evident is students' reasoning at this age. As Confrey and Kieren[49] point out, halving and doubling have their roots in a primitive scheme that they call *splitting*. Splitting, they assert, is based on actions that are purely multiplicative in nature and are separate from those of additive structures and counting. Whereas in counting the actions are joining, annexing, and removing, in splitting the primitive action is creating simultaneous multiple versions of an original by dividing symmetrically, growing, magnifying, and folding.

Although one of these sets of understandings—proportional estimation—is primarily visual and nonnumerical, while the other, halving and doubling, is numeric, both have their grounding in multiplicative operations. It was our proposal that if we could help students merge these separate kinds of multiplicative understandings, we would allow them to construct a core conceptual grounding for rational numbers.[50]

Our strategy from the beginning was to develop what we called a "bridging context"[51] to help students first access and then integrate their knowledge of visual proportions and their flexibility in working with halving numbers. The context we chose was to have students work with percents and linear measurement. As will be elaborated below, students were engaged from the start of the instructional sequence in estimating proportional relations based on length and in using their knowledge of halving to compute simple percent quantities. In our view, the percent and measurement context allowed students to access these initial kinds of understandings and then integrate them in a natural fashion. We regarded the integration of initial intuitions and knowledge as a foundation for rational-number learning.

Why Percent As a Starting Point?

While we found that starting with percent was useful for highlighting proportionally, we also recognized that it was a significant departure from traditional practice. Percent, known as the most difficult representation for students, is usually introduced only after fractions and decimals. Several considerations, however, led to this decision. First, with percents students are always working with the denominator of 100. We therefore postpone the problems that arise when students must compare or manipulate ratios with different denominators. This allows students to concentrate on developing their own procedures for comparison and calculation rather than requiring them to struggle to master a complex set of algorithms or procedures for working with different denominators.

Second, a further simplification at this beginning stage of learning is that all percentages have a corresponding decimal or fractional equivalent that can be relatively easy to determine (e.g., 40 percent = 0.40 or 0.4 = 40/100 or 4/10 or 2/5). By introducing percents first, we allow children to make their preliminary conversions among the different rational-number representations in a direct and intuitive fashion while developing a general understanding of how the three representations are related.

Finally, children know a good deal about percents from their everyday experiences.[52] By beginning with percents rather than fractions or decimals, we are able to capitalize on children's preexisting knowledge of the meanings of these numbers and the contexts in which they are important.[53]

Curriculum Overview

The curriculum is divided into roughly three parts. First the students are introduced to a single form of rational number—percent—using concrete props that highlight linear measurement. After students have spent time working with percents in many contexts, we present our next form of rational number, the two-place decimal. We do this in the context of percent, illustrating that a two-place decimal number is like the percent of the way between two whole numbers. Finally, our focus turns to activities that promote comparing and ordering rational numbers and moving among decimals and percents. Fractions are also taught at this stage in relation to percents and decimals.[54] The sections that follow provide details of many of the activities we devised and include accounts of how fourth, fifth, and sixth graders from our research classrooms worked through these activities. These lessons are described in a fair amount of detail so that interested teachers can try some of these activities with their own students. I also include these details to illustrate the strategies that were used to foster students' pride and investment in and willingness to monitor their work.

Lessons Part 1: Introduction to Percents

Percents in Everyday Life

Imagine a typical fourth-, fifth-, or sixth-grade class, in which the students have received no formal instruction in percent. Thus each time we implemented our curriculum, we began the lessons with discussions that probed the students' everyday knowledge of this topic. These questions generated a great number of responses in each of our research classrooms. Not only were the students able to volunteer a number of different contexts in which percents appear (e.g., siblings' school marks, price reductions in stores, and taxes on restaurant bills), but they also had a strong qualitative understanding of what different numerical values "mean." For example, students commented that 100 percent means "everything," 99 percent means "almost everything," 50 percent means "exactly half," and 1 percent means "almost nothing." As one student remarked, "You know if you are on a diet you should drink 1 percent milk instead of 4 percent milk."

Pipes and Tubes: A Representation for Fullness

To further explore students' intuitions and informal understandings, we presented them with a set of props specifically designed for the lessons. The set included a series of black drainage pipes (of varying heights) with white venting tubes[55] on the outside that could be raised or lowered, simulating the action of water filling them to different levels (see Figures 7-4a and 7-4b). To discover more about the students' understanding of percents and proportion, we asked them to consider how they would use these props to teach percent to a younger child. Again the students were full of ideas, many of which are central to the knowledge network for rational number.

First students demonstrated their understanding of the unit whole, as mentioned earlier, a concept that is often elusive in traditional instruction: "Each of these pipes is 100 percent." They also demonstrated understanding of the part–whole construct: "If you raise the tube up here [pointing to three-quarters of the length of the pipe], then the part that is covered is 75 percent, and the part that is left over is 25 percent." Students also naturally displayed their sense of rational number as operator: "This is 50 percent of the tube, and if we cut it in half again it is 25 percent." In addition, students demonstrated insights for proportions: "50 percent on this bigger pipe is bigger than 50 percent on this little pipe, but they're both still 50 percent." The idea of rational number as a measure was also embedded in the students' reasoning! "I know this is about 75 percent covered, because this first bit is 25 percent, and if you move the 25 percent piece along the tube three times, you get 75 percent." Clearly, they had strong intuitions about the general properties and interpretations of rational numbers in their informal understandings of percent.

We also were interested to see whether the use of these props could generate ideas about another difficult concept—the elusive idea of percents greater than 100.[56] Sam, an eager student, attempted to demonstrate this to his classmates. He first held up a tall pipe (80 cm): "We know that this whole pipe is 100 percent." Next, he picked up a second, shorter pipe (20 cm) and stood it beside the taller one, estimating that it was about 25 percent of the taller pipe. To confirm this conjecture, he moved the smaller pipe along the taller one, noting that it fit exactly four times. "Okay," he declared, "this is definitely 25 percent of the longer pipe. So, if you join the two [pipes] together like this [laying both pipes on the ground and placing the shorter one end to end with the larger], this new pipe is 125 percent of the first one."

Percents on Number Lines: More Estimation

In addition to drainage pipes, we included activities with laminated, meter-long number lines calibrated in centimeters to provide students with another way of visualizing percent (see Figures 7-5a and 7-5b). For example, we incorporated exercises in which children went on "percent walks." Here the number lines, which came to be known as "sidewalks," were lined up end to end on the classroom floor with small gaps between them. Students challenged each other to walk a given distance (e.g., "Can you please walk 70 percent of the first sidewalk? Now, how about 3 whole sidewalks and 65

FIGURE 7-4a

FIGURE 7-4b

FIGURE 7-5a

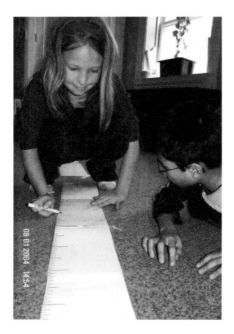

FIGURE 7-5b

percent of the fourth?"). The number-line activities were used to consolidate percent understandings and to extend the linear measurement context.

Computing with Percent

Next we introduced beakers of water with varying degrees of fullness (see Figures 7-6a and 7-6b). In keeping with the previous lessons, the students used percent terminology to estimate the "fullness" of these containers: "Approximately what percent of this beaker do you think is full?" or "How high will the liquid rise when it is 25 percent full?" As it turned out, the children's natural tendency when confronted with fullness problems was to use a repeated halving strategy. That is, they determined where a line representing 50 percent would go on the cylinder, then 25 percent, then 12 1/2 percent, and so on. These activities with fullness estimates led naturally to a focus on computation and measurement. For example, if it was discovered on measuring a beaker that it was 8 cm tall, then 4 cm from the bottom was the 50 percent point, and 2 cm was the 25 percent point. The halving strategies exemplified in these calculations became the basis for the computations the students tackled next.

Invented Procedures

Despite the move to calculating, the children were not given any standard rules to perform these operations, and so they naturally employed a series of strategies of their own invention using halves, quarters, and eighths as benchmarks to guide their calculations. For example, to calculate 75 percent of the length of a 60 cm desktop, the students typically considered this task in a series of steps: Step 1, find half, and then build up as necessary (50 percent of 60 = 30); Step 2, use a halving strategy to find 25 percent of 60, and if 50 percent of 60 = 30, then 25 percent of 60 = 15); and Step 3, sum the parts (30 + 15 = 45).

String Challenges: Guessing Mystery Objects

String measurement activities also proved to be an excellent way of considering percent quantities and calculating percentages using benchmarks. A string challenge that became a regular feature of classroom life was what we called "The Mystery Object Challenge." In this activity, which often started the lessons, the teacher held up a piece of string that was cut to the percent of the length of a certain object in the room. The routine went something like this:

FIGURE 7-6a

FIGURE 7-6b

Teacher	I have here a length of string that is 25 percent of the height of a mystery object in the class-room. Any ideas as to what the mystery object might be?
Student	I think that it is the desktop or maybe the poster on the wall.
Teacher	How did you figure that out?
Student	Well, I just imagined moving the string along the desk four times and I think it works. [The student, then, carefully moving the string along the desk, was able to confirm her assertion.]

Since these kinds of challenges were so popular with the children, we went on to invite pairs of students to find their own mystery object to challenge their classmates. Students went around the room, measured their chosen object, and then cut a piece of string to a percent of the total. As a culminating activity, the students made what they called "percent families" of strings using the length of their mystery object as a base. Each pair of children was given a large piece of cardboard on which they pasted lengths of string to represent the benchmarks of 100 percent, 50 percent, 25 percent, 75 percent, and 12 1/2 percent of the height of the object. These activities provided opportunities for calculating percents (e.g., if the object was 70 cm long, students would have to calculate and then measure and cut strings of 50 percent lengths, or 35 cm; of 25 percent lengths, or 17.5 cm; of 75 percent lengths, or 52.5 cm; etc.). Furthermore, the visual displays thus produced proved helpful in reinforcing the idea of proportion for the students. As students often remarked, "Our string lengths are different even though all of our percents are the same."

Summary of Lessons Part 1

The first phase of the lessons began with estimations and then calculations of percent quantities. These initial activities were all presented in the context of linear measurement of our specially designed pipes and tubes, beakers of water, string, and number lines. Students were not given formal instruction in specific calculating procedures; rather, they naturally employed procedures of their own that involved percent benchmarks and repeated halving. While percent was the only form of rational number that we officially introduced at this point, students often referred to fractions when working on these initial activities. At the beginning, all of the children naturally used the term "one-half" interchangeably with "fifty percent," and most knew that 25 percent (the next split) could be expressed as "one-quarter."

We also told them that the 12 1/2 percent split was called "one-eighth" and showed them the fraction symbol 1/8.

Although the props were enjoyable to the students, they also served an important function. The activities consistently helped students integrate their sense of visual proportion with their ability to do repeated halving. Our goal in all of these initial activities was to create situations in which these two kinds of informal understandings could become linked and serve as a foundation for the students' further learning of this number system.

Lessons Part 2: Introduction of Decimals

While the first phase of the lessons was designed to extend and elaborate students' knowledge of percent, the next phase moved the students to a new developmental level. At this point in our instructional program, we introduced students to a new form of rational number—the two-place decimal. The initial decimal lessons also had a strong focus on measurement and proportion.

Research has confirmed that a solid conceptual grounding in decimal numbers is difficult for students to achieve.[57] The similarities between the symbol systems for decimals and whole numbers lead to a number of misconceptions and error types.[58] Grasping the proportional nature of decimals is particularly challenging. In our program, we made a direct link from percents—which by now the students thought of in proportional terms—to decimals. In fact, we told the students that since they were now "percent experts," they could become "decimal experts." What we did with the students at this point was show that a two-place decimal number represents a percentage of the way between two adjacent whole numbers. In this way of thinking, a decimal represents an intermediate *distance* between two numbers (e.g., 5.25 is a distance that is 25 percent of the way between 5 and 6).

Decimals and Stopwatches

To begin the lessons in decimals, the students were given LCD stopwatches with screens that displayed seconds and hundredths of seconds (the latter indicated by two small digits to the right of the numbers; see Figure 7-7). The students were asked to consider what the two "small numbers" might mean and how these small numbers related to the bigger numbers to the left (seconds). After experimenting with the stopwatches, the children noted that there were 100 of these small time units in 1 second. With this observation, they made the connection to percents: "It's like they are percents of a second." After considerable discussion of what to name these small time intervals (e.g., some suggested that they were milliseconds), the students came to refer to these hundredths of seconds as

FIGURE 7-7

"centiseconds," a quantity they understood to be the percentage of time that had passed between any 2 whole seconds. We continued our work with decimals and stopwatches, with a focus on ordering numbers.

Magnitude and Order in Decimal Numbers

To illuminate the difficult concepts of magnitude and order (recall Wyatt's assertion that 2/3 = 3/4 and others' comments that 0.2 is smaller than 0.059), we devised many activities to help the students work with ordering decimals. The first of these activities was the "Stop-Start Challenge." In this exercise, students attempted to start and stop the watch as quickly as possible, several times in succession. After discussion, they learned to record their times as decimals. So, for example, 20 centiseconds was written as .20, 9 centiseconds as 0.09, and so on. Next, the students compared their personal quickest reaction time with that of their classmates, then ordered the times from quickest to slowest. In this exercise, the students could learn from their experience of trying to get the quickest time that, for example, 0.09 is a smaller number than .10 and eventually realize that .09 is smaller than .1. Another stopwatch game designed to actively engage students in issues of magnitude was "Stop the Watch Between": "Can you stop the watch between 0.45 and 0.50?" We also explored decimals through the laminated number lines, whereby students were asked to indicate parts of 100 using decimal representations: "Please put a mark where 0.09 is on this number line."

Summary of Lessons Part 2

In this second level of the instructional program, the students were introduced to decimals for the first time. Students worked on many activities that helped them first understand how decimals and percents are related and then learn how to represent decimals symbolically. As the decimal lessons proceeded, we moved on to activities designed to help students to consider and reflect on magnitude. Thus the final activities included situations in which students engaged in comparing and ordering decimals. This level of the program was the first step in students' learning to translate among the representations of rational number and gain fluency with different kinds of operations.

Lessons Part 3: Fractions and Mixed Representations of Rational Numbers

Fractions First: Equivalencies

As noted earlier, although the curriculum began with percents as the initial representation of rational numbers, we found that the students made many references to fractions. Now, at this final level of the program, our goal was to give students a chance to work with fractions more formally and then provide them with opportunities to translate flexibly among fractions, decimals, and percents. In a first series of activities, students worked on tasks in which they were asked to represent a fraction in as many ways as they could. Thus, for example, if their assignment was to show 3/4, students typically responded by presenting fraction equivalencies, such as 6/8 and 75/100. Students were also asked to compose "word problems" that incorporated fractions and were in turn given to their classmates to solve. Another activity that students enjoyed a great deal was challenging others to find the answers to equations of their own invention with questions such as "How much more to make one whole? (for example, 1/8 + 1/2 + 1/16 + 1/4 + ? = 1)," or "Is the following equation true or false? (1/4 + 1/8 + 5/10 + 1/8 = 1)." The reasoning of a fifth grader as he attempted to answer this question is typical of the reasoning of many of his classmates: "Well, 5/10 is 1/2. If you add 1/4 that makes three-quarters, so you need another quarter to make a whole and you have two-eighths, so it does equal one whole and so it is true!"

While students initially used fractions in these equations, they soon incorporated the other representations in challenges they composed. For example, one student posed the following question: "Here is my equation: 1/8 + 12.5 percent + 1/4 + .25 percent + ? = 1. How much more to make one whole?" To discover the missing quantity, the students' reasoning (anchored in percents and decimals) sounded something like this: "Well 12 1/2 (1/8) and 12 1/2 is 25 percent and another 25 percent (1/4) makes 50 percent and another .25 makes 75 percent so you would need another 25 percent to make a whole."

Crack the Code

The students carried out further work on conversions with the LCD stopwatches used earlier in the program. In a favorite game called "Crack the Code," students moved between representations of rational numbers as they were challenged to stop the watch at the decimal equivalent of different fractions and percents. For example, given a relatively simple secret code, e.g., 2/5, students stopped the watch at close to 40 centiseconds or 0.40 seconds as possible. Similarly with slightly more complex secret codes, such as "1/4 + 10 percent," students had to stop the watch at .35 seconds. This allowed them to increase their understanding of the possibility of fluid movement between representations.

Card Games

In one set of lessons, I gave the students a set of specially designed cards depicting various representations of fractions, decimals, and percents (e.g., there was a 3/8 card, a card with .375, and a card that read 37 1/2 percent). The students used the cards to design games that challenged their classmates to make comparisons among and between representations.

In the first game, the leader dealt the cards to the students, who in turn placed one card from their hand face up on the classroom floor. The challenge was to place the cards in order of increasing quantity. Students who disagreed with the placement of a particular card challenged the student who had gone before. This led to a great deal of debate. Sarah, for instance, had a card on which was written 5/9. This was a fraction that the students had not previously encountered in their lessons, and Sarah was not sure where to place it. Finally, she put the 5/9 card before a card on which was 50 percent, thus revealing that she thought that 5/9 was less than 50 percent. "That can't be right," asserted Jules. "In order to get 1/2 (50 percent) you would have to have 4 point 5 ninths and that is less than 5/9 so, 5/9 is larger than 1/2." The game ended when the children reached consensus and the teacher confirmed that all of the cards had been ordered correctly. The cards took up the entire length of the classroom by the time every student had placed his or her cards on the floor!

A second card game employing the same deck of cards, invented by a pair of students, had as its goal not only the comparison of decimals, fractions, and percents in mixed representations, but also the addition and subtraction of the differences between these numbers. This game again used the LCD stopwatches introduced earlier in the lessons. The two students who invented the game, Claire and Maggie, based it on the popular card game War. The students dealt the whole deck into two "hands," then simultaneously turned over the top card. The winner's score is increased by the difference in value of the two cards. In one turn, for example, Maggie's card had .20 written on it and Clare's had 1/8. What happened next is transcribed from the videotape of their play:

Claire	OK, now we have to figure out who has more.
Maggie	I do. 'Cause *you* only have $12\frac{1}{2}$ percent [one-eighth] but *I* have 20 percent. So *mine* is more.
Claire	Yeah, you're right; Ok I have to write down your score. . . . Hum . . .
	So that's 20 percent take away $12\frac{1}{2}$ percent so that's 7 1/2 [percent]. [Claire then took a pencil, and finding Maggie's place in the score column, wrote .075.]

At this point in the lessons, most of the students were comfortable thinking about percents, decimals, and fractions together. In fact, they assumed a shorthand way of speaking about quantities as they translated from fraction to percent. To illustrate this, I present a short excerpt from a conversation held by a visiting teacher who had watched the game the two girls had started and asked them to explain their reasoning.

Teacher	I was interested to know how you figured out which of the numbers is more, .20 or one-eighth. First of all, how did you know that one-eighth is equal to 12 1/2 percent?
Maggie	Ok, it is like this. One-eighth is half of one-fourth, and one-fourth is 25 percent. So, half of that is 12 1/2 percent.
Teacher	Well, you certainly know percents very well. But what about decimals? Do you know what 12 1/2 percent is as a decimal?

Claire: You see, 12 1/2 percent is like point 12 and a
               half and that's the same as point 12 point 5,
               because the point five is like half.

Maggie: Yeah, but in decimals you have to say it's really
               point 125.

Summary of Lessons Part 3

In the third part of the curriculum, we focused primarily on students' uses of mixed representations. We began with some formal activities with fractions and equivalencies, including tasks in which students had to work with and devise lengthy equations. We also had the students make up their own games and challenges to help them gain more practice in this kind of flexible movement from one operation to another. One of our primary goals here was to provide students with habits of mind regarding multiple representations that will be with them throughout their learning and lay the foundations for their ability to solve mathematical problems.

Results from Our Studies

To date, variations of our curriculum have been implemented and assessed in four experimental classrooms. From the very first lessons, students demonstrated and used their everyday knowledge of percents and worked successfully with percents in situations that called on their understanding of proportion. Our particular format also allowed students to express their informal knowledge of other concepts and meanings that are central to rational number understanding. Recall that when working with the pipes and tubes and the beakers of water, students successfully incorporated ideas of the rational-number subconstructs of measure, operator, and ratio. What was also evident was that they had a strong understanding of the unit whole and its transformations. Similarly, when decimals were introduced in the context of stopwatches, the students readily made sense of this new representation and were able to perform a variety of computations. Finally, by the end of the experimental sessions, the students had learned a flexible approach to translating among the representations of rational numbers using familiar benchmarks and halving and doubling as a vehicle of movement.

While the class as a whole appeared to be engaged and motivated by the lessons, we needed to look at the improvement made by individual students at the end of the experimental intervention. We were also interested to see how the performance of students in the experimental group compared with that of students who had traditional classroom instruction. To these ends, we assessed the experimental students on a variety of tasks before and after the course of instruction and administered these same tasks to students from classrooms in which textbook instruction had been pro-vided.[59]

Briefly, we found that students in the experimental group had improved significantly.[60] Further, the scores that they obtained after instruction were often higher than those of children who had received instruction in conventional classrooms and who were many years older. Not only were students in the experimental classrooms able to answer more questions than did the "textbook" students, but the quality of their answers was better. Specifically, the experimental group made more frequent reference to proportional concepts in justifying their answers than did the students in the nonexperimental group. What follows are some examples of changes in students' reasoning following participation in the experimental program, consisting of selections from interviews that were conducted following the conclusion of the experimental classes.

Children's Thinking After Instruction

Let us return to the question posed to Wyatt at the start of the program (and excerpted at the beginning of this chapter) and look at the responses of two students, Julie and Andy, whose reasoning was typical of that of the other students at the end of the program.

Interviewer	Here are three numbers: 2/3, 0.5, and 3/4. Could you please put these numbers in order from smallest to largest?
Julie	Well, let's see. Point 5 is the smallest because 3/4 is 75 percent. I am not exactly sure what 2/3 is as a percent *but* it is definitely more than a half. Can I use this paper to try it out? [Julie took two pieces of paper. Holding them horizontally, she first folded one in four equal parts and then pointed to three sections, remarking that this was 3/4. Next she folded the second sheet in three pieces and then lined the two pages up together to compare the differences between the 2/3 and 3/4]. So 3/4 is the biggest.

Andy responded to this same question differently.

Andy	It's easy: .5 is 50 percent and 2/3 is 66 percent, and so it goes first .5 then 2/3 and then 3/4 cause that's 75 percent.

As can be seen, both Andy and Julie correctly ordered the numbers using their knowledge of percent as a basis for their reasoning. Andy, a high-achieving student, simply converted these quantities to percents. Julie, identified as a lower achiever, used paper folding as a way of finding the bigger fraction. Both used multiplicative solutions, one concrete and one abstract.

Another example taken from posttest interviews illustrates not only the students' understanding of order and magnitude, but also their understanding of the density property of rational numbers—that there is an infinite number of numbers between any two rational numbers.

Interviewer	Can any fractions fit between one-fourth and two-fourths? And if so, can you name one?
Maggie	Well, I know that one-quarter is 25 percent and so two quarters is a half, so that's 50 percent. So, there's tons of numbers between them like 40 percent. So that would be 40/100.
Jed	One-quarter is the same as 2/8 and 2/4 is the same as 4/8, so the answer is three-eighths.

The above answers are in sharp contrast to those of children before our instruction or those from traditional classrooms, the majority of whom claimed no numbers could come between 1/4 and 2/4.

In a final example, students were asked to compute a percent of a given quantity—65 percent of 160. Although this type of computation was performed regularly in our classrooms, 65 percent of 160 was a significantly more difficult calculation than those the students had typically encountered in their lessons. Furthermore, this item required that students work with 10 percent as well as with the familiar benchmarks (25 percent, 50 percent, 75 percent, and 12 1/2 percent) that served as a basis for most of their classroom work. Despite these differences, students found ways to solve this difficult problem.

Interviewer	What is 65 percent of 160?
Sascha	Okay, 50 percent of 160 is 80. Half of 80 is 40, so that is 25 percent. So if you add 80 and 40 you get 120. But that (120) is too much because that's 75 percent. So you need to minus 10 percent (of 160) and that's 16. So, 120 take away 16 is 104.
Neelam	The answer is 104. First I did 50 percent, which was 80.

> Then I did 10 percent of 160, which is 16. Then
> I did 5 percent, which was 8. I added them [16
> + 8] to get 24, and added that to 80 to get 104.

For anyone who has seen a colleague pause when asked to compute a percentage, as one must, say, to calculate a tip, the ease with which these students worked through these problems is striking.

Knowledge Network

These are only a few examples from the posttest interviews that illustrate the kinds of new understandings and interconnections students had been able to develop through their participation in the curriculum. Overall, our analyses of the children's thinking revealed that students had gained (1) an overall understanding of the number system, as illustrated by their ability to use the representations of decimals, fractions, and percents interchangeably; (2) an appreciation of the magnitude of rational numbers, as seen in their ability to compare and order numbers within this system; (3) an understanding of the proportional- and ratio-based constructs of this domain, which underpins their facility with equivalencies; (4) an understanding of percent as an operator, as is evident in their ability to invent a variety of solution strategies for calculating with these numbers; and (5) general confidence and fluency in their ability to think about the domain using the benchmark values they had learned, which is a hallmark of number sense.

Our research is still in an early stage. We will continue to pursue many questions, including the potential limitations of successive halving as a way of operating with rational numbers, downplaying of the important understandings associated with the quotient subconstruct, as well as a limited view of fractions. Furthermore, we need to learn more about how students who have been introduced to rational numbers in this way will proceed with their ongoing learning of mathematics.

While we acknowledge that these questions have not yet been answered, we believe certain elements of our program contributed to the students' learning, elements that may have implications for other rational-number curricula. First, our program began with percents, thus permitting children to take advantage of their qualitative understanding of proportions and combine that understanding with their knowledge of the numbers from 1 to 100, while avoiding (or at least postponing) the problems presented by fractions. Second, we used linear measurement as a way of promoting the multiplicative ideas of relative quantities and fullness. Finally, our program emphasized benchmark values—of halves, quarters, eighths, etc.—for moving among equivalencies of percents, decimals, and fractions, which allowed students to be flexible and develop confidence in relying on their own procedures for problem solving.

CONCLUSION: HOW STUDENTS LEARN RATIONAL NUMBER

Principle #1: Prior Understandings

For years mathematics researchers have focused their attention on understanding the complexities of this number system and how to facilitate students' learning of the system. One well-established insight is that rational-number teaching focused on pie charts and part–whole understandings reinforces the primary problem students confront in learning rational number: the dominance of whole-number reasoning. One response is to place the multiplicative ideas of relative quantity, ratio, and proportion at the center of instruction.

However, our curriculum also builds on our theory and research findings pointing to the knowledge students typically bring to the study of rational number that can serve as a foundation for conceptual change. Two separate kinds of understandings that 10-year-olds typically possess have a multiplicative orientation. One of these is visual proportional estimation; for children, this understanding usually functions independently of numbers, at least initially. The second important kind of understanding is the numerical procedure for repeated halving. By strengthening and merging these two understandings, students can build a solid foundation for working flexibly with rational numbers.

Our initial instructional activities are designed to elicit these informal understandings and to provide instructional contexts that bring them together. We believe this coordination produces a new interlinked structure that serves both as foundation for the initial learning of rational number and subsequently as the basis on which to build a networked understanding of this domain.

Principle #2: Network of Concepts

At the beginning of this chapter, I outlined the complex set of core concepts, representations, and operations students need to acquire to gain an initial grounding in the rational-number system. As indicated above, the central conceptual challenge for students is to master proportion, a concept grounded in multiplicative reasoning. Our instructional strategy was to design a learning sequence that allowed students to first work with percents and proportion in linear measurement and next work with decimals and fractions. Extensive practice is incorporated to assure that students become fluent in translating between different forms of rational number. Our intention was to create a percent measurement structure that would become a central network to which all subsequent mathematical learning could be linked. This design is significantly different from traditional instruction in rational number, in which topics are taught separately.

Principle #3: Metacognition

In this chapter, I have not made detailed reference to students' developing metacognition. Yet the fostering of metacognition is in fact central to our curriculum. First, as the reader may have noted, we regularly engaged the students in whole-group discussions in which they were asked to explain their reasoning and share invented procedures with their classmates. We also designed the lessons so that students worked in small groups to collaborate in solving problems and constructing materials; we thereby provided students with a forum to express and refine their developing understandings. There were also many opportunities for students to consider how they would teach rational number to others, either younger students or their own classmates, by designing their own games and producing teaching plans for how these new concepts could be taught. In all these ways, we allowed students to reflect on their own learning and to consider what it meant for them and others to develop an understanding of rational number. Finally, we fostered metacognition in our program through the overall design and goals of the experimental curriculum, with its focus on interconnections and multiple representations. This focus, I believe, provided students with an overview of the number system as a whole and thus allowed them to make informed decisions on how best to operate with rational numbers.

Final Words

I conclude this chapter with an interchange, recorded verbatim, between a fourth-grade student and a researcher. Zach, the fourth grader, was being interviewed by the researcher as part of a posttest assessment. The conversation began when Zach had completed two pages of the six-page posttest and remarked to the interviewer, "I have just done 1/3 of the test;...that is 33.3 percent." When he finished the third page, he noted, "Now I have finished 1/2 or 50 percent of the test." On completing the fourth page he remarked, "Okay, so I have now done 2/3 of the test, which is the same as 66 percent." When he had completed the penultimate page, he wondered out loud what the equivalent percentage was for 5/6: "Okay, let's see; it has got to be over 66.6 percent and it is also more than 75 percent. I'd say that it is about 80 percent....No, wait; it can't be 80 percent because that is 4/5 and this [5/6] is more than 4/5. It is 1/2 plus 1/3...so it is 50 percent plus 33.3 percent, 83.3 percent. So I am 83.3 percent finished."

This exchange illustrates the kind of metacognitive capability that our curriculum is intended to develop. First, Zach posed his own questions, unprompted. Further, he did not expect that the question had to be answered by the teacher. Rather, he was confident that he had the tools, ideas, and concepts that would help him navigate his way to the answer. We also see that Zach rigorously assessed the reasonableness of his answers and that he used his knowledge of translating among the various representations to help him solve the problem. I conclude with this charming vignette as an illustration of the potential support our curriculum appears to offer to students beginning their learning of rational number.

Students then go on to learn algorithms that allow them to calculate a number like 83.3 percent from $^5/_6$ efficiently. But the foundation in mathematical reasoning that students like Zach possess allow them to use those algorithms with understanding to solve problems when an algorithm has been forgotten and to double check their answers using multiple methods. The confidence created when a student's mathematical reasoning is secure bodes well for future mathematics learning.

NOTES

1. Armstrong and Bezuk, 1995; Ball, 1990; Post et al., 1991.
2. Moss, 2000.
3. Carpenter et al., 1980.
4. Ball, 1993; Hiebert and Behr, 1988; Kieren, 1993.
5. Lamon, 1999.
6. Hiebert and Wearne, 1986; Wearne and Hiebert, 1988.
7. Hiebert and Behr, 1988.
8. Kerslake, 1986.
9. Heibert, 1992.
10. National Research Council, 2001.
11. Carpenter et al., 1993.
12. Lamon, 1999.
13. Lesh et al., 1988.
14. Baroody, 1999.
15. Lamon, 1999.
16. National Council of Teachers of Mathematics, 1989, 2000.
17. Markovits and Sowder, 1991, 1994; Sowder, 1995.
18. Cramer et al., 1989.
19. Sowder, 1995.
20. Sowder, 1992.
21. Hiebert and Behr, 1988.
22. Behr et al., 1983, 1984, 1992, 1993; Kieren, 1994, 1995; Ohlsson, 1988.
23. Hiebert and Behr, 1988.
24. Kerslake, 1986.
25. Behr et al., 1984; Case, 1998; Hiebert and Behr, 1988; Lamon, 1995; Mack, 1990, 1993, 1995; Resnick and Singer, 1993.

26. Hart, 1988; Karplus and Peterson, 1970; Karplus et al., 1981, 1983; Cramer et al., 1993; Noelting, 1980a, 1980b.
27. National Council of Teachers of Mathematics, 1989, 2000; National Research Council, 2001.
28. Ball, 1993.
29. Sowder, 1988.
30. Baroody, 1999; Heibert, 1992; Hiebert and Wearne, 1986; Moss and Case, 1999; Post et al., 1993.
31. Armstrong and Bezuk, 1995; Ball, 1993; Hiebert and Wearne, 1986; Mack, 1990, 1993; Markovits and Sowder, 1991, 1994; Sowder, 1995.
32. Confrey, 1994, 1995; Kieren, 1994, 1995; Post et al., 1993; Streefland, 1991, 1993.
33. Kieren, 1994, 1995; Mack, 1993, 1995; Sowder, 1995; Streefland, 1993.
34. Kieren, 1994, p. 389.
35. Kieren, 1992, 1995.
36. Confrey, 1995.
37. Lachance and Confrey, 1995.
38. Streefland, 1991, 1993.
39. Mack, 1990, 1993.
40. Lamon, 1993, 1994, 1999.
41. As of this writing, this curriculum is being implemented with students of low socioeconomic status in a grade 7 and 8 class. Preliminary analyses have shown that it is highly effective in helping struggling students relearn this number system and gain a stronger conceptual understanding.
42. Kalchman et al., 2000; Moss, 1997, 2000, 2001, 2003; Moss and Case, 1999.
43. National Research Council, 2001.
44. Parker and Leinhardt, 1995.
45. Case, 1985; Noelting, 1980a; Nunes and Bryant, 1996; Spinillo and Bryant, 1991.
46. Confrey, 1994; Kieren, 1994.
47. Resnick and Singer, 1993.
48. Case, 1985.
49. Confrey, 1994; Kieren, 1993.
50. Case and Okomoto, 1996.
51. Case, 1998; Kalchman et al., 2000.
52. Parker and Leinhardt, 1995.
53. Lembke and Reys, 1994.
54. While the activities and lessons we designed are organized in three phases, the actual order of the lessons and the pacing of the teaching, as well as the particular content of the activities described below, varied in different classrooms depending on the needs, capabilities, and interests of the participating students.
55. These materials are available at any building supply store.
56. Parker and Leinhardt, 1995.
57. Hiebert et al., 1991.
58. Resnick et al., 1989.

59. Kalchman et al., 2000; Moss, 1997, 2000, 2001; Moss and Case, 1999.
60. From pre- to posttest, achieving effect sizes between and 1 and 2 standard deviations.

REFERENCES

Armstrong, B.E., and Bezuk, N. (1995). Multiplication and division of fractions: The search for meaning. In J.T. Sowder and B.P. Schappelle (Eds.), *Providing a foundation for teaching mathematics in the middle grades* (pp. 85-120). Albany, NY: State University of New York Press.

Ball, D.L. (1990). The mathematics understanding that prospective teachers bring to teacher education elementary school. *Journal, 90,* 449-466.

Ball, D.L. (1993). Halves, pieces and twoths: Constructing and using representational contexts in teaching fractions. In T.P. Carpenter, E. Fennema, and T.A. Romberg (Eds.), *Rational numbers: An integration of research* (pp. 157-196). Mahwah, NJ: Lawrence Erlbaum Associates.

Baroody, A.J. (1999). *Fostering children's mathematical power: An investigative approach to K-8 mathematics instruction.* Mahwah, NJ: Lawrence Erlbaum Associates.

Behr, M.J., Lesh, R., Post, T.R., and Silver, E.A. (1983). Rational-number concepts. In R. Lesh and M. Landau (Eds.), *Acquisition of mathematics concepts and processes* (pp. 91-126). New York: Academic Press.

Behr, M.J., Wachsmuth, I., Post, T.R., and Lesh, T. (1984). Order and equivalence of rational numbers: A clinical teaching experiment. *Journal for Research in Mathematics Education, 15*(4), 323-341.

Behr, M.J., Harel, G., Post, T.R, and Lesh, R. (1992). Rational number, ratio, and proportion. In D.A. Grouws (Ed.), *Handbook of research on mathematics teaching and learning* (pp. 296-333). New York: Macmillan.

Behr, M.J., Harel, G., Post, T.R, and Lesh, R. (1993). Rational numbers: Towards a semantic analysis: Emphasis on the operator construct. In T.P. Carpenter, E. Fennema, and T.A. Romberg (Eds.), *Rational numbers: An integration of research* (pp. 13-48). Mahwah, NJ: Lawrence Erlbaum Associates.

Carpenter, T.P., Kepner, H., Corbitt, M.K., Lindquist, M.M., and Reys, R.E. (1980). Results of the NAEP mathematics assessment: Elementary school. *Arithmetic Teacher, 27,* 10-12, 44-47.

Carpenter, T.P., Fennema, E., and Romberg, T.A. (1993). Toward a unified discipline of scientific inquiry. In T. Carpenter, E. Fennema, and T.A. Romberg (Eds.), *Rational numbers: An integration of research* (pp. 1-12). Mahwah, NJ: Lawrence Erlbaum Associates.

Case, R. (1985). *Intellectual development: Birth to adulthood.* New York: Academic Press.

Case, R. (1998, April). *A psychological model of number sense and its development.* Paper presented at the annual meeting of the American Educational Research Association, San Diego, CA.

Case, R., and Okamoto, Y. (1996). The role of central conceptual structures in the development of children's thought. *Monographs of the Society for Research in Child Development, 246*(61), 1-2. Chicago, IL: University of Chicago Press.

Confrey, J. (1994). Splitting, similarity, and the rate of change: A new approach to multiplication and exponential functions. In G. Harel and J. Confrey (Eds.), *The development of multiplicative reasoning in the learning of mathematics* (pp. 293-332). Albany, NY: State University of New York Press.

Confrey, J. (1995). Student voice in examining "splitting" as an approach to ratio, proportions and fractions. In L. Meira and D. Carraher (Eds.), *Proceedings of the 19th international conference for the Psychology of Mathematics Education* (vol. 1, pp. 3-29). Recife, Brazil: Universidade Federal de Pernambuco.

Cramer, K., Post, T., and Behr, M. (1989). Cognitive restructuring ability, teacher guidance and perceptual distractor tasks: An aptitude treatment interaction study. *Journal for Research in Mathematics Education, 20*(1), 103-110.

Cramer, K., Post, T., and Currier, D. (1993). Learning and teaching ratio and proportion: Research implications. In D. Owens (Ed.), *Research ideas for the classroom: Middle grade mathematics* (pp. 159-179). New York: Macmillan.

Hart, K. (1988). Ratio and proportion. In J. Hiebert and M. Behr (Eds.), *Number concepts and operations in the middle grades* (pp. 198-220). Mahwah, NJ: Lawrence Erlbaum Associates.

Hiebert, J. (1992). Mathematical, cognitive, and instructional analyses of decimal fractions. In G. Leinhardt, R. Putnam, and R.A. Hattrup (Eds.), *Analysis of arithmetic for mathematics teaching* (pp. 283-322). Mahwah, NJ: Lawrence Erlbaum Associates.

Hiebert, J., and Behr, J.M. (1988). Capturing the major themes. In J. Hiebert and M. Behr (Eds.), *Number concepts and operations in the middle grades* (vol. 2, pp. 1-18). Mahwah, NJ: Lawrence Erlbaum Associates.

Hiebert, J., and Wearne, D. (1986). Procedures over concepts: The acquisition of decimal number knowledge. In J. Hiebert (Ed.), *Conceptual and procedural knowledge: The case of mathematics* (pp. 199-244). Mahwah, NJ: Lawrence Erlbaum Associates.

Hiebert, J., Wearne, D., and Taber, S. (1991). Fourth graders' gradual construction of decimal fractions during instruction using different physical representations. *Elementary School Journal, 91,* 321-341.

Kalchman, M., Moss, J., and Case, R. (2000). Psychological models for the development of mathematical understanding: Rational numbers and functions. In S. Carver and D. Klahr (Eds.), *Cognition and Instruction: 25 years of progress.* Mahwah, NJ: Lawrence Erlbaum Associates.

Karplus, R., and Peterson, R.W. (1970). Intellectual development beyond elementary school II: Ratio, a survey. *School Science and Mathematics, 70*(9), 813-820.

Karplus, R., Pulos, S., and Stage, E.K. (1981). *Proportional reasoning of early adolescents.* Berkeley, CA: University of California, Lawrence Hall of Science.

Karplus, R., Pulos, S., and Stage, E.K. (1983). Proportional reasoning of early adolescents. In R. Lesh and M. Landau (Eds.), *Acquisition of mathematics concepts and processes* (pp. 45-90). Orlando, FL: Academic.

Kerslake, D. (1986). *Fractions: Children's strategies and errors.* Windsor, UK: NFER Nelson.

Kieren, T.E. (1992). Rational and fractional numbers as mathematical and personal knowledge. In G. Leinhardt, R. Putnam, and R.A. Hattrup (Eds.), *Analysis of arithmetic for mathematics teaching* (pp. 323-372). Mahwah, NJ: Lawrence Erlbaum Associates.

Kieren, T.E. (1993). Rational and fractional numbers: From quotient fields to recursive understanding. In T. Carpenter, E. Fennema, and T.A. Romberg (Eds.), *Rational numbers: An integration of research* (pp. 49-84). Mahwah, NJ: Lawrence Erlbaum Associates.

Kieren, T.E. (1994). Multiple views of multiplicative structure. In G. Harel and J. Confrey (Eds.), *The development of multiplicative reasoning in the learning of mathematics* (pp. 387-397). Albany, NY: State University of New York Press.

Kieren, T.E. (1995). Creating spaces for learning fractions. In J.T. Sowder and B.P. Schappelle (Eds.), *Providing a foundation for teaching mathematics in the middle grades.* Albany, NY: State University of New York Press.

Lachance, A., and Confrey, J. (1995). Introducing fifth graders to decimal notation through ratio and proportion. In D.T. Owens, M.K. Reed, and G.M. Millsaps (Eds.), *Proceedings of the seventeenth annual meeting of the North American chapter of the International Group for the Psychology of Mathematics Education* (vol. 1, pp. 395-400). Columbus, OH: ERIC Clearinghouse for Science, Mathematics and Environmental Education.

Lamon, S.J. (1993). Ratio and proportion: Children's cognitive and metacognitive processes. In T.P. Carpenter, E. Fennema, and T.A. Romberg, (Eds.), *Rational numbers: An integration of research* (pp. 131-156). Mahwah, NJ: Lawrence Erlbaum Associates.

Lamon S.J. (1994). Ratio and proportion: Cognitive foundations in unitizing and norming. In G. Harel and J. Confrey (Eds.), *The development of multiplicative reasoning in the learning of mathematics* (pp. 89-122). Albany, NY: State University of New York Press.

Lamon, S.J. (1995). Ratio and proportion: Elementary didactical phenomenology. In J.T. Sowder and B.P. Schappelle (Eds.), *Providing a foundation for teaching mathematics in the middle grades.* Albany, NY: State University of New York Press.

Lamon, S.J. (1999). *Teaching fractions and ratios for understanding: Essential content knowledge and instructional strategies for teachers.* Mahwah, NJ: Lawrence Erlbaum Associates.

Lembke, L.O., and Reys, B.J. (1994). The development of, and interaction between, intuitive and school-taught ideas about percent. *Journal for Research in Mathematics Education, 25*(3), 237-259.

Lesh, R., Post, T., and Behr, M. (1988). Proportional reasoning. In M. Behr and J. Hiebert (Eds.), *Number concepts and operations in the middle grades* (pp. 93-118). Mahwah, NJ: Lawrence Erlbaum Associates.

Mack, N.K. (1990). Learning fractions with understanding: Building on informal knowledge. *Journal for Research in Mathematics Education, 21,* 16-32.

Mack, N.K. (1993). Learning rational numbers with understanding: The case of informal knowledge. In T.P. Carpenter, E. Fennema, and T.A. Romberg (Eds.), *Rational numbers: An integration of research* (pp. 85-105). Mahwah, NJ: Lawrence Erlbaum Associates.

Mack, N.K. (1995). Confounding whole-number and fraction concepts when building on informal knowledge. *Journal for Research in Mathematics Education, 26*(5), 422-441.

Markovits, Z., and Sowder, J.T. (1991). Students' understanding of the relationship between fractions and decimals. *Focus on Learning Problems in Mathematics, 13*(1), 3-11.

Markovits, Z., and Sowder, J.T. (1994). Developing number sense: An intervention study in grade 7. *Journal for Research in Mathematics Education, 25*(1), 4-29, 113.

Moss, J. (1997). *Developing children's rational number sense: A new approach and an experimental program.* Unpublished master's thesis, University of Toronto, Toronto, Ontario, Canada.

Moss, J. (2000). *Deepening children's understanding of rational numbers.* Dissertation Abstracts.

Moss, J. (2001). Percents and proportion at the center: Altering the teaching sequence for rational number. In B. Littweiller (Ed.), *Making sense of fractions, ratios, and proportions. The NCTM 2002 Yearbook* (pp. 109-120). Reston, VA: National Council of Teachers of Mathematics.

Moss, J. (2003). On the way to computational fluency: Beginning with percents as a way of developing understanding of the operations in rational numbers. In *Teaching children mathematics* (pp. 334-339). Reston, VA: National Council of Teachers of Mathematics.

Moss, J., and Case, R. (1999). Developing children's understanding of rational numbers: A new model and experimental curriculum. *Journal for Research in Mathematics Education, 30*(2), 119, 122-147.

National Council of Teachers of Mathematics. (1989). *Curriculum and evaluation standards for school mathematics.* Reston, VA: National Council of Teachers of Mathematics.

National Council of Teachers of Mathematics. (2000). *Curriculum and evaluation standards for school mathematics.* Reston, VA: National Council of Teachers of Mathematics.

National Research Council. (2001). *Adding it up: Helping children learn mathematics.* Mathematics Learning Study Committee, J. Kilpatrick, J., Swafford, J., and B. Findell (Eds.). Center for Education. Division of Behavioral and Social Sciences and Education. Washington, DC: National Academy Press.

Noelting, G. (1980a). The development of proportional reasoning and the ratio concept. Part I: Differentiation of stages. *Educational Studies in Mathematics, 11,* 217-253.

Noelting, G. (1980b). The development of proportional reasoning and the ratio concept. Part II: Problem-structure at successive stages: Problem-solving strategies and the mechanism of adaptive restructuring. *Educational Studies in Mathematics, 11,* 331-363.

Nunes, T., and Bryant, P. (1996). *Children doing mathematics.* Cambridge, MA: Blackwell.

Ohlsson, S. (1988). Mathematical meaning and applicational meaning in the semantics of fractions and related concepts. In J. Hiebert and M. Behr (Eds.), *Number concepts and operations in the middle grades* (vol. 2, pp. 53-92). Mahwah, NJ: Lawrence Erlbaum Associates.

Parker, M., and Leinhardt, G. (1995). Percent: A privileged proportion. *Review of Educational Research, 65*(4), 421-481.

Post, T., Harel, G., Behr, M., and Lesh, R. (1991). Intermediate teachers' knowledge of rational number concepts. In E. Fennema, T. Carpenter, and S. Lamon (Eds.), *Integrating research on teaching and learning mathematics* (pp. 177-198). Albany, NY: State University of New York Press.

Post, T.R., Cramer, K.A., Behr, M., Lesh, R., and Harel, G. (1993). Curriculum implications of research on the learning, teaching and assessing of rational number concepts. In T.P. Carpenter, E. Fennema, and T.A. Romberg (Eds.), *Rational numbers: An integration of research* (pp. 327-362). Mahwah, NJ: Lawrence Erlbaum Associates.

Resnick, L.B., and Singer, J.A. (1993). Protoquantitative origins of ratio reasoning. In T.P. Carpenter, E. Fennema, and T.A. Romberg (Eds.), *Rational numbers: An integration of research* (pp. 107-130). Mahwah, NJ: Lawrence Erlbaum Associates.

Resnick, L.B., Nesher, P., Leonard, F., Magone, M., Omanson, S., and Peled I. (1989). Conceptual bases of arithmetic errors: The case of decimal fractions. *Journal for Research in Mathematics Education, 20*(1), 8-27.

Sowder, J.T. (1988). Mental computation and number comparison: Their roles in the development of number sense and computational estimation. In J. Hiebert and M. Behr (Eds.), *Number concepts and operations in the middle grades* (vol. 2, pp. 182-198). Mahwah, NJ: Lawrence Erlbaum Associates.

Sowder, J.T. (1992). Making sense of numbers in school mathematics. In G. Leinhardt, R. Putnam, and R. Hattrup, (Eds.), *Analysis of arithmetic for mathematics* (pp. 1-51). Mahwah, NJ: Lawrence Erlbaum Associates.

Sowder, J.T. (1995). Instructing for rational number sense. In J.T. Sowder and B.P. Schappelle (Eds.), *Providing a foundation for teaching mathematics in the middle grades*. Albany, NY: State University of New York Press.

Spinillo, A.G., and Bryant, P. (1991). Children's proportional judgements: The importance of "half." *Child Development, 62,* 427-440.

Streefland, L. (1991). Fractions: An integrated perspective. In L. Streefland (Ed.), *Realistic mathematics education in primary school* (pp. 93-118). Utrecht, The Netherlands: Freudenthal Institute.

Streefland, L. (1993). Fractions: A realistic approach. In T.P. Carpenter, E. Fennema, and T.A. Romberg (Eds.), *Rational numbers: An integration of research* (pp. 289-327). Mahwah, NJ: Lawrence Erlbaum Associates.

Wearne, D., and Hiebert, J. (1988). Constructing and using meaning for mathematical symbols: The case of decimal fractions. In J. Hiebert and M. Behr (Eds.), *Number concepts and operations in the middle grades* (vol. 2, pp. 220-235). Mahwah, NJ: Lawrence Erlbaum Associates.

8

Teaching and Learning Functions

Mindy Kalchman and Kenneth R. Koedinger

This chapter focuses on teaching and learning mathematical functions.[1] Functions are all around us, though students do not always realize this. For example, a functional relationship between quantities is at play when we are paying for gasoline by the gallon or fruit by the pound. We need functions for financial plans so we can calculate such things as accrued income and interest. Functions are important as well to interpretations of local and world demographics and population growth, which are critical for economic planning and development. Functions are even found in such familiar settings as baseball statistics and metric conversions.

Algebraic tools allow us to express these functional relationships very efficiently; find the value of one thing (such as the gas price) when we know the value of the other (the number of gallons); and display a relationship visually in a way that allows us to quickly grasp the direction, magnitude, and rate of change in one variable over a range of values of the other. For simple problems such as determining gas prices, students' existing knowledge of multiplication will usually allow them to calculate the cost for a specific amount of gas once they know the price per gallon (say, $2) with no problem. Students know that 2 gallons cost $4, 3 gallons cost $6, 4 gallons cost $8, and so on. While we can list each set of values, it is very efficient to say that for all values in gallons (which we call x by convention), the total cost (which we call y by convention), is equal to 2x. Writing y = 2x is a simple way of saying a great deal.

As functional relationships become more complex, as in the growth of a population or the accumulation of interest over time, solutions are not so easily calculated because the base changes each period. In these situations, algebraic tools allow highly complex problems to be solved and displayed in a way that provides a powerful image of change over time.

Many students would be more than a little surprised at this description. Few students view algebra as a powerful toolkit that allows them to solve complex problems much more easily. Rather, they regard the algebra itself as the problem, and the toolkit as hopelessly complex. This result is not surprising given that algebra is often taught in ways that violate all three principles of learning set forth in *How People Learn* and highlighted in this volume.

The first principle suggests the importance of building new knowledge on the foundation of students' existing knowledge and understanding. Because students have many encounters with functional relationships in their everyday lives, they bring a great deal of relevant knowledge to the classroom. That knowledge can help students reason carefully through algebra problems. Box 8-1 suggests that a problem described in its everyday manifestation can be solved by many more students than the same problem presented only as a mathematical equation. Yet if the existing mathematics understandings students bring to the classroom are not linked to formal algebra learning, they will not be available to support new learning.

The second principle of *How People Learn* argues that students need a strong conceptual understanding of function as well as procedural fluency. The new and very central concept introduced with functions is that of a *dependent relationship:* the value of one thing depends on, is determined by, or is a function of another. The kinds of problems we are dealing with no longer are focused on determining a specific value (the cost of 5 gallons of gas). They are now focused on the *rule* or expression that tells us how one thing (cost) is related to another (amount of gas). A "function" is formally defined in mathematics as "a set of ordered pairs of numbers (x, y) such that to each value of the first variable (x) there corresponds a unique value of the second variable (y)."[2] Such a definition, while true, does not signal to students that they are beginning to learn about a new class of problems in which the value of one thing is determined by the value of another, and the rule that tells them how they are related.

Within mathematics education, function has come to have a broader interpretation that refers not only to the formal definition, but also to the multiple ways in which functions can be written and described.[3] Common ways of describing functions include tables, graphs, algebraic symbols, words, and problem situations. Each of these representations describes how the value of one variable is determined by the value of another. For instance, in a verbal problem situation such as "you get two dollars for every kilometer you walk in a walkathon," the dollars earned depend on, are determined by, or are a function of the distance walked. Conceptually, students need to understand that these are different ways of describing the same relationship.

Good instruction is not just about developing students' facility with performing various procedures, such as finding the value of *y* given *x* or creating a graph given an equation. Instruction should also help students develop a conceptual understanding of function, the ability to represent a function in a variety of ways, and fluency in moving among multiple representations of functions. The slope of the line as represented in an equation, for example, should have a "meaning" in the verbal description of the relationship between two variables, as well as a visual representation on a graph.

The third principle of *How People Learn* suggests the importance of students' engaging in metacognitive processes, monitoring their understanding as they go. Because mathematical relationships are generalized in algebra, students must operate at a higher level of abstraction than is typical of the mathematics they have generally encountered previously. At all levels of mathematics, students need to be engaged in monitoring their problem solving and reflecting on their solutions and strategies. But the metacognitive engagement is particularly important as mathematics becomes more abstract, because students will have few clues even when a solution has gone terribly awry if they are not actively engaged in sense making.

When students' conceptual understanding and metacognitive monitoring are weak, their efforts to solve even fairly simple algebra problems can, and often do, fail. Consider the problem in Figure 8-1a. How might students approach and respond to this problem? What graph-reading and table-building skills are required? Are such skills sufficient for a correct solution? If students lack a conceptual understanding of linear function, what errors might they make? Figure 8-1b shows an example student solution.

What skills does this student exhibit? What does this student understand and not understand about functions? This student has shown that he knows how to construct a table of values and knows how to record in that table coordinate points he has determined to be on the graph. He also clearly recalls that an algorithm for finding the slope of the function is dividing the change in y(Δy) by the change in x(Δx). There are, however, significant problems with this solution that reveal this student's weak conceptual understanding of functions.

Problem: Make a table of values that would produce the function seen on page 356.

First, and most superficially, the student (likely carelessly) mislabeled the coordinate for the y-intercept (0, 3) rather than (0, –3). This led him to make an error in calculating Δy by subtracting 0 from 3 rather than from –3. In so doing, he arrived at a value for the slope of the function that was negative—an impossible solution given that the graph is of an increasing linear function. This slip, by itself, is of less concern than the fact that the

BOX 8-1 Linking Formal Mathematical Understanding to Informal Reasoning

Which of these problems is most difficult for a beginning algebra student?

Story Problem

When Ted got home from his waiter job, he multiplied his hourly wage by the 6 hours he worked that day. Then he added the $66 he made in tips and found he had earned $81.90. How much does Ted make per hour?

Word Problem

Starting with some number, if I multiply it by 6 and then add 66, I get 81.9. What number did I start with?

Equation

Solve for x:
x * 6 + 66 = 81.90

Most teachers and researchers predict that students will have more difficulty correctly solving the story or word problem than the equation.[4] They might explain this expectation by saying that a student needs to read the verbal problems (story and word) and then translate them into the equation. In fact, research investigating urban high school students' performance on such problems found that on average, they scored 66 percent on the story problem, 62 percent on the word problem, and only 43 percent on the equation.[5] In other words, students were more likely to solve the verbal problems correctly than the equation. Investigating students' written work helps explain why.

Students often solved the verbal problems without using the equation. For instance, some students used a generate-and-test strategy: They estimated a value for the hourly rate (e.g., $4/hour), computed the corresponding pay (e.g., $90), compared it against the given value ($81.90), and repeated as needed. Other students used a more efficient unwind or working backwards strategy. They started with the final value of 81.9 and subtracted 66 to undo the last step of adding 66. Then they took the resulting 15.9 and divided by 6 to undo the first step of multiplying by 6. These strategies made the verbal problems easier than expected. But why were the equations difficult for students? Although experts in algebra may believe no reading is involved in equation solving, students do in fact need to learn how to read equations. The majority of student errors on equations can be attributed to difficulties in correctly comprehending the meaning of the equation.[6] In the above equation, for example, many students added 6 and 66, but no student did so on the verbal problems.

Besides providing some insight into how students think about algebraic problem solving, these studies illustrate how experts in an area such as algebra may have an "expert blind spot" for learning challenges beginners may experience. An expert blind spot occurs when someone skilled in an area overestimates the ease of learning its formalisms or jargon and underestimates learners' informal understanding of its key ideas. As a result, too little attention is paid to linking formal mathematical understanding to informal reasoning. Looking closely at students' work, the strategies they employ, and the errors they make, and even comparing their performance on similar kinds of problems, are some of the ways we can get past such blind spots and our natural tendency to think students think as we do.

Such studies of student thinking contributed to the creation of a technology-enhanced algebra course, originally Pump Algebra Tutor and now Cognitive Tutor Algebra.[7] That course includes an intelligent tutor that provides students with individualized assistance as they use multiple representations (words, tables, graphs, and equations) to analyze real-world problem situations. Numerous classroom studies have shown that this course significantly improves student achievement relative to alternative algebra courses (see www.carnegielearning.com/research). The course, which was based on basic research on learning science, is now in use in over 1,500 schools.

a

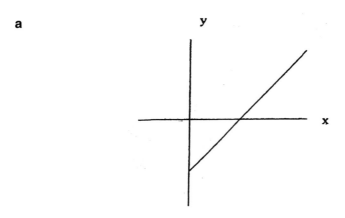

b

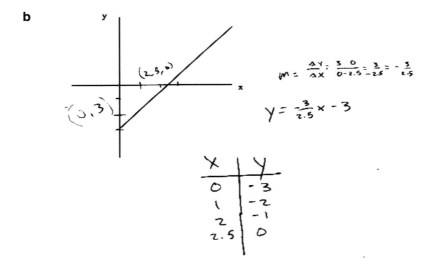

$$m = \frac{\Delta y}{\Delta x} : \frac{3 - 0}{0 - 2.5} = \frac{3}{-2.5} = -\frac{3}{2.5}$$

$$y = \frac{-3}{2.5} x - 3$$

X	Y
0	-3
1	-2
2	-1
2.5	0

FIGURE 8-1

student did not recognize the inconsistency between the positive slope of the line and the negative slope in the equation. Even good mathematicians could make such a mistake, but they would likely monitor their work as they went along or reflect on the plausibility of the answer and detect the inconsistency. This student could have caught and corrected his error had he acquired both fluency in interpreting the slope of a function from its equation (i.e., to see that it represents a decreasing function) and a reflective strategy for comparing features of different representations.

A second, more fundamental error in the student's solution was that the table of values does not represent a linear function. That is, there is not a constant change in y for every unit change in x. The first three coordinates in the student's table were linear, but he then recorded (2.5, 0) as the fourth coordinate pair rather than (3, 0), which would have made the function linear. He appears to have estimated and recorded coordinate points by visually reading them off the graph without regard for whether the final table embodied linearity. Furthermore, the student did not realize that the equation he produced, $y = \frac{-3}{2.5}x - 3$, translates not only into a decreasing line, but also into a table of numbers that decreases by $\frac{-3}{2.5}$ for every positive unit change in x.

At a surface level, this student's solution reflects some weaknesses in procedural knowledge, namely, getting the sign wrong on the y-intercept and imprecisely reading x-y coordinates off the graph. More important, however, these surface errors reflect a deeper weakness in the student's conceptual understanding of function. The student either did not have or did not apply knowledge for interpreting key features (e.g., increasing or decreasing) of different function representations (e.g., graph, equation, table) and for using strategies for checking the consistency of these interpretations (e.g., all should be increasing). In general, the student's work on this problem reflects an incomplete conceptual framework for linear functions, one that does not provide a solid foundation for fluid and flexible movement among a function's representations.

This student's work is representative of the difficulties many secondary-level students have with such a problem after completing a traditional textbook unit on functions. In a study of learning and teaching functions, about 25 percent of students taking ninth- and eleventh-grade advanced mathematics courses made errors of this type—that is, providing a table of values that does not reflect a constant slope—following instruction on functions.[8] This performance contrasts with that of ninth- and eleventh-grade mathematics students who solved this same problem after receiving instruction based on the curriculum described in this chapter. This group of students had an 88 percent success rate on the problem. Because these students had developed a deeper understanding of the concept of function, they knew that the y-values in a table must change by the same amount for every unit change in x for the function to be linear. The example in Figure 8-1c shows such thinking.

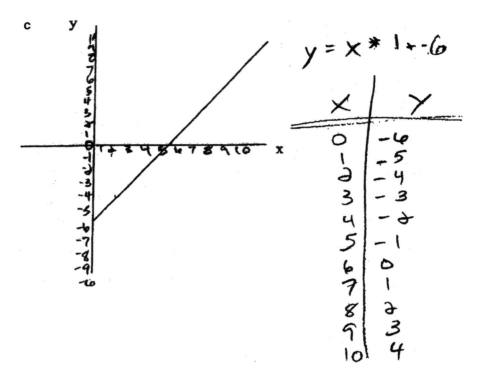

FIGURE 8-1

Problem: Make a table of values that would produce the function seen above.

This student identified a possible y-intercept based on a reasonable scale for the y-axis. She then labeled the x- and y-axes, from which she determined coordinate pairs from the graph and recorded them in a table of values. She determined and recorded values that show a constant increase in y for every positive unit change in x. She also derived an equation for the function that not only corresponds to both the graph and the table, but also represents a linear relationship between x and y.

How might one teach to achieve this kind of understanding? The goal of this chapter is to illustrate approaches to teaching functions that foster deep understanding and mathematical fluency. We emphasize the importance of designing thoughtful instructional approaches and curricula that reflect the principles of *How People Learn* (as outlined in Chapter 1), as well as recent research on what it means to learn and understand functions in particular. We first describe our approach to addressing each of the three principles. We then provide three sample lessons that emphasize those principles in sequence. We hope that these examples provide interesting activities to try with students. More important, these activities incorporate important discoveries about student learning that teachers can use to design other instructional activities to achieve the same goals.

ADDRESSING THE THREE PRINCIPLES

Principle #1: Building on Prior Knowledge

Principle 1 emphasizes the importance of students and teachers continually making links between students' experiences outside the mathematics classroom and their school learning experiences. The understandings students bring to the classroom can be viewed in two ways: as their everyday, informal, experiential, out-of-school knowledge, and as their school-based or "instructional" knowledge. In the instructional approach illustrated here, students are introduced to function and its multiple representations by having their prior experiences and knowledge engaged in the context of a walkathon. This particular context was chosen because (1) students are familiar with money and distance as variable quantities, (2) they understand the contingency relationship between the variables, and (3) they are interested in and motivated by the rate at which money is earned.

The use of a powerful instructional context, which we call a "bridging context," is crucial here. We use this term because the context serves to bridge students' numeric (equations) and spatial (graphic) understandings and to link their everyday experiences to lessons in the mathematics classroom. Following is an example of a classroom interaction that occurred during students' first lesson on functions, showing how use of the walkathon context as an introduction to functions in multiple forms—real-world situation (walkathon), table, graph, verbal ("$1.00 for each kilometer"), situation-specific symbols ($ = 1 * km), and generic symbolic (y = x * 1)—accomplishes these bridging goals. Figures 8-2a through 8-2c show changes in the whiteboard as the lesson proceeded.

Teacher	What we're looking at is, we're looking at what we do to numbers, to one set of numbers, to get other numbers. . . . So how many of you have done something like a walkathon? A readathon? A swimathon? A bikeathon?

	[Students raise their hands or nod.] So most of you...So I would say "Hi Tom [talking to a student in class], I'm going to raise money for such and such a charity and I'm going to walk ten kilometers."
Tom	OK.
Teacher	Say you're gonna sponsor me one dollar for every kilometer that I walk. So that's sort of the first way that we can think about a function. It's a rule. One dollar *for* every kilometer walked. So you have one dollar for each kilometer [writing "$1.00 for each kilometer" on the board while saying it]. So then what I do is I need to calculate how much money I'm gonna earn. And I have to start somewhere. So at zero kilometers how much money do I have Tom? How much are you gonna pay me if I collapse at the starting line? [Fills in the number 0 in the left-hand column of a table labeled "km"; the right-hand column is labeled "$".]
Tom	None.
Teacher	So Tom, I managed to walk one kilometer [putting a "1" in the "km" column of the table of values below the "0"]. . . .
Tom	One dollar.
Teacher	One dollar [moving to the graph]. So I'm going to go over one kilometer and up one dollar [see Figure 8-2a].

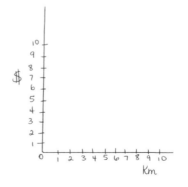 

FIGURE 8-2a Graphing a point from the table: "Over by one kilometer and up by one dollar." The teacher uses everyday English ("up by") and maintains connection with the situation by incorporating the units "kilometer" and "dollar."

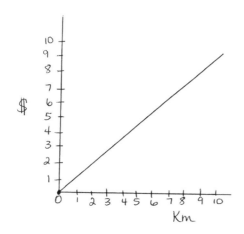

Km	$
0	0
1	1
2	2
3	3
4	4
5	5
6	6

FIGURE 8-2b *The teacher and students construct the table and graph point by point, and a line is then drawn.*

[Students continue to provide the dollar amounts for each of the successive kilometer values. Simple as it is, students are encouraged to describe the computation—"I multiply two kilometers by one to get two dollars." The teacher fills in the table and graphs each coordinate pair. [The board is now as shown in Figure 8-2b.]

Teacher   Now, what I want you to try and do, first I want you to look at this [pointing to the table that goes from x = 0 to x = 10 for y = x] and tell me what's happening here.

Melissa   You, like, earn one dollar every time you go up. Like it gets bigger by one every time.

Teacher   So every time you walk one kilometer you get one more dollar, right? [Makes "> 1" marks between successive "$" values in the table—see Figure 8-2c.] And if you look on the graph, every time I walk one kilometer I get one more dollar. [Makes "step" marks on the graph.] So now I want to come up with an equation, I want to come up with some way of using this symbol [pointing to the "km" header in the left-hand column of the table] and this symbol [pointing to the "$" header in the right-hand column of the table] to say the same thing, that for every kilometer I walk, let's put it this way, the money I earn is gonna be equal to one times the number of kilometers I walk. Someone want to try that?

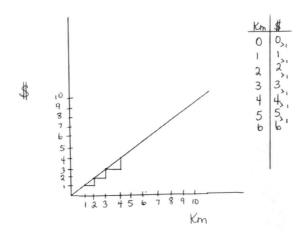

FIGURE 8-2c *The teacher highlights the "up by" amount in the table (">1" marks), graph (over and up "step" marks), and symbolic equation (pointing at "* 1").*

Alana	Um, kilometers times one equals money. [The teacher writes "km x 1 = $" and "y = x * 1"; see Figure 8-2c.]
Teacher	So this equation, this table, and this graph are all the same function. They all mean the same thing. They all mean that you're multiplying each of these numbers (pointing to the values along the x-axis of the graph) by one to get new numbers.

Another way of building on students' prior knowledge is to engage everyday experiential knowledge. Students frequently know things through experience that they have not been taught explicitly. They can often solve problems in ways we do not teach them or expect if, and this is an important qualification, the problems are described using words, drawings, or notations they understand. For example, the topic of slope is typically reserved for ninth-grade mathematics, and is a part of students' introduction to relations and functions in general and to linear functions in particular. It is generally defined as the ratio of vertical distance to horizontal distance, or "rise to run." The rise is the change in the vertical distance, and the run is the change in the horizontal distance so that $slope = \frac{rise}{run}$. Once the equation for a straight line, $y = mx + b$, has been introduced, m is defined as the slope of that line and is calculated using the formula $m = \frac{y_2 - y_1}{x_2 - x_1}$.

For students to understand slope in these definitional and symbolic ways, they must already have in place a great deal of formal knowledge, including the meaning of ratio, coordinate graphing, variables, and subscripts, and such skills as solving equations in two variables and combining arithmetic operations. Knowing algorithms for finding the slope of a function, however, does not ensure that the general *meaning* of slope will be understood. As illustrated in Figure 8-1a, a student can know the algorithm for finding the slope, but not understand that the slope of a line characterizes its relative steepness on a graph and tells something about the rate of change in covarying, dependent quantities.

We have found that younger students have intuitive and experiential understandings of slope that can be used to underpin the formal learning that involves conventional notations, algorithms, and definitions. To illustrate, we gave a class of fifth and sixth graders the following situation:

> Jane is in a walkathon. A rule or "function" tells us how much Jane will earn depending on how many kilometers she walks. We don't know what the function is. It is a mystery. We do know that if Jane walks 1 kilometer she will earn 4 dollars and if she walks 3 kilometers she will earn 8 dollars.

Students were asked to figure out the slope of the function that tells how much Jane will earn. Half of the students were provided with the formal rise-over-run ratio definition of slope; the other half were given a definition of slope that reflected more familiar, student language, being told that the slope of a function is the amount by which the answer goes up for every change of one in the start value.

We found that many of these younger students were able to describe informally the slope of the function given in the story problem by figuring out how much Jane's earnings go up by for every kilometer she walks. They noticed that when Jane walks three kilometers instead of one, she earns four more dollars; thus she earns two more dollars for every extra kilometer she walks. In this way, these prealgebra students identified the slope of the mystery function as 2 without receiving instruction on formal definitions or procedures. In contrast, students who were given the textbook definition of slope were not able to determine the slope in this example.

Our point is not that all problems should be phrased in "student language." It is important for students to learn formal mathematics terminology and abstract algebraic symbolism. Our point, instead, is that using student language is one way of first assessing what knowledge students are bringing to a particular topic at hand, and then linking to and building on what they already know to guide them toward a deeper understanding of formal mathematical terms, algorithms, and symbols.

In sum, students' prior knowledge acts as a building block for the development of more sophisticated ways of thinking mathematically. In some cases, we may underestimate the knowledge and skills students bring to the learning of functions. Topics and activities we presume to be challenging and difficult for students may in fact have intuitive or experiential underpinnings, and it is important to discover these and use them for formalizing students' thinking.

Principle #2: Building Conceptual Understanding, Procedural Fluency, and Connected Knowledge

The focus of Principle 2 is on simultaneously developing conceptual understanding and procedural fluency, and helping students connect and organize knowledge in its various forms. Students can develop surface facility with the notations, words, and methods of a domain of study (e.g., functions) without having a foundation of understanding. For students to understand such mathematical formalisms, we must help them connect these formalisms with other forms of knowledge, including everyday experience, concrete examples, and visual representations. Such connections form a conceptual framework that holds mathematical knowledge together and facilitates its retrieval and application.

As described previously, we want students to understand the core concept of a fuctional relationship: that the value of one variable is dependent on the value of another. And we want them to understand that the relationship between two variables can be expressed in a variety of ways—in words, equations, graphs, tables—all of which have the same meaning or use the same "rule" for the relationship. Ultimately, we want students' conceptual understanding to be sufficiently secure, and their facility with representing functions in a variety of ways and solving for unknown variables sufficiently fluid, that they can tackle sophisticated problems with confidence. To this end, we need an instructional plan that deliberately builds and secures that knowledge. Good teaching requires not only a solid understanding of the content domain, but also specific knowledge of student development of these conceptual understandings and procedural competencies. The developmental model of function learning that provides the foundation for our instructional approach encompasses four levels—0 to 3—as summarized in Table 8-1. Each level describes what students can typically do at a given developmental stage. The instructional program is then designed to build those competences.

Level 0

Level 0 characterizes the kinds of numeric/symbolic and spatial understandings students typically bring to learning functions. Initially, the numeric and spatial understandings are separate. The initial numeric understanding is one whereby students can iteratively compute *within* a single string of whole numbers. That is, given a string of positive, whole numbers such as 0,

TABLE 8-1 A Developmental Model for Learning Functions

Level	General Description	Example Tasks and Understandings
0	Students have separate numeric and spatial understandings.	
	• Initial numeric understanding: students iteratively compute (e.g., "add 4") *within* a string of positive whole numbers.	Extend the pattern 3, 7, 11, 15, ___, ____, ____.
	• Initial spatial understanding: students represent the relative sizes of quantities as bars on a graph and perceive patterns of qualitative changes in amount by a left-to-right visual scan of the graph, but cannot quantify those changes.	Notice in a bar graph of yearly population figures that each bar is taller than the previous bar.
1	Spatial and numeric understandings are elaborated and integrated, forming a central conceptual structure.	
	• Elaboration of numeric understanding: — Iteratively apply a single operation to, rather than within, a string of numbers to generate a second string of numbers. — Construct an algebraic expression for this repeated operation.	Multiply each number in the sequence 0, 1, 2, ... by 2 to get a set of pairs: 0-0, 1-2, 2-4, ... Generalize the pattern and express it as $y = 2x$.
	• Elaboration of spatial understanding: — Use continuous quantities along the horizontal axis. — Perceive emergent properties, such as linear or increasing, in the shape of the line drawn between points. • Integration of elaborated understandings:	Notice that a graph of daily plant growth must leave spaces for unmeasured Saturday and Sunday values. For every 1 km, a constant "up by" $2 in both the y-column of a table and the y-axis in a graph generates a linear pattern (spatial) with a slope of 2 (numeric). $y = 2x$ can be read

Continued

TABLE 8-1 Continued

Level	General Description	Example Tasks and Understandings
	— See the relationship between the differences in the y-column in a table and the size of the step from one point to the next in the associated graph. • Interpret algebraic representations both numerically and spatially.	from, or produced in, both a table and a graph.
2	• Elaborate initial integrated numeric and spatial understandings to create more sophisticated variations. • Integrate understanding of $y = x$ and $y = x + b$ to form a mental structure for linear functions. • Integrate rational numbers and negative integers. • Form mental structures for other families of functions, such as $y = x^n + b$.	Look at the function below. Could it represent $y = x - 10$? Why or why not? If you think it could not, sketch what you think it looks like.
3	• Integrate variant (e.g., linear and nonlinear) structures developed at level 2 to create higher-order structures for understanding more-complex functions, such as polynomials and exponential and reciprocal functions. • Elaborate understanding of graphs and negative integers to differentiate the four quadrants of the Cartesian plane. • Understand the relationship of these quadrants to each other.	At what points would the function $y = 10x - x^2$ cross the x axis? Please show all of your work.

2, 4, 6, 8, ..., students are able to see the pattern of adding 2 to each successive number. The initial spatial understanding is one whereby students can represent the relative sizes of quantities as bars on a graph. Students can easily see differences in the sizes of bars (how tall they are) and can use this spatial information to draw inferences about associated quantities. Students can read bar graphs that, for instance, show daily measurements of the growth of a plant in the classroom. They can see that each bar is taller than the previous one, that the plant is taller on Friday than on Thursday, but cannot easily quantify those changes.

Level 1

At level 1, students begin to elaborate and integrate their initial numeric and spatial understandings of functions. They elaborate their numeric understanding in two steps. First, whereas students at level 0 can extend a single sequence of numbers such as 0, 2, 4, 6, ..., at level 1 they can operate on one sequence of numbers to produce a second sequence. For example, students can multiply each number in the sequence 0, 1, 2, 3, ... by 2 and form the resulting pairs of values: 0-0, 1-2, 2-4, 3-6, ... Students learn to record these pairs of values in a table and to construct an algebraic equation for this repeated operation by generalizing the pattern into an equation such as $y = 2x$.

Students' spatial understanding is also improving. They come to understand that maintaining equal distances between values on the x-axis is critical to having a meaningful graph of a function. They also progress from understanding graphs with verbal or categorical values along the x-axis, such as cities (with their populations on the y-axis), to understanding graphs with quantitative values along the x-axis, such as time quantified as days (with the height of a plant on each successive day on the y-axis). The example of graphing plant growth is an interesting one because it is an activity at the cusp of this transition. Students initially view values on the x-axis as categorical, not sequenced (so that Thursday, Friday, Monday is okay). Later they come to view these values as quantitative, in a sequence with a fixed distance between the values (such that Thursday, Friday, Monday is not okay because Saturday and Sunday must be accounted for).

Without being able to view the x-axis as quantitative, students cannot see graphs as representing the relationship between two changing quantities. Drawing a line to join the points provides a visual representation of the relationship between the quantities. The line offers a way of packaging key properties of the function or pattern of change that can be perceived quickly and easily. For example, students can see how much earnings change per kilometer by looking at the steepness of the line.

As their initial numeric and spatial understandings are elaborated, students at level 1 also begin to connect, or integrate, these understandings. They make connections between tables and graphs of x-y pairs, using one representation to generate inferences that can be checked by the other. The overall pattern of a function can be understood both in the size of the increments in the y-column of the table and in the steepness of the line moving from one point to another in the graph. The constant "up-by" 1 seen, for example, in Figure 8-2c in the right-hand column of a table is the same as the constant "up-by" 1 in a line of a graph (see the same figure). As these views become integrated, students develop a deeper and more flexible understanding of functions, in this case, a linear pattern with a rise of 1. With this new integrated mental structure for functions, students can support numeric and spatial understandings of algebraic representations such as $y = 1x$.

Grasping why and how the line on a graph maps onto the relationship described in a word problem or an equation is a core conceptual understanding. If students' understanding is only procedural, they will not be well prepared for the next level (see Box 8-2). To ensure that students master the concepts at this level, complex content is avoided. Students are not required to operate with negative or rational numbers or carry out more than one operation in a single function (such as multiplying x by any value and adding or subtracting a constant, as in the general $y = mx + b$ form). Such limiting of these complicating factors is intended to minimize loads on processing and working memory, thus enabling students to focus on the essence of the integration of numeric and spatial understandings of function. Students learn more complex content during levels 2 and 3.

Level 2

As students progress to level 2, they begin to elaborate their initial integrated numeric and spatial understandings. In doing so, they begin to combine operations and develop fluency with functions in the form $y = mx + b$, where m and b can be positive or negative rational numbers. They also work with $y = x^n + b$, where n is a positive whole number, and b is any positive or negative rational number. For a full elaboration to occur, it is necessary for students to understand integers and rational numbers and have facility in computing with both of these number systems. Finally, students differentiate families of functions to see differences in the shapes and characteristics of linear, quadratic, and cubic functions.

Level 3

At level 3, students learn how linear and nonlinear terms can be related and understand the properties and behaviors of the resulting entities by analyzing these relations. To achieve this understanding, students must have well-constructed and differentiated models of different sorts of functions, such as quadratics in the form $y = ax^2 + bx + c$ or $y = a(x - p)^2 + q$; polynomials; and reciprocal, exponential, and growth functions. They must also have the necessary facility with computational, algebraic, and graphing operations to interrelate the numeric/symbolic and spatial representations of these complex functions. Furthermore, students must elaborate their understanding of graphs so they differentiate the four quadrants of the Cartesian plane, understand the relationship of these quadrants to each other, and relate these quadrants to negative numbers.

Recall Figure 8-1a and the difficulties the student had in producing a table of values for an increasing linear function with a negative y-intercept. This student did not recognize, or at least did not acknowledge, why it is impossible for the given function to have a negative slope and to have a table of values without a constant rate of change. These are the sorts of problems that occur when students experience instruction that fails to promote the development of a sound conceptual framework for functions. Now consider the solution to the problem in Box 8-3, in which a student introduces a table (without prompting) to help solve a problem about interpreting a graph in terms of an equation.

This student exhibited an integrated concept of function. He generated a response that showed consistency between the spatial (graph) and numeric (table and equation) representations of the function. He explained why the function has a slope of −2 as per its numeric (tabular) and spatial (graphic) representations and correctly symbolized that rationale in the equation.

Such integration can be supported in the classroom. For example, throughout the walkathon classroom exchange reported earlier, the teacher is moving fluidly and rapidly between numeric and spatial representations of a function (the table and equation and the graph, respectively). Such movement helps students simultaneously build understandings of each of these representations in isolation, and of the integrated nature of the representations in particular and the concept in general. This integration helps students begin to understand and organize their knowledge in ways that facilitate the retrieval and application of relevant mathematical concepts and procedures.

If students' numeric and spatial understandings are not integrated, they may not notice when a conclusion drawn from one understanding is inconsistent with a conclusion drawn from another. The inconsistencies found in the student's work in Figure 8-1a illustrate such a lack of reflective recognition.

BOX 8-2 **The Devil's in the Details: The 3-Slot Schema for Graphing a Line**

What students glean from instruction is often very different from what we as teachers intend. This observation is nicely illustrated by the research of Schoenfeld and colleagues.[9] They detail the surprising misunderstandings of a 16-year old advanced algebra student who is grappling with conceptual questions about equations and graphs of linear functions.

Most standard algebra instruction is intended to guide students toward developing what Schoenfeld and colleagues[10] call the "2-slot schema" for understanding and graphing an equation for a line. This schema says that knowing the slope of a line and its y-intercept enables one to obtain a complete description of the line, both graphically and algebraically. Call the line L; let its slope be m and its y-intercept b. Algebraically, the line L has equation $y = mx + b$ if and only if the line has slope m and y-intercept b. Graphically, the line L passes through the point $(0, b)$ and rises m units vertically for each unit it traverses horizontally.

The student in Schoenfeld's study, called IN, was relatively sophisticated in understanding aspects of the above schema. However, IN's knowledge was not fully integrated, and she exhibited a surprising misunderstanding. She initially believed that three quantities must be known to graph an equation of a line: (1) slope, (2) y-intercept, and (3) x-intercept. After having solved the equation $2 = 4x + 1$ to get $x = 1/4$, she was asked to the graph the function $4x + 1$ on the right side of this equation. She responded as follows: "the slope, which is 4, . . . the y-intercept, which is 1,...and...the x-intercept, which is 1/4, so we've found everything." Note that IN said that to find "everything," she needed the slope, y-intercept, *and* x-intercept. In other words, she appeared to have a 3-slot schema for understanding and graphing a linear equation instead of the 2-slot schema described above.

Clearly this student had received extensive instruction in linear functions. For instance, in an earlier exchange, when asked for an equation of

Principle #3: Building Resourceful, Self-Regulating Problem Solvers

As discussed above, teaching aimed at developing robust and fluent mathematical knowledge of functions should build on students' existing real-world and school knowledge (Principle 1) and should integrate procedural

a straight line, she immediately said, "y = mx + b." However, IN lacked a well-integrated understanding of the relationships between the features of the equation and graphical forms of a line. Schoenfeld and colleagues[11] explain:

When a person knowledgeable about the domain determines that the slope of a particular line is some value (say, 1. . .) and that its intercept is some other value (say, 3), then the job is done. The equation of the line must be y = (1)x + 3. IN had no such procedure. Although she believed that the slope, x-intercept, and y-intercept were all important (and she could read the values of the slope and y-intercept off equations of the form y = mx + b), she did not have a stable procedure for determining the values of those entities from a graph and did not know what to do with the values when she had them.

As other researchers have shown,[12] learners often struggle to tell the difference between the surface features of a subject, which are easy to see but can be misleading, and the deep features, which are difficult to see but are needed for understanding and accurate performance. In this case, three "entities" or aspects of the graph of a line stood out when IN looked at a graph: namely, where it crossed the x-axis, where it crossed the y-axis, and the steepness of the line. All three are important, but IN had the surface understanding that all three are *necessary*. She appeared to lack the deeper understanding that only two of these three are needed to draw a line. She did not understand how using the y-intercept and slope, in particular, facilitate an efficient graphing strategy because they can be read immediately off the standard form of an equation.

Schoenfeld and colleagues' fine-grained analysis of learning nicely illustrates how subtle and easily overlooked misconceptions can be—even among our best students.[13]

skill and conceptual understanding (Principle 2). However, instruction should assist students not only in thinking *with* mathematical procedures and concepts, but also in thinking *about* procedures and concepts and in reflecting on and articulating their own thinking and learning. This kind of thinking about thinking, or metacognition, is the focus of Principle 3. Encouraging students to reflect on and communicate their ideas about functions supports

BOX 8-3 An Integrated Understanding of Functions

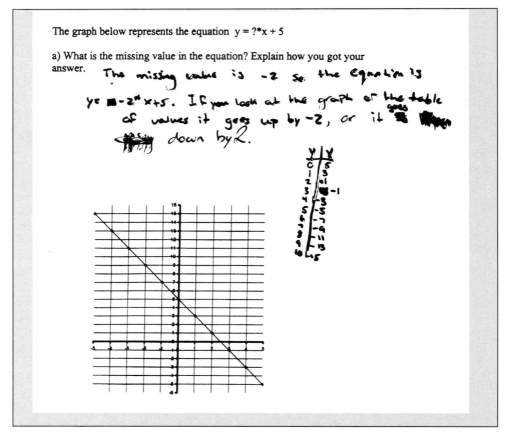

The graph below represents the equation $y = ?*x + 5$

a) What is the missing value in the equation? Explain how you got your answer.

The missing value is -2 so the equation is $y = -2*x+5$. If you look at the graph of the table of values it goes up by -2, or it goes down by 2.

them in making the connections among representations that are necessary for flexible, fluent, and reliable performance.

A particularly important type of metacognitive thinking in mathematics is coordinating conclusions drawn from alternative mathematical representations or strategies. Teachers will recognize one form of such coordination in the well-known recommendation that students solve problems in more than one way (e.g., add up and add down) to check whether the same answer is found. A more subtle form of such coordination was exemplified in the earlier discussion of desired student performance on the assessment item shown in Figure 8-1a. In this example, good metacognitive thinking was not about checking the consistency of *numeric answers* obtained using different *strategies*, but about checking the consistency of *verbal interpretations* (e.g., increasing vs. decreasing) of different *representations*. In other words, we want to encourage students to think about problems not only in multiple ways (strategies), but also with multiple tools (representations), and to draw conclusions that are not only quantitative (numeric answers), but also qualitative (verbal interpretations).

Supporting metacognitive thinking and attitudes goes beyond reflection and coordination of alternative mathematical representations and strategies. It includes creating a classroom atmosphere in which students feel comfortable to explore, experiment, and take risks in problem solving and learning. It also includes helping students develop a tolerance for the difficulties mathematics sometimes presents and a will to persevere when, for example, they are unable to detect the pattern in the table of values that identifies the relationship between x and y in a particular function. Yet another type of instructional support for metacognitive thinking involves helping students become better help seekers. Students need to learn to recognize when they have reached the limits of their understanding and to know how to obtain the support they need, including asking the teacher or a fellow student; consulting reference materials; and using such tools as computer software, the Internet, or a graphing calculator.

TEACHING FUNCTIONS FOR UNDERSTANDING

Good teaching requires more than knowledge of the content to be taught and of a developmental model for how students acquire an understanding of that content. It also requires a set of instructional strategies for moving students along that developmental pathway and for addressing the obstacles and opportunities that appear most frequently along the way. Below we describe a unit of instruction, based on the developmental model described above, that has been shown experimentally to be more effective than traditional instruction in increasing understanding of functions for eighth and tenth graders.[14] In fact, sixth-grade students taught with this instructional approach were more successful on a functions test than eighth and tenth graders who had learned functions through conventional instruction. At the secondary level, tenth graders learning with this approach demonstrated a deeper understanding of complex nonlinear functions. For instance, they performed significantly better on a test item requiring them to draw a "qualitative" graph (no scale on the axes) of the function $y = x^3$ in relation to a given graph of $y = x^4$.

Curriculum for Moving Students Through the Model

This section summarizes the key features and activities of a curriculum that was developed for moving students through the four-level learning sequence described above. We believe such theory-based instruction encourages students (1) to build on and apply their prior knowledge (Principle 1),

(2) to construct an integrated conceptual framework for understanding functions (principle 2), and (3) to apply metacognitive skills to their learning (principle 3). An overview of this curriculum is presented in Table 8-2, followed by a more detailed description. Example lessons are provided in the next section.

The curricular sequence we suggest has been used effectively with students in sixth, eighth, tenth, and eleventh grades. Because timetables and scheduling vary from school to school and from grade to grade, the amount of material per lesson will also vary depending on the available class time. This unit requires approximately 650 minutes of class time to complete. We recommend that it be taught as a whole and in the sequence suggested, even if students are in an upper secondary-level grade and require the more advanced level 3 material. We emphasize implementing the full sequence of topics because the concepts addressed in the level 3 material are supported by a deep and flexible understanding of the ideas found in the level 1 and 2 material, an understanding that is often insufficiently developed in earlier grades. Students in the senior grades will likely move more quickly through the beginning part of the unit than will junior students, and the extra time allotted for the unit can then be used for working through more-advanced ideas that are likely beyond younger students' capabilities.

The instructional approach we are suggesting is different from some more traditional approaches in many ways. First, the latter approaches often use different contexts or situations for introducing the individual topics within the domain, rather than the single bridging context of the walkathon we use. Within one curriculum, for example, the gradient of a hill may be used for introducing slope, and fixed cost in production may be used for introducing y-intercept. Mixing contexts can make understanding $y = mx + b$ as an integrated concept more difficult than is the case if slope and y-intercept are introduced within the same context.

The use of multiple representations is another significant feature of the suggested curriculum, one that again distinguishes it from more traditional approaches. In many traditional approaches, instruction may be focused on a single representation (e.g., equation or graph) for weeks before multiple representations are related. In our curricular approach, tables, graphs, equations, and verbal rules are copresented within seconds, and students are encouraged to see them as equivalent representations of the same mathematical relationship. Emphasis is placed on moving among these representations and on working to understand how they relate to each other.

Our approach also engages students in the construction of functional notation, and thus helps them build notations and meanings for such constructs as slope and y-intercept into equations. This approach contrasts with many existing curricula, which give students the formal notation and then focus on introducing them to procedures for finding, for example, the slope of a linear function or the vertex of a quadratic function. Over the course of our instruction, students progressively formalize their own initial notations until those notations correspond with conventional general equations, such as $y = mx + b$ or $y = ax^2 + bx + c$.

Finally, the kinds of follow-up activities we suggest may differ from those of more traditional approaches. We suggest activities that allow students to remain situated in the context of instruction for the first part of the unit (that is, related to a walkathon) until they are confident and competent with the concepts on a more abstract basis. Then, when students move to the computer environment, they engage in activities in which no new concepts are introduced at first. Rather, students have time to consolidate the individual concepts addressed in the first part of the unit, and then move on to more challenging activities that advance their thinking and understanding in the domain. These more challenging activities involve the addition of new features to familiar structures. For example, the left-hand quadrants of the Cartesian plane are eventually included in activities, and linear terms are added to $y = x^2 + b$ to generate equations in the form $y = ax^2 + bx + c$. Students also give presentations on a particular kind of function (e.g., linear, quadratic, reciprocal, cubic) to their classmates. In these presentations, students share their understanding of and expertise in key characteristics and behaviors of these functions.

Example Lessons

In the following sections, we elaborate on three specific lessons that highlight the role of the three principles of *How People Learn* in the curriculum described in Table 8-2. Although we do not provide a complete description of these lessons, the example activities should be sufficient to suggest how the lessons might be used in other classrooms. The three lessons and their companion activities illustrate the principles of *How People Learn* in three key topic areas: slope, y-intercept, and quadratic functions. Example lesson 1, "Learning Slope," illustrates principle 1, building on students' prior knowledge. Example lesson 2, "Learning y-intercept," illustrates principle 2, connecting students' factual/procedural and conceptual knowledge. Example lesson 3, "Operating on $y = x^2$," illustrates principle 3, fostering reflective thinking or metacognition in students. Although each of the selected lessons is used to highlight one of the principles in particular, the reader should keep in mind that all three principles interact simultaneously throughout each lesson.

TABLE 8-2 Suggested Curricular Sequence

Topic	Description	Activities
Level 1 Introduction	The walkathon bridging context is introduced. Students record in tables the money earned for each kilometer walked and plot each pair of values for a variety of rules. Using kilometers and dollars, an equation is constructed based on the rule of sponsorship.	Student partners each invent at least two of their own sponsorship arrangements, for which their partner constructs tables, graphs, and equations.
Slope	Slope is introduced as the constant numeric up-by (or down-by) amount between successive dollar values in a table or a graph. It is a relative measure of the steepness of a function. It is the amount by which each kilometer (x – value) is multiplied.	Students are asked to find the slope of several different functions expressed in tables, graphs, and equations.
y-Intercept	y-Intercept is introduced as the "starter offer," that is, a fixed starting bonus students receive before the walkathon begins. It affects only the vertical starting point of the numeric sequence and graph. It does not affect the steepness or shape of the line.	Students invent two linear functions that allow them to earn exactly $153.00 after walking 10 kilometers. Students record the slope and y-intercept of each function and explain how the y-intercept of each function can be found in its table, graph, and equation.
Curving functions	Nonlinear functions are introduced as those having up-by amounts that increase (or decrease) after each kilometer walked. They are	Students are asked to decide which of four functions expressed in tables are nonlinear and to explain their reasoning. They are also

TABLE 8-2 Continued

Topic	Description	Activities
	derived by multiplying the kilometers (x) by itself at least . once The more times x is multiplied by itself, the greater is the difference between dollar values and thus the steeper the curve.	asked to write an equation for and to sketch and label the graph of each function. Students are asked to come up with a curved-line function for earning $153.00 over 10 kilometers.
Levels 2 and 3 Computer activities	Level 2 students use spreadsheet technology and prepared files and activity sheets to consolidate and extend the understandings they constructed about slope, y-intercept, and linearity in the first part of the curriculum. Level 3 extensions include working in all four quadrants to transform quadratic and cubic functions and to explore the properties, behaviors, and characteristics of exponential, reciprocal, and other polynomial functions.	Students change the steepness, y-intercept, and direction of $y = x$ and $y = x^2$ to make the function go through preplotted points. They record the numeric, algebraic, and graphic effects of their changes. They also invent functions with specific attributes, such as parallel to $y = 4x$ and a y-intercept below the x-axis, or an inverted parabola that is compressed and in the lower left-hand quadrant.
Presentations	Groups of students investigate and then prepare a presentation about a particular type of function. Presentations stimulate discussion and summarizing of key concepts and serve as a partial teacher assessment for evaluating students' post-instruction understanding about functions.	Groups of students use computer-generated output of graphs, equations, and tables to illustrate a particular type of function's general properties and behaviors. Students give presentations about their function and share their expertise with classmates.

Example Lesson 1: Learning Slope

The classroom interaction recounted below took place during students' first lesson on slope. The students had already worked through the construction of representations for the introductory rule of the walkathon—earning one dollar for every kilometer walked. In this interaction we can see how Katya quickly grasps the idea of slope as relative steepness, as defined by the variable relationship between two quantities (distance walked and money earned in this case):

Teacher	I want to think of a way, let's see, Katya, how might you sponsor me that would make a line that is steeper than this [y = x is already drawn on graph, as in Figure 8-2b]?
Katya	Steeper? Alright . . . every kilometer you walk you get two dollars.
Teacher	Two dollars. So let's try that. So at zero kilometers how much am I going to have?
Katya	At zero kilometers you'll have zero.
Teacher	At one?
Katya	You'll have two.
Teacher	And what happens at ten?
Katya	At ten you'll have twenty.
Teacher	So Katya, what have you done each time?
Katya:	I've just multiplied by two.
Teacher	You've multiplied each one of these [pointing to the numbers in the left column of the table] by two, right? Zero times two, one times two [moving finger back and forth between columns]. If I graph that, where's it going to start, Katya?
Katya	It's going to start at zero.
Teacher	So at zero kilometers, zero money. At one?
Katya	At one it's going to go to two.
Teacher	At two it's going to go to?
Katya	Four.
Teacher	Over two up to four. At three?
Katya	It's going to go to six.
Teacher	What do you see on the graph? What do you see happening?

Katya	It's going higher. It's steeper than the other one.
Teacher	So it's steeper and it's going up by how much?
Katya	Two.
Teacher	So Katya, since this is your function, what would the equation for this function be?
Katya	Kilometers times two equals money.
Teacher	That's absolutely right. And what do you notice about these values [pointing to dollar values in the table and making ">" marks between successive values]?
Katya	They're going up by 2.

The Lesson. The lesson on slope is the second lesson suggested in the overall sequence of instruction, after the walkathon has been introduced. It requires about two class periods, or 90 minutes. We introduce slope as the constant numeric up-by amount that is found between successive y-values for every unit change in x. This up-by amount can be seen in a function's table or its graph. The up-by terminology was invented by students who were asked to describe the meaning of slope using their own words. When introducing this up-by idea to students, we suggest beginning with the graph and the table for the rule of earning one dollar for every kilometer walked ($ = 1 x km) and having students see that in each of these representations, the dollar amount goes up by one for each kilometer walked. To show this on the graph, the teacher may draw a staircase-like path from point to point that goes over one and then up one (see Figure 8-2c). In the table, a third column may be created to show the constant up-by difference between successive y-values, as also illustrated in Figure 8-2c. We then suggest drawing students' attention to the facts that this up-by amount corresponds to the mathematical concept of slope and that slope is a relative measure of a function's steepness. That is, the greater the up-by amount, the steeper is the function. From this point on, y = x (y = 1 • x with a slope of 1) may be employed as a landmark function for students to use in qualitative reasoning, by comparison, about the slopes (and later the y-intercepts) of other functions. Conceptual landmarks are crucial tools to support learners in making sense of, catching, and correcting their own and others' errors.

After having created tables and graphs for the one dollar per kilometer context, we challenge students such as Katya to provide sponsorship rules (or functions) having slopes that are steeper and less steep than y = x. To facilitate the comparison of graphs of functions with different slopes, we encourage students to plot functions on the same set of axes. Before each rule is graphed, we ask the students to predict the steepness of the line relative to y = x. We also have them invent other rules and make tables and graphs for those rules. These explorations in multiple contexts and representations develop students' deeper understanding of slope. After all, the essence of understanding is being able to apply a concept flexibly in different contexts and with different representations. After having worked with functions having varying degrees of steepness, we ask the students to summarize their findings about slope and to explain that steeper lines are the result of functions having bigger up-by amounts.

In our instruction, we do not provide students at the outset with an algorithm for finding the slope of a function. However, we do suggest that students be asked for their ideas about how the steepness, or slope, of a function can be quantified—that is, represented as a number—and how they can obtain that number from any of the representations of a function they have seen. This is illustrated by the following teacher–student exchange from a ninth-grade class:

Teacher	This line [pointing to a graph of y = x] has a certain steepness to it. . . . If you had to give a number to this steepness, what would you give it? Look at these numbers (pointing to the corresponding table of values).
Aaron	One.
Teacher	Why one?
Aaron	'Cause they all go up by one.

Introducing and working with functions having negative slopes is also important to show that the way the students have been constructing slope as the up-by amount is applicable to all straight-line functions, whether they increase or decrease. We generally introduce negative values along the y-axis by asking students to think about how the negative values along the y-axis can be used. One situation we employ is from the perspective of the donor or sponsor, who loses money as the participant walks. In our experience, students generally recognize that these lines have a down-by amount when a fixed amount of money is given away for each kilometer walked.

Summary of Principle #1 in the Context of Learning Slope. We have used a lesson on slope to illustrate how students' initial knowledge of a topic can be used for building formal or conventional mathematical knowledge and notation structures. In this case, we draw on three sorts of prior knowledge. First, students' prior knowledge of familiar situations such as earning money in a walkathon can be used to elicit and extend the students' informal, intuitive ideas about a difficult topic such as slope. Second, students' prior knowledge of natural language, such as "up-by," can be used to build a sound foundation of understanding for explaining and working with more formal concepts and procedures, such as finding slope from a graph. Third, prior knowledge with respect to initial numeric and spatial understandings can be integrated through instruction to help students construct a conceptual understanding of slope within a broader framework for understanding functions in general.

Example Lesson 2: Learning y-Intercept

This example lesson focuses on learning and teaching y-intercept. It illustrates the effect of theory-based instructional design in connecting students' factual/procedural and conceptual knowledge (principle 2).

A commonly taught procedure for finding the y-intercept of a function is to substitute x = 0 into the function's equation, with the result being the y-intercept. Instead of starting by formally introducing this method, this lesson begins by having students explore situations in which a nonzero starting amount is used. This approach appears to do a better job of helping students learn the formal procedure in the context of a robust conceptual understanding.

The Lesson. The lesson on y-intercept follows that on slope in the overall curricular sequence. Two class periods of about 90 minutes are suggested for working with y-intercept. We introduce the y-intercept by suggesting the idea of a starting bonus or an initial amount of money that may be contributed before the walkathon even begins. Students have termed this starting amount the "starter offer" or "starter upper." These phrases have repeatedly been shown to be simple for students to understand first in the walkathon context and then in more abstract situations.

We again begin this lesson with a sponsorship arrangement of earning one dollar for every kilometer walked. We then have students graph this function, construct a table of values, and write a symbolic representation for the function. We then tell students they will be given a five-dollar starter offer just for participating in the walkathon. That is, before they have walked at all, they will already have earned five dollars. In addition to this starting bonus, they will still be earning one dollar for every kilometer walked. Students are then asked to construct a table for this function and to calculate how much money they will have earned at zero kilometers, one kilometer, two kilometers, and so on. After the table has been constructed, students are asked to graph the function and to make an equation for it. Having students verbally describe the relationship between the kilometers and dollars helps them formulate an equation. For example, a student might say, "I think it would be five plus the kilometers equals money." That description could then be translated into the situation-specific symbolic expression 5 + km = $, and that expression, in turn, formalized into the general expression, y = x + 5.

As the lesson proceeds, we suggest other rules whereby students earn one dollar per kilometer but have different starter offer amounts, such as two dollars, ten dollars, and three and a half dollars. We ask the students first to predict where on a graph each new function will be relative to the first example given (y = x + 5) and then to construct tables, graphs, and equations for each new function. Students are asked to describe any patterns or salient characteristics they see in this group of functions. What we want students to see, both literally and figuratively, is that all of the functions are parallel, with a slope of 1, but their starting point on the graph changes in accordance with the starting bonus offered. Furthermore, the distance between points on any two graphs is equal to the difference in starting bonuses. For example, the functions 5 + km = $ and 10 + km = $ are five units apart at every point along the line of each function. Likewise, in examining the tables for each of the functions, we want students to see that all of the functions go up by one (accounting for the parallel lines), but the first value in the dollar column of each of the tables is equal to the starting bonus. We then connect the "starting points" of the graphs and tables with the structure of the equations to show that the starting bonus is indeed added to each x-value.

Emphasizing that the only effect of changing the starter offer is a vertical shift in a function is crucial because a number of researchers have found that students regularly confuse the values for slope and y-intercept in equations. That is, in an equation such as y = 2x + 7, many students are unsure of which "number" is the y-intercept and which is the slope. Initially, students of all ages and grades in our program often predict that changing the starter offer will also change the steepness (slope) of a function. However, working through many examples for which the amount earned per kilometer (the slope) is held constant will help students see, in context, that changing the starting bonus does not affect the amount being earned per kilometer, which is how the steepness or slope of the function is determined. Ultimately, by establishing the meaning of y-intercept in the context of the walkathon and by applying that meaning to the different representations of a function, the confusion of slope and y-intercept is significantly minimized for students.

Negative y-intercepts are introduced using the idea of debt. In this case, students have to pay off a starter offer amount. For example, a student in one of our studies suggested that if she owed ten dollars on her credit card and paid off one dollar every time she walked a kilometer, she would have to start at minus ten dollars. Then after one kilometer, she would pay off one dollar and still be nine dollars in debt, then eight, then seven, etc. Students can construct tables, graphs, and equations for such situations that they invent and perhaps share with a partner or the class. The writing of the equations for these functions may take different forms at first. Many students choose to adhere to the notion that the starter offer is "added" in the equation. Thus an equation for a function such as that described above would look like $\$ = 1 \bullet km + -10$. While students are consolidating the concept of y-intercept and distinguishing it from slope, we recommend that they be allowed to write equations in this way. An alternative, more conventional format may be suggested by repeating the function and writing it in conventional notation alongside the student-constructed expression. Again, we stress the importance of students' developing a conceptual framework for these difficult concepts, which can be formalized over time once the ideas are firmly in place.

Following is a short classroom exchange between a teacher and a student. The context of earning five dollars per day for a paper route had already been developed by the teacher for an earlier teaching example. The teacher continued with this context in introducing linear functions with negative y-intercepts and positive slopes.

Teacher	We owe 90 dollars, so think of it as a negative amount we have and over time we're coming up toward zero. We're coming toward breaking even; towards no longer being in debt. So every day that goes 5 dollars toward zero [referring to and constructing both a graph and a table]. So up by 5, up by 5, up by 5, and so on. What are these differences [referring to the y values in the table]?
Justin	Positive 5.
Teacher	Ya, we're going up by 5 so as we go across 1 we go up by 5.

In the lessons on nonlinear functions, the starter offer idea is also applied. Generally, students quickly see that including the starter offer in a curved-line function has the same effect as it does on straight-line functions. That is, the steepness of the line (or curve) is not altered by changing the starter offer, only the place at which the function meets the vertical axis in a graph. The result is that each point on the curve is shifted up (or down) by the starter offer amount.

A suggested follow-up activity that addresses both slope and y-intercept is to have students, either individually or in pairs, invent two functions that will allow them to earn exactly $153 upon completing a ten-kilometer walkathon. Both strategies must produce straight lines. We ask students to construct tables, graphs, and equations to show their work, and also ask them to identify the slope and y-intercept of each function. Individuals or pairs of students then show their functions to the whole group. Samples of student work are shown in Box 8-4. We also challenge students to work "backwards," that is, to find what the starter offer would have to be if the slope were 10, or what the slope would have to be if the starter offer were 20.

Summary of Principle #2 in the Context of Learning y-Intercept. We have used a lesson on y-intercept to illustrate how students connect their factual/procedural and conceptual knowledge within the instructional bridging context of a walkathon. The walkathon context is intended to help students relate their new and existing knowledge within an organized conceptual framework in ways that facilitate efficient retrieval of that knowledge. The idea of a "starter offer" gives students a reasonably familiar situation that provides a context for learning y-intercept—ordinarily a relatively abstract and difficult mathematical topic that is often confused with slope in students' understanding of linear function. In our approach, students still learn the notations, symbols, words, and methods necessary for identifying the y-intercept of a function (linear or nonlinear). However, they acquire that knowledge in context and initially without algorithms, and with a depth of understanding and attribution of meaning that minimize the procedural and conceptual difficulties many students experience with the topic.

Example Lesson 3: Operating on $y = x^2$

After the first four lessons, which take place in the classroom, students move to a computer environment where they work with spreadsheet technology to consolidate and apply the concepts introduced in the classroom instruction and to extend their understandings to new situations. The particular lesson we use for illustrating principle 3, developing metacognitive skills, is the fourth in the series of computer activities.

The Lesson. Pairs of students use prepared spreadsheet files to work with a computer screen such as that seen in Figure 8-3. Students are asked to change specific parameters in the function $y = ax^2 + b$ to move the graph through preplotted colored points. The file is designed so the students can change the value of just the exponent, the coefficient of x^2, the y-intercept, or any combination of these. With each change, the graph and table of values change instantly and automatically to reflect the numeric (tabular) and graphic (spatial) implications of that change. For example, students are asked to describe and record what happens to the graph and the "Y" column of the table of values when the exponent in $y = x^2$ is changed to 3, to 4, and then more generally to any number greater than 2. Students are then asked to describe and record what happens to the curve when x^2 is multiplied by

BOX 8-4 Two Different Student Solutions to an Open-Ended Problem

Think of a straight-line function that would allow you to earn exactly that amount in a 10 km walkathon. Consider that you might be given an initial donation ("starter offer") from the school.

a. Make a table of values for your function.

Student 1

x	Y
0	133
1	135
2	137
3	139
4	141
5	143
6	145
7	147
8	149
9	151
10	153

Student 2

km	$
0	3
1	18
2	33
3	48
4	63
5	78

km	$
6	93
7	108
8	123
9	138
10	153

b. *Sketch* the graph of your function.

Student 1

Student 2

	Student 1	Student 2
Write the equation for your function:	y = 2 * x + 133	km * 15 + 3 = $
What is the slope of your function?	2	15
Where is the y-intercept of your function?	$ 133	3

a value larger than 1, smaller than 1 but greater than 0, and less than 0. They are then asked to compare the tables and graphs for $y = x^2$, $y = 2 * x^2$, $y = 3 * x^2$, $y = 4 * x^2$, etc. and to describe in words what patterns they find. Finally, students are asked to compare the table of values for $y = 2 * x^2$ and $y = -2 * x^2$ and describe what they notice.

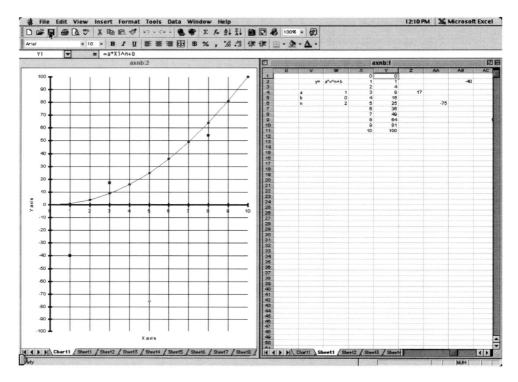

FIGURE 8-3 Sample computer screen. In this configuration, students can change the value of a, n, or b to effect immediate and automatic changes in the graph and the table. For example, if students change the value of b, just the y-intercept of the curve will change. If students change a or n to a positive value other than 1, the degree of steepness of the curve will change. If students change the value of a to a negative value, the curve will come down. All graphic patterns will be reflected in the table of values.

Students must employ effective metacognitive strategies to negotiate and complete these computer activities. Opportunities for exploring, persevering, and knowing when and how to obtain help are abundant. Metacognitive activity is illustrated in the following situation, which has occurred among students from middle school through high school who have worked through these activities.

When students are asked to change the parameters of $y = x^2$ to make it curve down and go through a colored point that is in the lower right quadrant, their first intuition is often to make the exponent rather than the coefficient negative. When they make that change, they are surprised to find that the graph changes shape entirely and that a negative exponent will not satisfy their needs. By trying a number of other possible alterations (persevering), some students discover that they need to change the coefficient of x^2 rather than the exponent to a negative number to make the function curve down. It is then a matter of further exploration and discovery to find the correct value that will make the graph pass through the point in question. Some students, however, require support to discover this solution. Some try to subtract a value from x^2 but are then reminded by the result they see on the computer screen that subtracting an amount from x^2 causes a downward vertical shift of the graph. Drawing students' attention to earlier exercises in which they multiplied the x in $y = x$ by a negative number to make the numeric pattern and the graph go down encourages them to apply that same notion to $y = x^2$. To follow up, we suggest emphasizing for students the numeric pattern in the tables of values for decreasing curves to show how the number pattern decreases with a negative coefficient but not with a negative exponent.

Following is a typical exchange between the circulating teacher and a pair of students struggling with flipping the function $y = x^2$ (i.e., reflecting it in the x-axis). This exchange illustrates the use of metacognitive prompting to help students supervise their own learning by suggesting the coordination of conclusions drawn from one representation (e.g., slope in linear functions) with those drawn from another (e.g., slope in power functions).

Teacher	How did you make a straight line come down or change direction?
John	We used minus.
Teacher	How did you use "minus"?
Pete	Oh yeah, we times it by minus something.
Teacher	So . . . how about here [pointing at the x^2]?
John	We could times it by minus 2 [typing in $x^2 \cdot -2$]. There! It worked.

Without metacognitive awareness and skills, students are at risk of missing important inconsistencies in their work and will not be in a position to self-correct or to move on to more advanced problem solving. The example shown earlier in Figure 8-1a involves a student not reflecting on the inconsistency between a negative slope in his equation and a positive slope in his graph. Another sort of difficulty may arise when students attempt to apply "rules" or algorithms they have been taught for simplifying a solution to a situation that in fact does not warrant such simplification or efficiency.

For example, many high school mathematics students are taught that "you only really need two points to graph a straight line" or "if you know it's a straight line, you only need two points." The key phrase here is "if you know it's a straight line." In our research, we have found students applying

What shape would the graph of the function $y = x^2 + 1$ have? Draw it below.

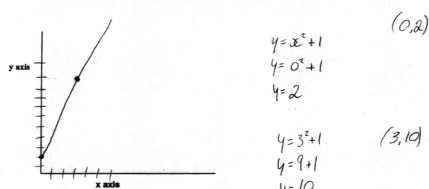

$(0,2)$

$y = x^2 + 1$
$y = 0^2 + 1$
$y = 2$

$y = 3^2 + 1$ $(3, 10)$
$y = 9 + 1$
$y = 10$

FIGURE 8-4

that two-point rule for graphing straight lines to the graphing of curved-line functions. In the example shown in Figure 8-4, an eleventh-grade advanced mathematics student who had been learning functions primarily from a textbook unit decided to calculate and plot only two points of the function $y = x^2 + 1$ and then to join them incorrectly with a straight line. This student had just finished a unit that included transformations of quadratic functions and thus presumably *knew* that $y = x^2$ makes a parabola rather than a straight line. What this student did not know to perform, or at least exercise, was a metacognitive analysis of the problem that would have ruled out the application of the two-points rule for graphing this particular function.

Summary of Principle #3 in the Context of Operating on y = x². The general metacognitive opportunities for the computer activities in our curriculum are extensive. Students must develop and engage their skills involving prediction, error detection, and correction, as well as strategies for scientific inquiry such as hypothesis generating and testing. For instance, because there are innumerable combinations of y-intercept, coefficient, and exponent that will move $y = x^2$ through each of the colored points, students must recognize and acknowledge alternative solution paths. Some students may fixate on the steepness of the curve and get as close to the colored points as possible by adjusting just the steepness of the curve (by changing either the exponent or the coefficient of x^2) and then changing the y-intercept. Others may begin by selecting a manageable y-intercept and then adjust the steepness of the curve by changing the exponent or the coefficient. Others may use both strategies equally. Furthermore, students must constantly be predicting the shapes and behaviors of the functions with which they are working and adjusting and readjusting their expectations with respect to the mathematical properties and characteristics of linear and nonlinear functions.

SUMMARY

Sometimes mathematics instruction can lead to what we refer to as "ungrounded competence." A student with ungrounded competence will display elements of sophisticated procedural or quantitative skills in some contexts, but in other contexts will make errors indicating a lack of conceptual or qualitative understanding underpinning these skills. The student solution shown earlier in Figure 8-1a illustrates such ungrounded competence. On the one hand, the student displays elements of sophisticated skills, including the slope formula and negative and fractional coefficients. On the other hand, the student displays a lack of coordinated conceptual understanding of linear functions and how they appear in graphical, tabular, and symbolic representations. In particular, he does not appear to be able to extract qualitative features such as linearity and the sign of the slope and to check that all three representations share these qualitative features.

The curricular approach described in this chapter is based on cognitive principles and a detailed developmental model of student learning. It was designed to produce grounded competence whereby students can reason with and about multiple representations of mathematical functions flexibly and fluently. Experimental studies have shown that this curriculum is effective in improving student learning beyond that achieved by the same teachers using a more traditional curriculum. We hope that teachers will find the principles, developmental model, and instructional examples provided here useful in guiding their curriculum and teaching choices.

We have presented three example lessons that were designed within one possible unifying context. Other lessons and contexts are possible and desirable, but these three examples illustrate some key points. For instance, students may learn more effectively when given a gradual introduction to ideas. Our curriculum employs three strategies for creating such a gradual introduction to ideas:

- Starting with a familiar context: Contexts that are familiar to students, such as the walkathon, allow them to draw on prior knowledge to think through a mathematical process or idea using a concrete example.
- Starting with simple content: To get at the essence of the idea while avoiding other, distracting difficulties, our curriculum starts with mathematical content that is as simple as possible—the function "you get one dollar for every kilometer you walk" ($y = x$).

- Focusing on having students express concepts in their own language before learning and using conventional terminology: To the extent that a curriculum initially illustrates an idea in an unfamiliar context or with more-complex content, students may be less likely to be able to construct or invent their own language for the idea. Students may better understand and explain new ideas when they progress from thinking about those ideas using their own invented or natural language to thinking about them using formal conventional terms.

A risk of simplicity and familiarity is that students may not acquire the full generality of relevant ideas and concepts. Our curriculum helps students acquire correct generalizations by constructing multiple representations for the same idea for the same problem at the same time. Students make comparisons and contrasts across representations. For example, they may compare the functions $y = .5x$, $y = 2x$, and $y = 10x$ in different representations and consider how the change in slope looks in the graph and how the table and symbolic formula change from function to function. We also emphasize the use of multiple representations because it facilitates the necessary bridging between the spatial and numerical aspects of functions. Each representation has both spatial and numerical components, and students need experience with identifying and constructing how they are linked.

As illustrated earlier in Figure 8-1a, a curriculum that does not take this multiple-representation approach can lead students to acquire shallow ideas about functions, slope, and linearity. The student whose response is shown in that figure had a superficial understanding of how tables and graphs are linked: he could read off points from the graph, but he lacked a deep understanding of the relationship between tables and graphs and the underlying idea of linearity. He did not see or "encode" the fact that because the graph is linear, equal changes in x must yield equal changes in y, and the values in the table must represent this critical characteristic of linearity.

The curriculum presented in this chapter attempts to focus limited instructional time on core conceptual understanding by using multiple representations and generalizing from variations on just a few familiar contexts. The goal is to develop robust, generalizable knowledge, and there may be multiple pathways to this end. Because instructional time is limited, we decided to experiment with a primary emphasis on a single simple, real-world context for introducing function concepts instead of using multiple contexts or a single complex context. This is not to say that students would not benefit from a greater variety of contexts and some experience with rich, complex, real-world contexts. Other contexts that are relevant to students' *current* real-world experience could help them build further on prior knowledge. Moreover, contexts that are relevant to students' *future* real-world experiences, such as fixed and variable costs of production, could help them in their later work life. Since our lessons can be accomplished in anywhere from 3 to 6 weeks (650 minutes), there is sufficient time for other activities to supplement and extend students' experience.

In addition to providing a gradual introduction to complex ideas, a key point illustrated by our lessons is that curriculum should be mathematically sound and targeted toward high standards. Although the lessons described here start gradually, they quickly progress to the point at which students work with and learn about sophisticated mathematical functions at or beyond what is typical for their grade level. For instance, students progress from functions such as $y = x$ to $y = 10 - .4x$ in their study of linear functions across lessons 1 to 3, and from $y = x^2$ to $y = (x - 2)^2 + 4$ in their study of nonlinear functions across lessons 4 to 8.

We do not mean to suggest that this is the only curriculum that promotes a deep conceptual understanding of functions or that illustrates the principles of *How People Learn*. Indeed, it has important similarities, as well as differences, with other successful innovations in algebra instruction, such as the Jasper Woodbury series and Cognitive Tutor Algebra (previously called PUMP), both described in *How People Learn*. All of these programs build on students' prior knowledge by using problem situations and making connections among multiple representations of function. However, whereas the Jasper Woodbury series emphasizes rich, complex, real-world contexts, the approach described in this chapter keeps the context simple to help students perceive and understand the richness and complexity of the underlying mathematical functions. And whereas Cognitive Tutor Algebra uses a wide variety of real-world contexts and provides intelligent computer tutor support, the approach described here uses spreadsheet technology and focuses on a single context within which a wide variety of content is illustrated.

All of these curricula, however, stand in contrast to more traditional textbook-based curricula, which have focused on developing the numeric/symbolic and spatial aspects of functions in isolation and without particular attention to the out-of-school knowledge that students bring to the classroom. Furthermore, these traditional approaches do not endeavor to connect the two sorts of understandings, which we have tried to show is an essential part of building a conceptual framework that underpins students' learning of functions and ultimately their learning in related areas.

ACKNOWLEDGMENTS

Thanks to Ryan Baker, Brad Stephens, and Eric Knuth for helpful comments. Thanks to the McDonnell Foundation for funding.

NOTES

1. The study of functions, as we define it here, overlaps substantially with the topic of "algebra" traditionally taught in the United States in ninth grade, though national and many state standards now recommend that aspects of algebra be addressed in earlier grades (as is done in most other countries). Although functions are a critical piece of algebra, other aspects of algebra, such as equation solving, are not addressed in this chapter.
2. Thomas, 1972, p. 17.
3. Goldenberg, 1995; Leinhardt et al., 1990; Romberg et al., 1993.
4. Nathan and Koedinger, 2000.
5. Koedinger and Nathan, 2004.
6. Koedinger and Nathan, 2004.
7. Koedinger et al., 1997.
8. Kalchman, 2001.
9. Schoenfeld et al., 1993.
10. Schoenfeld et al., 1987.
11. Schoenfeld et al., 1998, p. 81.
12. Chi et al., 1981.
13. Chi et al., 1981; Schoenfeld et al., 1993.
14. Kalchman, 2001.

REFERENCES

Chi, M.T.H., Feltovich, P.J., and Glaser, R. (1981). Categorization and representation of physics problems by experts and novices. *Cognitive Science, 5,* 121-152.

Goldenberg, E.P. (1995). Multiple representations: A vehicle for understanding. In D. Perkins, J. Schwartz, M. West, and M. Wiske (Eds.), *Software goes to school: Teaching for understanding with new technologies* (pp. 155-171). New York: Oxford University Press.

Kalchman, M. (2001). *Using a neo-Piagetian framework for learning and teaching mathematical functions.* Doctoral Dissertation, Toronto, Ontario, University of Toronto.

Koedinger, K.R., and Nathan, M.J. (2004). The real story behind story problems: Effects of representations on quantitative reasoning. *Journal of the Learning Sciences, 13*(2).

Koedinger, K.R., Anderson, J.R., Hadley, W.H., and Mark, M.A. (1997). Intelligent tutoring goes to school in the big city. *International Journal of Artificial Intelligence in Education, 8,* 30-43.

Leinhardt, G., Zaslavsky, O., and Stein, M. (1990). Functions, graphs, and graphing: Tasks, learning, and teaching. *Review of Educational Research, 60*(1), 1-64.

Nathan, M.J., and Koedinger, K.R. (2000). Teachers' and researchers' beliefs of early algebra development. *Journal for Research in Mathematics Education, 31*(2), 168-190.

Romberg, T., Fennema, E., and Carpenter, T.P. (1993). *Integrating research on the graphical representation of functions.* Mahwah, NJ: Lawrence Erlbaum Associates.

Schoenfeld, A.H. (1987). *Cognitive science and mathematics education.* Mahwah, NJ: Lawrence Erlbaum Associates.

Schoenfeld, A.H. (1998). Reflections on a course in mathematical problem solving. In A.H. Schoenfeld, J. Kaput, and E. Dubinsky (Eds.), *CBMS issues in mathematics education* (vol. 7, pp. 81-99.) Washington, DC: Conference Board of the Mathematical Sciences.

Schoenfeld, A.H., Smith J., and Arcavi A. (1993). Learning: The microgenetic analysis of one student's evolving understanding of a complex subject matter. In R. Glaser (Ed.), *Advances in Instructional Psychology* (vol. 4, pp. 55-175). Mahwah, NJ: Lawrence Erlbaum Associates.

Thomas, G.B. (1972). *Calculus and analytic geometry.* Reading, MA: Addison-Wesley.

OTHER RELEVANT READINGS

Bednarz, N., Kieran, C., and Lee, L. (1996). *Approaches to algebra. Perspectives for research and teaching.* Dordrecht, The Netherlands: Kluwer Academic Press.

Confrey, J., and Smith, E. (1995). Splitting, co-variation, and their role in the development of exponential functions. *Journal for Research in Mathematics Education, 26*(1), 66-86.

Janvier, C. (1987). *Problems of representation in the teaching and learning of mathematics.* Mahwah, NJ: Lawrence Erlbaum Associates.

Kaput, J.J. (1989). Linking representations in the symbol systems of algebra. In S. Wagner and C. Kieran (Eds.), *Research issues in the learning and teaching of algebra* (pp. 167-181). Reston, VA: National Council of Teachers of Mathematics.

A FINAL SYNTHESIS:
REVISITING THE THREE LEARNING PRINCIPLES

Pages 395-566 are not printed in this volume.
They are on the CD attached to the back cover.

13

Pulling Threads

M. Suzanne Donovan and John D. Bransford

What ties the chapters of this volume together are the three principles from *How People Learn* (set forth in Chapter 1) that each chapter takes as its point of departure. The collection of chapters in a sense serves as a demonstration of the second principle: that a solid foundation of detailed knowledge and clarity about the core concepts around which that knowledge is organized are both required to support effective learning. The three principles themselves are the core organizing concepts, and the chapter discussions that place them in information-rich contexts give those concepts greater meaning. After visiting multiple topics in history, math, and science, we are now poised to use those discussions to explore further the three principles of learning.

ENGAGING RESILIENT PRECONCEPTIONS

All of the chapters in this volume address common preconceptions that students bring to the topic of focus. Principle one from *How People Learn* suggests that those preconceptions must be engaged in the learning process, and the chapters suggest strategies for doing so. Those strategies can be grouped into three approaches that are likely to be applicable across a broad range of topics.

1. Draw on knowledge and experiences that students commonly bring to the class-room but are generally not activated with regard to the topic of study.

This technique is employed by Lee, for example, in dealing with students' common conception that historical change happens as an *event*. He points out that students bring to history class the everyday experience of "nothing much happening" until an event changes things. Historians, on the other hand, generally think of change in terms of the *state of affairs*. Change in this sense may include, but is not equivalent to, the occurrence of events. Yet students have many experiences in which things change gradually—experiences in which "nothing happening" is, upon reflection, a mischaracterization. Lee suggests, as an example, students might be asked to "consider the change from a state of affairs in which a class does not trust a teacher to one in which it does. There may be no event that could be singled out as marking the change, just a long and gradual process."

There are many such experiences on which a teacher could draw, such as shifting alliances among friends or a gradual change in a sports team's status with an improvement in performance. Each of these experiences has characteristics that support the desired conception of history. Events are certainly not irrelevant. A teacher may do particular things that encourage trust, such as going to bat for a student who is in a difficult situation or postponing a quiz because students have two other tests on the same day. Similarly, there may be an incident in a group that changes the dynamic, such as a less popular member winning a valued prize or taking the blame for an incident to prevent the whole group from being punished. But in these contexts students can see, perhaps with some guided discussion, that single events are rarely the sole explanation for the state of affairs.

It is often the case that students have experiences that can support the conceptions we intend to teach, but instructional guidance is required to bring these experiences to the fore. These might be thought of as "recessive" experiences. In learning about rational number, for example, it is clear that whole-number reasoning—the subject of study in earlier grades—is dominant for most students (see Chapter 7). Yet students typically have experience with thinking about percents in the context of sale items in stores, grades in school, or loading of programs on a computer. Moss's approach to teaching rational number as described in Chapter 7 uses that knowledge of percents to which most students have easy access as an alternative path to learning rational number. She brings students' recessive understanding of proportion in the context of reasoning about percents to the fore and strengthens their knowledge and skill by creating multiple contexts in which proportional reasoning is employed (pipes and tubes, beakers, strings). As with events in history, students do later work with fractions, and that work at times presents them with problems that involve dividing a pizza or a pie into discrete parts—a problem in which whole-number reasoning often dominates. Because a facility with proportional reasoning is brought to bear, however, the division of a pie no longer leads students so easily into whole-number traps.

Moss reinforces proportional reasoning by having students play games in which fractions (such as $\frac{1}{4}$) must be lined up in order of size with decimals (such as .33) and percents (such as 40 percent). A theme that runs throughout the chapters of this volume, in fact, is that students need many opportunities to work with a new or recessive concept, especially when doing so requires that powerful preconceptions be overturned or modified.

Bain, for example, writes about students' tendency to see "history" and "the past" as the same thing: "No one should think that merely pointing out conceptual distinctions through a classroom activity equips students to make consistent, regular, and independent use of these distinctions. Students' habits of seeing history and the past as the same do not disappear overnight." Bain's equivalent of repeated comparisons of fractions, decimals, and percents is the ever-present question regarding descriptions and materials: is this "history-as-event"—the description of a past occurrence—or "history-as-account"—an explanation of a past occurrence. Supporting conceptual change in students requires repeated efforts to strengthen the new conception so that it becomes dominant.

2. Provide opportunities for students to experience discrepant events that allow them to come to terms with the shortcomings in their everyday models.

Relying on students' existing knowledge and experiences can be difficult in some instances because everyday experiences provide little if any opportunity to become familiar with the phenomenon of interest. This is often true in science, for example, where the subject of study may require specialized tools or controlled environmental conditions that students do not commonly encounter.

In the study of gravity, for example, students do not come to the classroom with experiences that easily support conceptual change because gravity is a constant in their world. Moreover, experiences they have with other forces often support misconceptions about gravity. For example, students can experience variation in friction because most have opportunities to walk or run an object over such surfaces as ice, polished wood, carpeting, and gravel. Likewise, movement in water or heavy winds provide experiences with resistance that many students can easily access. Minstrell found his students believed that these forces with which they had experience explained why they did not float off into space (see Chapter 11). Ideas about buoyancy and air pressure, generally not covered in units on gravity, influenced these students' thinking about gravity. Television images of astronauts floating in space reinforced for the students the idea that, without air to hold things down, they would simply float off.

Minstrell posed to his students a question that would draw out their thinking. He showed them a large frame from which a spring scale hung and placed an object on the scale that weighed 10 pounds. He then asked the students to consider a situation in which a large glass dome would be placed over the scale and all the air forced out with a vacuum pump. He asked the students to predict (imprecisely) what would happen to the scale reading. Half of Minstrell's students predicted that the scale reading would drop to zero without air; about a third thought there would be no effect at all on the scale reading; and the remainder thought there would be a small change. That students made a prediction and the predictions differed stimulated engagement. When the experiment was carried out, the ideas of many students were directly challenged by the results they observed.

In teaching evolution, Stewart and colleagues found that students' everyday observations led them to underestimate the amount of variation in common species. In such cases, student observations are not so much "wrong" as they are insufficiently refined. Scientists are more aware of variation because they engage in careful measurement and attend to differences at a level of detail not commonly noticed by the lay person. Stewart and colleagues had students count and sort sunflower seeds by their number of stripes as an easy route to a discrepant event of sorts. The students discovered there is far more variation among seeds than they had noticed. Unless students understand this point, it will be difficult for them to grasp that natural selection working on natural variation can support evolutionary change.

While discrepant events are perhaps used most commonly in science, Bain suggests they can be used productively in history as well (see Chapter 4). To dislodge the common belief that history is simply factual accounts of events, Bain asked students to predict how people living in the colonies (and later in the United States) would have marked the anniversary of Columbus's voyage 100 years after his landing in 1492 and then each hundred years after that through 1992. Students wrote their predictions in journals and were then given historical information about the changing Columbian story over the 500-year period. That information suggests that the first two anniversaries were not really marked at all, that the view of Columbus's "discovery of the new world" as important had emerged by 1792 among former colonists and new citizens of the United States, and that by 1992 the Smithsonian museum was making no mention of "discovery" but referred to its exhibit as the "Columbian Exchange." If students regard history as the reporting of facts, the question posed by Bain will lead them to think about *how* people might have celebrated Columbus's important discovery, and not *whether* people would have considered the voyage a cause for celebration at all. The discrepancy between students' expectation regarding the answer to the question and the historical accounts they are given in the classroom lecture cannot help but jar the conception that history books simply report events as they occurred in the past.

3. Provide students with narrative accounts of the discovery of (targeted) knowledge or the development of (targeted) tools.

What we teach in schools draws on our cultural heritage—a heritage of scientific discovery, mathematical invention, and historical reconstruction. Narrative accounts of how this work was done provide a window into change that can serve as a ready source of support for students who are being asked to undergo that very change themselves. How is it that the earth was discovered to be round when nothing we casually observe tells us that it is? What is place value anyway? Is it, like the round earth, a natural phenomenon that was discovered? Is it truth, like e = mc², to be unlocked? There was a time, of course, when everyday notions prevailed, or everyday problems required a solution. If students can witness major changes through narrative, they will be provided an opportunity to undergo conceptual change as well.

Stewart and colleagues describe the use of such an approach in teaching about evolution (see Chapter 12). Darwin's theory of natural selection operating on random variation can be difficult for students to grasp. The beliefs that all change represents an advance toward greater complexity and sophistication and that changes happen in response to use (the giraffe's neck stretching because it reaches for high leaves, for example) are widespread and resilient. And the scientific theory of evolution is challenged today, as it was in Darwin's time, by those who believe in intelligent design—that all organisms were made perfectly for their function by an intelligent creator. To allow students to differentiate among these views and understand why Darwin's theory is the one that is accepted scientifically, students work with three opposing theories as they were developed, supported, and argued in Darwin's day: William Paley's model of intelligent design, Jean Baptiste de Lamarck's model of acquired characteristics based on use, and Darwin's theory of natural selection. Students' own preconceptions are generally represented somewhere in the three theories. By considering in some depth the arguments made for each theory, the evidence that each theorist relied upon to support his argument, and finally the course of events that led to the scientific community's eventually embracing Darwin's theory, students have an opportunity to see their own ideas argued, challenged, and subjected to tests of evidence.

Every scientific theory has a history that can be used to the same end. And every scientific theory was formulated by particular people in particular circumstances. These people had hopes, fears, and passions that drove their work. Sometimes students can understand theories more readily if they learn about them in the context of those hopes, fears, and passions. A narrative that places theory in its human context need not sacrifice any of the technical material to be learned, but can make that material more engaging and meaningful for students.

The principle, of course, does not apply only to science and is not restricted to discovery. In mathematics, for example, while some patterns and relationships were discovered, conventions that form our system of counting were *invented*. As the mathematics chapters suggest, the use of mathematics with understanding—the engagement with problem solving and strategy use displayed by the best mathematics students—is undermined when students think of math as a rigid application of given algorithms to problems and look for surface hints as to which algorithm applies. If students can see the nature of the problems that mathematical conventions were designed to solve, their conceptions of what mathematics is can be influenced productively.

Historical accounts of the development of mathematical conventions may not always be available. For purposes of supporting conceptual change, however, fictional story telling may do just as well as history. In *Teaching as Story Telling*, Egan[1] relates a tale that can support students' understanding of place value:

A king wanted to count his army. He had five clueless counselors and one ingenious counselor. Each of the clueless five tried to work out a way of counting the soldiers, but came up with methods that were hopeless. One, for example, tried using tally sticks to make a count, but the soldiers kept moving around, and the count was confused. The ingenious counselor told the king to have the clueless counselors pick up ten pebbles each. He then had them stand behind a table that was set up where the army was to march past. In front of each clueless counselor a bowl was placed. The army then began to march past the end of the table.

As each soldier went by, the first counselor put one pebble into his bowl. Once he had put all ten pebbles into the bowl, he scooped them up and then continued to put one pebble down for each soldier marching by the table. He had a very busy afternoon, putting down his pebbles one by one and then scooping them up when all were in the bowl. Each time he scooped up the ten pebbles, the clueless counselor to his left put one pebble into her bowl [gender equity]. When her ten pebbles were in her bowl, she too scooped them out again, and continued to put one back into the bowl each time the clueless counselor to her right picked his up.

The clueless counselor to her left had to watch her through the afternoon, and he put one pebble into his bowl each time she picked bers up. And so on for the remaining counselors. At the end of the afternoon, the counselor on the far left had only one pebble in his bowl, the next counselor had two, the next had seven, the next had six and the counselor at the other end of the table, where the soldiers had marched by, had three pebbles in his bowl. So we know that the army had 12,763 soldiers. The king was delighted that his ingenious counselor had counted the whole army with just fifty pebbles.[2]

When this story is used in elementary school classrooms, Egan encourages the teacher to follow up by having the students count the class or some other, more numerous objects using this method.

The story illustrates nicely for students how the place-value system allows the complex problem of counting large numbers to be made simpler. Place value is portrayed not as a truth but as an invention. Students can then change the base from 10 to other numbers to appreciate that base 10 is not a "truth" but a "choice." This activity supports students in understanding that what they are learning is designed to make number problems raised in the course of human activity manageable.

That imaginative stories can, if effectively designed, support conceptual change as well as historical accounts is worth noting for another reason: the fact that an historical account is an *account* might be viewed as cause for excluding it from a curriculum in which the nature of the account is not the subject of study. Historical accounts of Galileo, Newton, or Darwin written for elementary and secondary students can be contested. One would hope that students who study history will come to understand these as accounts, and that they will be presented to students as such. But the purpose of the accounts, in this case, is to allow students to experience a time when ideas that they themselves may hold were challenged and changed, and that purpose can be served even if the accounts are somewhat simplified and their contested aspects not treated fully.

ORGANIZING KNOWLEDGE AROUND CORE CONCEPTS

In the *Fish Is Fish* story discussed in Chapter 1, we understand quite easily that when the description of a human generates an image of an upright fish wearing clothing, there are some key missing concepts: adaptation, warm-blooded versus cold-blooded species, and the difference in mobility challenges in and out of water. How do we know which concepts are "core?" Is it always obvious?

The work of the chapter authors, as well as the committee/author discussions that supported the volume's development, provides numerous insights about the identification of core concepts. The first is observed most explicitly in the work of Peter Lee (see Chapter 2): that two distinct types of core concepts must be brought to the fore simultaneously. These are concepts about the nature of the discipline (what it means to engage in doing history, math, or science) and concepts that are central to the understanding of the subject matter (exploration of the new world, mathematical functions, or gravity). Lee refers to these as first-order (the discipline) and second-order (the subject) concepts. And he demonstrates very persuasively in his work that students bring preconceptions about the discipline that are just as powerful and difficult to change as those they bring about the specific subject matter.

For teachers, knowing the core concepts of the discipline itself—the standards of evidence, what constitutes proof and disproof, and modes of reasoning and engaging in inquiry—is clearly required. This requirement is undoubtedly at the root of arguments in support of teachers' course work in the discipline in which they will teach. But that course work will be a blunt instrument if it focuses only on second-order knowledge (of subject) but not on first-order knowledge (of the discipline). Clarity about the core concepts of the discipline is required if students are to grasp what the discipline— history, math, or science—is about.

For identifying both first- and second-order concepts, the obvious place to turn initially is to those with deep expertise in the discipline. The concepts that organize experts' knowledge, structure what they see, and guide their problem solving are clearly core. But in many cases, exploring expert knowledge directly will not be sufficient. Often experts have such facility with a concept that it does not even enter their consciousness. These "expert blind spots" require that "knowledge packages"[3]—sets of related concepts and skills that support expert knowledge—become a matter for study.

A striking example can be found in Chapter 7 on elementary mathematics. For those with expertise in mathematics, there may appear to be no "core concept" in whole-number counting because it is done so automatically. How one first masters that ability may not be accessible to those who did so long ago. Building on the work of numerous researchers on how children come to acquire whole-number knowledge, Griffin and Case's[4] research conducted over many years suggests a core conceptual structure that supports the development of the critical concept of *quantity*. Similar work has been done by Moss and Case[5] (on the core conceptual structure for rational number) and by Kalchman, Moss, and Case[6] (on the core conceptual structure for functions). The work of Case and his colleagues suggests the important role cognitive and developmental psychologists can play in extending understanding of the network of concepts that are "core" and might be framed in less detail by mathematicians (and other disciplinary experts).

The work of Stewart and his colleagues described in Chapter 12 is an-other case in which observations of student efforts to learn help reshape understanding of the package of related core concepts. The critical role of natural selection in understanding evolution would certainly be identified as a core concept by any expert in biology. But in the course of teaching about natural selection, these researchers' realization that students underestimated the variation in populations led them to recognize the importance of this concept that they had not previously identified as core. Again, experts in evolutionary biology may not identify population variation as an important concept because they understand and use the concept routinely—perhaps without conscious attention to it. Knowledge gleaned from classroom teaching, then, can be critical in defining the connected concepts that help support core understandings.

But just as concepts defined by disciplinary experts can be incomplete without the study of student thinking and learning, so, too, the concepts as defined by teachers can fall short if the mastery of disciplinary concepts is shallow. Liping Ma's study of teachers' understanding of the mathematics of subtraction with regrouping provides a compelling example. Some teachers had little conceptual understanding, emphasizing procedure only. But as Box 13-1 suggests, others attempted to provide conceptual understanding without adequate mastery of the core concepts themselves. Ma's work provides many examples (in the teaching of multidigit multiplication, division of fractions, and calculation of perimeter and area) in which efforts to teach for understanding without a solid grasp of disciplinary concepts falls short.

SUPPORTING METACOGNITION

A prominent feature of all of the chapters in this volume is the extent to which the teaching described emphasizes the development of metacognitive skills in students. Strengthening metacognitive skills, as discussed in Chapter 1, improves the performance of all students, but has a particularly large impact on students who are lower-achieving.[7]

Perhaps the most striking consistency in pedagogical approach across the chapters is the ample use of classroom discussion. At times students discuss in small groups and at times as a whole class; at times the teacher leads the discussion; and at times the students take responsibility for questioning. A primary goal of classroom discussion is that by observing and engaging in questioning, students become better at monitoring and questioning their own thinking.

In Chapter 5 by Fuson, Kalchman, and Bransford, for example, students solve problems on the board and then discuss alternative approaches to solving the same problem. The classroom dialogue, reproduced in Box 13-2, supports the kind of careful thinking about why a particular problem-solv-

BOX 13-1 Conceptual Explanation Without Conceptual Understanding

Liping Ma explored approaches to teaching subtraction with regrouping (problems like 52 – 25, in which subtraction of the 5 ones from the 2 ones requires that the number be regrouped). She found that some teachers took a very procedural approach that emphasized the order of the steps, while others emphasized the concept of composing a number (in this case into 5 tens and 2 ones) and decomposing a number (into 4 tens and 12 ones). Between these two approaches, however, were those of teachers whose intentions were to go beyond procedural teaching, but who did not themselves fully grasp the concepts at issue. Ma[8] describes one such teacher as follows:

> *Tr. Barry, another experienced teacher in the procedurally directed group, mentioned using manipulatives to get across the idea that "you need to borrow something." He said he would bring in quarters and let students change a quarter into two dimes and one nickel: "a good idea might be coins, using money because kids like money. . . . The idea of taking a quarter even, and changing it to two dimes and a nickel so you can borrow a dime, getting across that idea that you need to borrow something."*
> *There are two difficulties with this idea. First of all, the mathematical problem in Tr. Barry's representation was 25 – 10, which is not a subtraction with regrouping. Second, Tr. Barry confused borrowing in everyday life—borrowing a dime from a person who has a quarter—with the "borrowing" process in subtraction with regrouping—to regroup the minuend by rearranging within place values. In fact, Tr. Barry's manipulative would not convey any conceptual understanding of the mathematical topic he was supposed to teach.*

Another teacher who grasps the core concept comments on the idea of "borrowing" as follows:[9]

> *Some of my students may have learned from their parents that you "borrow one unit form the tens and regard it as 10 ones". . . . I will explain to them that we are not borrowing a 10, but decomposing a 10. "Borrowing" can't explain why you can take a 10 to the ones place. But "decomposing" can. When you say decomposing, it implies that the digits in higher places are actually composed of those at lower places. They are exchangeable . . . borrowing one unit and turning it into 10 sounds arbitrary. My students may ask me how can we borrow from the tens? If we borrow something, we should return it later on.*

ing strategy does or does not work, as well as the relative benefits of different strategies, that can support skilled mathematics performance.

Similarly, in the science chapters students typically work in groups, and the groups question each other and explain their reasoning. Box 13-3 reproduces a dialogue at the high school level that is a more sophisticated version of that among young mathematics students just described. One group of students explains to another not only what they concluded about the evolutionary purpose of different coloration, but also the thinking that led them to that conclusion and the background knowledge from an earlier example that supported their thinking. The practice of bringing other knowledge to bear in the reasoning process is at the heart of effective problem solving, but can be difficult to teach directly. It involves a search through one's mental files for what is relevant. If teachers simply give students the knowledge to incorporate, the practice and skill development of doing one's own mental search is shortchanged. Group work and discussions encourage students to engage actively in the mental search; they also provide examples from other students' thinking of different searches and search results. The monitoring of consistency between explanation and theory that we see in this group discussion (e.g., even if the male dies, the genes have already been passed along) is preparation for the kind of self-monitoring that biologists do routinely.

Having emphasized the benefits of classroom discussion, however, we offer two cautionary notes. First, the discussion cited in the chapters is *guided* by teachers to achieve the desired learning. Using classroom discussion well places a substantial burden on the teacher to support skilled discussion, respond flexibly to the direction the discussion is taking, and steer it productively. Guiding discussion can be a challenging instructional task. Not all questions are good ones, and the art of questioning requires learning on the part of both students and teachers.[10] Even at the high school level, Bain (see Chapter 4) notes the challenge a teacher faces in supporting good student questioning:

Sarena	Does anyone notice the years that these were written? About how old are these accounts? Andrew?
Andrew	They were written in 1889 and 1836. So some of them are about 112 years old and others are about 165 years old.
Teacher	Why did you ask, Sarena?
Sarena	I'm supposed to ask questions about when the source was written and who wrote it. So, I'm just doing my job.

BOX 13-2 Supporting Skilled Questioning and Explaining in Mathematics Problem Solving

In the dialogue below, young children are learning to explain their thinking and to ask questions of each other—skills that help students guide their own learning when those skills are eventually internalized as self-questioning and self-explaining.

Teacher	Maria, can you please explain to your friends in the class how you solved the problem?
Maria	Six is bigger than 4, so I can't subtract here [pointing] in the ones. So I have to get more ones. But I have to be fair when I get more ones, so I add ten to both my numbers. I add a ten here in the top [pointing] to change the 4 to a 14, and I add a ten here in the bottom in the tens place, so I write another ten by my 5. So now I count up from 6 to 14, and I get 8 ones (demonstrating by counting "6, 7, 8, 9, 10, 11, 12, 13, 14" while raising a finger for each word from 7 to 14). And I know my doubles, so 6 plus 6 is 12, so I have 6 tens left. [She thought, "1 + 5 = 6 and 6 + ? = 12 tens. Oh, I know 6 + 6 = 12, so my answer is 6 tens."]
Jorge	I don't see the other 6 in your tens. I only see one 6 in your answer.
Maria	The other 6 is from adding my 1 ten to the 5 tens to get 6 tens. I didn't write it down.
Andy	But you're changing the problem. How do you get the right answer?
Maria	If I make both numbers bigger by the same amount, the difference will stay the same. Remember we looked at that on drawings last week and on the meter stick.
Michelle	Why did you count up?

Palincsar[11] has documented the progress of students as they move beyond early, unskilled efforts at questioning. Initially, students often parrot the questions of a teacher regardless of their appropriateness or develop questions from a written text that repeat a line of the text verbatim, leaving a blank to be filled in. With experience, however, students become productive questioners, learning to attend to content and ask genuine questions.

Maria	Counting down is too hard, and my mother taught me to count up to subtract in first grade.
Teacher	How many of you remember how confused we were when we first saw Maria's method last week? Some of us could not figure out what she was doing even though Elena and Juan and Elba did it the same way. What did we do?
Rafael	We made drawings with our ten-sticks and dots to see what those numbers meant. And we figured out they were both tens. Even though the 5 looked like a 15, it was really just 6. And we went home to see if any of
	our parents could explain it to us, but we had to figure it out ourselves and it took us 2 days.
Teacher	Yes, I was asking other teachers, too. We worked on other methods too, but we kept trying to understand what this method was and why it worked.
	And Elena and Juan decided it was clearer if they crossed out the 5 and wrote a 6, but Elba and Maria liked to do it the way they learned at home. Any other questions or comments for Maria? No? Ok, Peter, can you explain your method?
Peter	Yes, I like to ungroup my top number when I don't have enough to subtract everywhere. So here I ungrouped 1 ten and gave it to the 4 ones to make 14 ones, so I had 1 ten left here. So 6 up to 10 is 4 and 4 more up to 14 is 8, so 14 minus 6 is 8 ones. And 5 tens up to 11 tens is 6 tens. So my answer is 68.
Carmen	How did you know it was 11 tens?
Peter	Because it is 1 hundred and 1 ten and that is 11 tens.

Similarly, students' answers often cannot serve the purpose of clarifying their thinking for classmates, teachers, or themselves without substantial support from teachers. The dialogue in Box 13-4 provides an example of a student becoming clearer about the meaning of what he observed as the teacher helped structure the articulation.

BOX 13-3 Questioning and Explaining in High School Science

The teacher passes out eight pages of case materials and asks the students to get to work. Each group receives a file folder containing the task description and information about the natural history of the ring-necked pheasant. There are color pictures that show adult males, adult females, and young. Some of the pages contain information about predators, mating behavior, and mating success. The three students spend the remainder of the period looking over and discussing various aspects of the case. By the middle of the period on Tuesday, this group is just finalizing their explanation when Casey, a member of another group, asks if she can talk to them.

Casey   What have you guys come up with? Our group was wondering if we could talk over our ideas with you.

Grace   Sure, come over and we can each read our explanations.

These two groups have very different explanations. Hillary's group is thinking that the males' bright coloration distracts predators from the nest, while Casey's group has decided that the bright coloration confers an advantage on the males by helping them attract more mates. A lively discussion ensues.

Ed   But wait, I don't understand. How can dying be a good thing?

Jerome   Well, you have to think beyond just survival of the male himself. We think that the key is the survival of the kids. If the male can protect his

Group work and group or classroom discussions have another potential pitfall that requires teacher attention: some students may dominate the discussion and the group decisions, while others may participate little if at all. Having a classmate take charge is no more effective at promoting metacognitive development—or supporting conceptual change—than having a teacher take charge. In either case, active engagement becomes unnecessary. One approach to tackling this problem is to have students rate their group effort in terms not only of their product, but also of their group dy-

	young and give them a better chance of surviving then he has an advantage.
Claire	Even if he dies doing it?
Grace	Yeah, because he will have already passed on his genes and stuff to his kids before he dies.
Casey	How did you come up with this? Did you see something in the packets that we didn't see?
Grace	One reason we thought of it had to do with the last case with the monarchs and viceroy.
Hillary	Yeah, we were thinking that the advantage isn't always obvious and sometimes what is good for the whole group might not seem like it is good for one bird or butterfly or whatever.
Jerome	We also looked at the data in our packets on the number of offspring fathered by brighter versus duller males. We saw that the brighter males had a longer bar.
Grace	See, look on page 5, right here.
Jerome	So they had more kids, right?
Casey	We saw that table too, but we thought that it could back up our idea that the brighter males were able to attract more females as mates.

The groups agree to disagree on their interpretation of this piece of data and continue to compare their explanations on other points. While it may take the involvement of a teacher to consider further merits of each explanation given the data, the students' group work and dialogue provide the opportunity for constructing, articulating, and questioning a scientific hypothesis.

namics.[12] Another approach, suggested by Bain (Chapter 4), is to have students pause during class discussion to think and write individually. As students discussed the kind of person Columbus was, Bain asked them to write a 2-minute essay before discussing further. Such an exercise ensures that students who do not engage in the public discussion nonetheless formulate their ideas.

Group work is certainly not the only approach to supporting the development of metacognitive skills. And given the potential hazard of group

BOX 13-4 Guiding Student Observation and Articulation

In an elementary classroom in which students were studying the behavior of light, one group of students observed that light could be both reflected and transmitted by a single object. But students needed considerable support from teachers to be able to articulate this observation in a way that was meaningful to them and to others in the class:

Ms. Lacey	I'm wondering. I know you have a lot of see-through things, a lot of reflect things. I'm wondering how you knew it was see-through.
Kevin	It would shine just, straight through it.
Ms. Lacey	What did you see happening?
Kevin	We saw light going through the . . .
Derek	Like if we put light . . .
Kevin	Wherever we tried the flashlight, like right here, it would show on the board.
Derek	And then I looked at the screen [in front of and to the side of the object], and then it showed a light on the screen. Then he said, come here, and look at the back. And I saw the back, and it had another [spot].
Ms. Lacey	Did you see anything else happening at the material?
Kevin	We saw sort of a little reflection, but we, it had mostly just see-through.
Derek	We put, on our paper we put reflect, but we had to decide which one to put it in. Because it had more of this than more of that.
Ms. Lacey	Oh. So you're saying that some materials . . .
Derek	Had more than others . . .

dynamics, using some individual approaches to supporting self-monitoring and evaluation may be important. For example, in two experiments with students using a cognitive tutor, Aleven and Koedinger[13] asked one group to explain the problem-solving steps to themselves as they worked. They found that students who were asked to self-explain outperformed those who spent the same amount of time on task but did not engage in self-explanation on transfer problems. This was true even though the common time limitation meant that the self-explainers solved fewer problems.

Ms. Lacey	. . . are doing, could be in two different categories.
Derek	Yeah, because some through were really reflection and see-through together, but we had to decide which.
	[Intervening discussion takes place about other data presented by this group that had to do with seeing light reflected or transmitted as a particular color, and how that color compared with the color of the object.]
	[at the end of this group's reporting, and after the students had been encouraged to identify several claims that their data supported among those that had been presented previously by other groups of students]
Ms. Lacey	There was something else I was kinda convinced of. And that was that light can do two different things. Didn't you tell me it went both see-through and reflected?
Kevin & Derek	Yeah. Mm-hmm.
Ms. Lacey	So do you think you might have another claim there?
Derek	Yeah.
Kevin	Light can do two things with one object.
Ms. Lacey	More than one thing?
Kevin	Yeah.
Ms. Lacey	Okay. What did you say?
Kevin & Derek	Light can do two things with one object.

See Chapter 10 for the context of this dialogue.

Another individual approach to supporting metacognition is suggested by Stewart (Chapter 12). Students record their thinking early in the treatment of a new topic and refer back to it at the unit's end to see how it has changed. This brings conscious attention to the change in a student's own thinking. Similarly, the reflective assessment aspect of the ThinkerTools curriculum described in Chapter 1 shifts students from group inquiry work to evaluating their group's inquiry individually. The results in the ThinkerTools case suggest that the combination of group work and individual reflective assessment is more powerful that the group work alone (see Box 9-5 in Chapter 9).

PRINCIPLES OF LEARNING AND CLASSROOM ENVIRONMENTS

The principles that shaped these chapters are based on efforts by researchers to uncover the rules of the learning game. Those rules as we understand them today do not tell us how to play the best instructional game. They can, however, point to the strengths and weakness of instructional strategies and the classroom environments that support those strategies. In Chapter 1, we describe effective classroom environments as learner-centered, knowledge-centered, assessment-centered, and community-centered. Each of these characteristics suggests a somewhat different focus. But at the same time they are interrelated, and the balance among them will help determine the effectiveness of instruction.

A community-centered classroom that relies extensively on classroom discussion, for example, can facilitate learning for several reasons (in addition to supporting metacognition as discussed above):

- It allows students' thinking to be made transparent—an outcome that is critical to a learner-centered classroom. Teachers can become familiar with student ideas—for example, the idea in Chapter 7 that two-thirds of a pie is about the same as three-fourths of a pie because both are missing one piece. Teachers can also monitor the change in those ideas with learning opportunities, the pace at which students are prepared to move, and the ideas that require further work—key features of an assessment-centered classroom.

- It requires that students explain their thinking to others. In the course of explanation, students develop a disposition toward productive interchange with others (community-centered) and develop their thinking more fully (learner-centered). In many of the examples of student discussion throughout this volume—for example, the discussion in Chapter 2 of students examining the role of Hitler in World War II—one sees individual students becoming clearer about their own thinking as the discussion develops.

- Conceptual change can be supported when students' thinking is challenged, as when one group points out a phenomenon that another group's model cannot explain (knowledge-centered). This happens, for example, in a dialogue in Chapter 12 when Delia explains to Scott that a flap might prevent more detergent from pouring out, but cannot explain why the amount of detergent would always be the same.

At the same time, emphasizing the benefits of classroom discussion in supporting effective learning does not imply that lectures cannot be excellent pedagogical devices. Who among us have not been witness to a lecture from which we have come away having learned something new and important? The Feynman lectures on introductory physics mentioned in Chapter 1, for example, are well designed to support learning. That design incorporates a strategy for accomplishing the learning goals described throughout this volume.[14] Feynman anticipates and addresses the points at which students' preconceptions may be a problem. Knowing that students will likely have had no experiences that support grasping the size of an atom, he spends time on this issue, using familiar references for relative size that allow students to envision just how tiny an atom is.

But to achieve effective learning by means of lectures alone places a major burden on the teacher to anticipate student thinking and address problems effectively. To be applied well, this approach is likely to require both a great deal of insight and much experience on the part of the teacher. Without such insight and experience, it will be difficult for teachers to anticipate the full range of conceptions students bring and the points at which they may stumble.[15] While one can see that Feynman made deliberate efforts to anticipate student misconceptions, he himself commented that the major difficulty in the lecture series was the lack of opportunity for student questions and discussion, so that he had no way of really knowing how effective the lectures were. In a learner-centered classroom, discussion is a powerful tool for eliciting and monitoring student thinking and learning.

In a knowledge-centered classroom, however, lectures can be an important accompaniment to classroom discussion—an efficient means of consolidating learning or presenting a set of concepts coherently. In Chapter 4, for example, Bain describes how, once students have spent some time working on competing accounts of the significance of Columbus's voyage and struggled with the question of how the anniversaries of the voyage were celebrated, he delivers a lecture that presents students with a description of current thinking on the topic among historians. At the point at which this lecture is delivered, student conceptions have already been elicited and explored. Because lectures can play an important role in instruction, we stress once again that the emphasis in this volume on the use of discussion to elicit students' thinking, monitor understanding, and support metacognitive development—all critical elements of effective teaching—should not be mistaken for a pedagogical recommendation of a single approach to instruction. Indeed, inquiry-based learning may fall short of its target of providing students with deep conceptual understanding if the teacher places the full burden of learning on the activities. As Box 1-3 in Chapter 1 suggests, a lecture that consolidates the lessons of an activity and places the activity in the conceptual framework of the discipline explicitly can play a critical role in supporting student understanding.

How the balance is struck in creating a classroom that functions as a learning community attentive to the learners' needs, the knowledge to be mastered, and assessments that support and guide instruction will certain vary from one teacher and classroom to the next. Our hope for this volume, then, is that its presentations of instructional approaches to addressing the key principles from *How People Learn* will support the efforts of teachers to play their own instructional game well. This volume is a first effort to elaborate those findings with regard to specific topics, but we hope it is the first of many such efforts. As teachers and researchers become more familiar with some common aspects of student thinking about a topic, their attention may begin to shift to other aspects that have previously attracted little notice. And as insights about one topic become commonplace, they may be applied to new topics.

Beyond extending the reach of the treatment of the learning principles of *How People Learn* within and across topics, we hope that efforts to incorporate those principles into teaching and learning will help strengthen and reshape our understanding of the rules of the learning game. With physics as his topic of concern, Feynman[16] talks about just such a process: "For a long time we will have a rule that works excellently in an overall way, even when we cannot follow the details, and then some time we may discover a *new rule*. From the point of view of basic physics, the most interesting phenomena are of course in the *new* places, the places where the rules do not work—not the places where they *do* work! That is the way in which we discover new rules."

We look forward to the opportunities created for the evolution of the science of learning and the professional practice of teaching as the principles of learning on which this volume focuses are incorporated into classroom teaching.

NOTES

1. Egan, 1986.
2. Story summarized by Kieran Egan, personal communication, March 7, 2003.
3. Liping Ma's work, described in Chapter 1, refers to the set of core concepts and the connected concepts and knowledge that support them as "knowledge packages."
4. Griffin and Case, 1995.
5. Moss and Case, 1999.
6. Kalchman et al., 2001.
7. Palincsar, 1986; White and Fredrickson, 1998.
8. Ma, 1999, p. 5.
9. Ma, 1999, p. 9.

10. Palincsar, 1986.
11. Palincsar, 1986.
12. National Research Council, 2005 (Stewart et al., 2005, Chapter 12).
13. Aleven and Koedinger, 2002.
14. For example, he highlights core concepts conspicuously. In his first lecture, he asks, "If, in some cataclysm, all of scientific knowledge were to be destroyed, and only one sentence passed on to the next generation of creatures, what statement would contain the most information in the fewest words? I believe it is the atomic hypothesis that all things are made of atoms—little particles that move around in perpetual motion, attracting each other when they are a little distance apart, but repelling upon being squeezed into one another.
15. Even with experience, the thinking of individual students may be unanticipated by the teacher.
16. Feynman, 1995, p. 25.

REFERENCES

Aleven, V., and Koedinger, K. (2002). An effective metacognitive strategy: Learning by doing and explaining with a computer-based cognitive tutor. *Cognitive Science, 26*, 147-179.

Egan, K. (1986). *Teaching as story telling: An alternative approach to teaching and curriculum in the elementary school* (vol. iii). Chicago, IL: University of Chicago Press.

Feynman, R.P. (1995). *Six easy pieces: Essentials of physics explained by its most brilliant teacher.* Reading, MA: Perseus Books.

Griffin, S., and Case, R. (1995). Re-thinking the primary school math curriculum: An approach based on cognitive science. *Issues in Education, 3*(1), 1-49.

Kalchman, M., Moss, J., and Case, R. (2001). Psychological models for the development of mathematical understanding: Rational numbers and functions. In S. Carver and D. Klahr (Eds.), *Cognition and instruction: Twenty-five years of progress* (pp. 1-38). Mahwah, NJ: Lawrence Erlbaum Associates.

Ma, L. (1999). *Knowing and teaching elementary mathematics.* Mahwah, NJ: Lawrence Erlbaum Associates.

Moss, J., and Case, R. (1999). Developing children's understanding of rational numbers: A new model and experimental curriculum. *Journal for Research in Mathematics Education, 30*(2).

Palincsar, A.S. (1986). *Reciprocal teaching: Teaching reading as thinking.* Oak Brook, IL: North Central Regional Educational Laboratory.

Stewart, J., Cartier, J.L., and Passmore, C.M. (2005). Developing understanding through model-based inquiry. In National Research Council, *How students learn: History, mathematics, and science in the classroom.* Committee on How People Learn, A Targeted Report for Teachers, M.S. Donovan and J.D. Bransford (Eds.). Division of Behavioral and Social Sciences and Education. Washington, DC: The National Academies Press.

White, B., and Fredrickson, J. (1998). Inquiry, modeling and metacognition: Making science accessible to all students. *Cognition and Instruction, 6*(1), 3-117.

OTHER RESOURCES

National Academy of Sciences. (1998). *Teaching about evolution and the nature of science.* Working Group on Teaching Evolution. Washington, DC: National Academy Press: Available: http://books.nap.edu/catalog/5787.html.

National Academy of Sciences. (2004). *Evolution in Hawaii: A supplement to teaching about evolution and the nature of science* by Steve Olson. Washington, DC: The National Academies Press. Available: http://www.nap.edu/books/0309089913/html/.

Biographical Sketches of Committee Members and Contributors

Rosalyn Ashby is a lecturer in education in the History in Education Unit in the School of Arts and Humanities in the University of London Institute of Education. Her work focuses on designing history curricula, assessment systems, and support materials for teachers. She now leads a history teacher-training course. Prior to becoming a university lecturer, Ashby taught history, politics and economics, and then worked as a history adviser with primary and secondary teachers. She has published numerous articles and book chapters, including many coauthored with Peter Lee regarding children's ideas about history. She is an editor of the *International Review of History Education*. She has a degree in American history and government from the University of Essex.

Robert B. Bain is assistant professor in the school of education at the University of Michigan. He teaches social studies education and investigates history education, the intersection between the disciplines and social studies instruction, and professional development. Previously, he spent more than 25 years as a high school history teacher. Among other publications, he has coauthored an article on professional development of elementary school teachers.

John D. Bransford (*Chair*) is James W. Mifflin university professor and professor of education at the University of Washington in Seattle. Previously, he was centennial professor of psychology and education and codirector of the Learning Technology Center at Vanderbilt University. Early work by Bransford and his colleagues in the 1970s included research in the areas of human learning and memory and problem solving; this research helped shape the "cognitive revolution" in psychology. An author of seven books and hundreds of articles and presentations, Bransford's work focuses on the areas of cognition and technology. He served as cochair of the National Research Council (NRC) committee that authored *How People Learn: Brain, Mind, Experience, and School*. He received a Ph.D. in cognitive psychology from the University of Minnesota.

Susan Carey is a professor of psychology at Harvard University. Carey's research concerns the evolutionary and ontogenetic origins of human knowledge in a variety of domains, including number, lexical semantics, physical reasoning, and reasoning about intentional states. She studies conceptual change involving older children, and focuses on three domains of knowledge: number, intuitive biology, and intuitive physics. She received a Ph.D. from Harvard University.

Jennifer L. Cartier is an assistant professor in the Department of Instruction and Learning at the University of Pittsburgh. Her research interests include student learning in classrooms where modeling is a focus and teacher education—particularly the ways in which hands-on curriculum materials can be implemented to engage elementary school students in realistic scientific practices. She has published articles describing students' reasoning in genetics in *Science and Education* and *BioQUEST Notes* and she has coauthored a book chapter describing the use of black-box activities to introduce students to aspects of scientific argumentation.

M. Suzanne Donovan (*Study Director*) is also director of the NRC's Strategic Education Research Partnership (SERP) and coeditor of the project's two reports, *Strategic Education Research Partnership* and *Learning and Instruction: A SERP Research Agenda*. At the NRC, she served as director of the previous study that produced *How People Learn: Bridging Research and Practice,* and she was coeditor for the NRC reports *Minority Students in Special and Gifted Education* and *Eager to Learn: Educating Our Preschoolers.* Previously, she was on the faculty of Columbia University. She has a Ph.D. in public policy from the University of California at Berkeley.

Kieran Egan is a professor in the Faculty of Education at Simon Fraser University in Burnaby, Canada. Dr. Egan was the 1991 winner of the Grawemeyer Award in Education for his analyses of children's imaginations. His recent books include *The Educated Mind: How Cognitive Tools Shape Our Understanding* (University of Chicago Press) and *Getting It Wrong from the Beginning: Our Progressivist Inheritance from Herbert Spencer, John Dewey, and Jean Piaget* (Yale University Press).

Karen C. Fuson is a professor emeritus in the School of Education and Social Policy and in the Psychology Department at Northwestern University. After teaching high school mathematics to Chicago inner-city African-American students for 3 years, she began research to ascertain how to help all students enter high school with more knowledge of mathematics. She has conducted extensive research regarding children's learning of mathematical concepts from ages 2 through 12, focusing in on the development of effective teaching and learning materials, including the "Children's Math World's K through 5" curriculum, supporting effective learning for children from various backgrounds, and ambitious accessible learning paths through school mathematics. Fuson was a member of the NRC committee that authored *Adding It Up: Helping Children Learn Mathematics.*

Sharon Griffin is an associate professor of education and an adjunct associate professor of psychology at Clark University. She is coauthor of "Number Worlds," a research-based mathematics program for young children, coauthor of *What Develops in Emotional Development?* (Plenum), and author of several articles on cognitive development and mathematics education. For the past 10 years, she has sought to improve mathematics learning and achievement for young children by developing and evaluating programs to "provide the central conceptual prerequisites for success in school math to children at risk for school failure." Griffin is currently participating in an advisory capacity on national projects, in Canada and the United States, to enhance the cognitive, mathematical, and language development of "high-need" preschool children, from birth to 5 years.

Mindy Kalchman is an assistant professor in the School of Education at DePaul University. Her research interests include children's learning of mathematics, theory-based curriculum design, and the effect of discoveries from the field of developmental cognitive psychology on classroom practice. She has coauthored numerous articles regarding mathematics education and curriculum and has conducted workshops on how to teach functions. Kalchman also served as a consulting content editor for the development of the Ontario mathematics curriculum for grades 9–12. She received her Ph.D. from the Ontario Institute for Studies in Education, University of Toronto.

Kenneth R. Koedinger is an associate professor in the Human Computer Interaction Institute and Psychology Department at Carnegie Mellon University. His research interests include cognitive modeling, problem solving and learning, intelligent tutoring systems, and educational technology. Earlier in his career, Koedinger was a teacher in an urban high school. He has developed computer simulations of student thinking that are used to guide the construction of educational materials and are the core of intelligent software systems that provide students with individualized interactive learning assistance. He has developed such "cognitive tutors" for mathematics that are now in use in over 1700 schools.

Pamela Kraus is a research scientist and cofounder of FACET Innovations. She is currently working on the Diagnoser projects and related professional development projects and she is helping conduct the research and organize the facet clusters in the physical sciences. In addition, Kraus works closely with the resource teachers from across the state as they produce assessment tools. She received a Ph.D. from the University of Washington.

Peter J. Lee is a senior lecturer in education in the History Education Unit of the School of Arts and Humanities at the Institute of Education of The University of London. Previously, he taught history in primary and secondary schools. Lee has directed several research and curriculum development projects (the latter with Denis Shemilt). He has edited five books on history education, and published numerous chapters and articles exploring children's ideas about history, many of them coauthored with Rosalyn Ashby. He is an editor of the *International Review of History Education*. He received a history degree at Oxford University.

Shirley J. Magnusson is the Cotchett Professor of Science and Mathematics Teacher Education at the California Polytechnic State University. She has taught science to students at the elementary, middle school, high school, and college levels since 1980. She joined the faculty at the University of Michigan in 1991 as a science teacher educator, specializing in learning and instruction in science at the elementary school level. She collaborated with Annemarie Palincsar on a program of research that has sought to define and study the outcomes from an approach to inquiry-based science instruction known as Guided Inquiry supporting Multiple Literacies (GIsML). Publications of Magnusson's work have appeared in the *Journal of the Learning Sciences, Teaching and Teacher Education*, the *Journal of Science Education and Technology*, and *Learning Disabilities Quarterly*, as well as a number of books such as *Science Teacher Knowledge, Cognition and Instruction: Twenty-five Years of Progress*, and *Translating Educational Theory into Practice*.

James Minstrell is cofounder and research scientist at FACET Innovations, LLC. This position followed a lengthy career as a science and mathematics teacher and classroom researcher in the learning of physical science and mathematics. He received the Presidential Award for Excellence in Science and Mathematics Teaching from the National Science Foundation. Minstrell served on the U.S. Department of Education's Expert Panel on Science and

Mathematics Education. He has published numerous articles, with a major focus on understanding of mathematics and physics.

Joan Moss is an assistant professor in the Department of Human Development and Applied Psychology at the Ontario Institute for Studies in Education at the University of Toronto. Previously she worked as a master teacher at the Institute of Child Study Laboratory School. Her research interests include children's development and understanding of rational numbers and proportional reasoning. More recently, Moss has been working on classroom-based studies of children's development of algebraic thinking. Her work in professional development includes preservice training, as well as coordination of learning opportunities with novice elementary school mathematics teachers using a Japanese lesson study approach. She has published widely and is an author of a mathematics textbook series. Moss carried out postdoctoral research at the University of California at Berkeley.

Annemarie Sullivan Palincsar is the Jean and Charles Walgreen professor of reading and literacy at the University of Michigan's School of Education. She has conduced extensive research on peer collaboration in problem-solving activity, instruction to promote self-regulation, acquisition and instruction of literacy with primary students at risk for academic difficulty, and how children use literacy in the context of guided inquiry experiences. She was a member of the NRC committees that produced the reports *How People Learn: Bridging Research and Practice,* and *Preventing Reading Difficulties in young Children.* Palincsar is currently coeditor of *Cognition and Instruction.*

Cynthia M. Passmore is an assistant professor in the School of Education at the University of California, Davis. She specializes in science education and is particularly interested in student learning and reasoning about scientific models. Her research also focuses on preservice and in-service teacher professional development. She teaches the science methods courses for single and multiple subjects credential candidates, as well as graduate courses in science education. Earlier in her career she worked as a high school science teacher in East Africa, Southern California, and Wisconsin.

Denis Shemilt has worked at the University of Leeds for more than 25 years, where he has been evaluator of the Schools History Project 13-16, and codirector of the Cambridge History Project. Until recently, he was head of the School of Education at Trinity and All Saints, a constituent college of the university, devoting time to educational management at the expense of real work. He is now focusing on training history teachers and pursuing a long-postponed interest in the development of students' historical frameworks.

He has published numerous contributions to history education, including the *History 13-16 Evaluation Study* and papers on students' ideas about change, evidence, and empathy in history. He received a degree in education from the University of Manchester.

James Stewart is a professor in the School of Education's Department of Curriculum and Instruction at the University of Wisconsin-Madison. His research interests include student understanding, reasoning, and problem solving in science, particularly in the biological sciences. Stewart's recent publications include articles on student understanding in genetics and evolutionary biology in *Science Education* and the *Journal of Research in Science Teaching* and a book chapter, "Teaching Science in a Multicultural Perspective."

Suzanne M. Wilson is a professor in the Department of Teacher Education and director of the Center for the Scholarship of Teaching at Michigan State University. She was a history and mathematics teacher for 6 years; directed the Teacher Assessment Project at Stanford University; taught third-grade social studies in a professional development school; and has directed several research projects exploring the relationship of teachers' practice to curriculum mandates. Wilson teaches prospective and practicing teachers, as well as prospective teacher educators and researchers.

Samuel S. Wineburg is professor of education at Stanford University, where he directs the Ph.D. program in History Education. His research explores the development of historical thinking among adolescents and the nature of historical consciousness. Wineburg's book, *Historical Thinking and Other Unnatural Acts: Charting the Future and Past,* was awarded the 2002 Frederic W. Ness Prize for the "most important contribution to the understanding and improvement of liberal education" by the Association of American Colleges and Universities. He was a member of the NRC committee that wrote *How People Learn: Brain, Mind, Experience, and School.* He received his Ph.D. from Stanford University.

Index

This index includes the text of the full version of *How Students Learn: History, Mathematics, and Science*, which can be found on the CD attached to the back cover.

A

Absolute difference, 311
Absolute thinking
    as additive, 311
Access to someone who saw for himself
    and textbook claims and the nature
    of sources, 93
Accounts, 59–61
    of Colombian voyages, 192–193
    different ideas about historical, 38–39
    historical, 59–61
    substantiated, 87
Actions at a distance
    exploring similarities and differences
        between, 492–493
Activity A1 worksheet, 483
Adams, John, 185
Adaptive reasoning, 218
Adding It Up, 218, 233, 241
Additive reasoning, 311, 321
    absolute thinking as, 311
Addressing preconceptions, 399–403
Advantage
    selective, 542
Adventure
    sense of, 71
Alternative instructional approaches, 321–322

American Association for the Advancement
    of Science
    guidelines of, 398
    textbook review by, 16
Analogs of number representations that
    children can actively explore
    hands-on, 292–296
    Rosemary's Magic Shoes game, 295–296
    Skating Party game, 292–295
Analogy to understand the benchmark
    experience, 489–490
Ancient views of the Earth as flat or round,
    196–197
    the Atlas Farnese, 196
    the story of Eratosthenes and the
        Earth's circumference, 196–197
Anglo-Saxons, 117
Anselm, St., 46
Arguments
    inadequacies in, 403
Ashby, Rosalyn, 79–178, 591
Assessment-centered, 415
Assessment-centered classroom
    environments, 13, 16–17, 267, 290,
        292, 555–558
    examples of students' critiques of
        their own Darwinian explanations,
        558

T